Other New Releases from IRM Press

- **Multimedia and Interactive Digital TV: Managing the Opportunities Created by Digital Convergence**/Margherita Pagani
  ISBN: 1-931777-38-1; eISBN: 1-931777-54-3 / US$59.95 / © 2003
- **Virtual Education: Cases in Learning & Teaching Technologies**/ Fawzi Albalooshi (Ed.), ISBN: 1-931777-39-X; eISBN: 1-931777-55-1 / US$59.95 / © 2003
- **Managing IT in Government, Business & Communities**/Gerry Gingrich (Ed.)
  ISBN: 1-931777-40-3; eISBN: 1-931777-56-X / US$59.95 / © 2003
- **Information Management: Support Systems & Multimedia Technology**/ George Ditsa (Ed.), ISBN: 1-931777-41-1; eISBN: 1-931777-57-8 / US$59.95 / © 2003
- **Managing Globally with Information Technology**/Sherif Kamel (Ed.)
  ISBN: 42-X; eISBN: 1-931777-58-6 / US$59.95 / © 2003
- **Current Security Management & Ethical Issues of Information Technology**/Rasool Azari (Ed.), ISBN: 1-931777-43-8; eISBN: 1-931777-59-4 / US$59.95 / © 2003
- **UML and the Unified Process**/Liliana Favre (Ed.)
  ISBN: 1-931777-44-6; eISBN: 1-931777-60-8 / US$59.95 / © 2003
- **Business Strategies for Information Technology Management**/Kalle Kangas (Ed.)
  ISBN: 1-931777-45-4; eISBN: 1-931777-61-6 / US$59.95 / © 2003
- **Managing E-Commerce and Mobile Computing Technologies**/Julie Mariga (Ed.)
  ISBN: 1-931777-46-2; eISBN: 1-931777-62-4 / US$59.95 / © 2003
- **Effective Databases for Text & Document Management**/Shirley A. Becker (Ed.)
  ISBN: 1-931777-47-0; eISBN: 1-931777-63-2 / US$59.95 / © 2003
- **Technologies & Methodologies for Evaluating Information Technology in Business**/ Charles K. Davis (Ed.), ISBN: 1-931777-48-9; eISBN: 1-931777-64-0 / US$59.95 / © 2003
- **ERP & Data Warehousing in Organizations: Issues and Challenges**/Gerald Grant (Ed.), ISBN: 1-931777-49-7; eISBN: 1-931777-65-9 / US$59.95 / © 2003
- **Practicing Software Engineering in the 21st Century**/Joan Peckham (Ed.)
  ISBN: 1-931777-50-0; eISBN: 1-931777-66-7 / US$59.95 / © 2003
- **Knowledge Management: Current Issues and Challenges**/Elayne Coakes (Ed.)
  ISBN: 1-931777-51-9; eISBN: 1-931777-67-5 / US$59.95 / © 2003
- **Computing Information Technology: The Human Side**/Steven Gordon (Ed.)
  ISBN: 1-931777-52-7; eISBN: 1-931777-68-3 / US$59.95 / © 2003
- **Current Issues in IT Education**/Tanya McGill (Ed.)
  ISBN: 1-931777-53-5; eISBN: 1-931777-69-1 / US$59.95 / © 2003

Excellent additions to your institution's library!
Recommend these titles to your Librarian!

To receive a copy of the Idea Group, Inc. catalog, please contact (toll free) 1/800-345-4332, fax 1/717-533-8661,or visit the IGI Online Bookstore at: [http://www.idea-group.com]!
Note: All IGI books are also available as ebooks on netlibrary.com as well as other ebook sources. Contact Ms. Carrie Skovrinskie at [cskovrinskie@idea-group.com] to receive a complete list of sources where you can obtain ebook information or IGP titles.

Managing IT in Government, Business & Communities

Table of Contents

Section II: Managing IT Across Regions and Countries

Section III: IT Addressing Globalization

Preface

Management of information technology in today's connected, information rich global marketplace is a far cry from management in the 1980s and 1990s. Today's computing environment is ubiquitous, networked, and systemically connected; yesterday's computing environment was distributed, centralized, and stovepiped. From selecting and designing systems to implementing and evaluating systems, an organization and its leadership are challenged to perform differently than in the past. The articles in this volume illustrate new organizational, leadership, and management approaches to information systems and technology. They are drawn from international governments, small and medium-sized enterprises (SMEs), and universities. The diversity and range of the articles underscores the pervasiveness of the trends that are changing today's global computing landscape.

Computing in today's world is ubiquitous. Increasing numbers of people have access to information technology; the variety of IT devices continues to proliferate; technology prices continue to fall; and people are educated and trained in the use of technology at increasingly younger and older ages. People around the world continue to access digital technology with increasing frequency. As rural areas decline in population and cities increase in population, people have greater and greater access to computing technology in the office and home, in airports, hotels, and coffeshops, and on the local street corner. Additionally, the variety of information technology devices is increasing. IT still assumes the traditional form of microcomputers, but it also appears in everything from palm pilots and cell phones to automobiles and traffic lights, to smart cards and facial scanners. And despite a predicted slowdown in the growth of computing power, the power of digital devices from year to year still continues to follow Moore's law and the price per megaflop continues to drop exponentially. Finally, individuals around the world interact with technology during periods of their lives that would be considered unusual 10-15 years ago. Child programmers and hackers are commonplace, and retired workers are turning to digital communications for second careers and hobbies and to keep up with the grandchildren. All of these trends – increasing access, increasing types of IT devices, decreasing prices, and increasing numbers of computer users – are helping to create a world of ubiquitous computing.

Computing is not only ubiquitous, it's networked. Computers were first connected locally with WANs and LANs in the 1980s, thus increasing the speed of communications within and across organizations. The growth of the Internet in the 1990s increased the number of those communications exponentially and expanded them around the world to include millions of players and organizations. Global communications now occur in near real-time, across a variety of economic, government, political, and social groups, and frequently between people and groups that previously were unknown to one another.

Until the advent of the Internet, global communications were confined primarily to financial institutions and the movement of money. These communications were dependent on the technology of magnetic tape traveling by "planes, trains, and automobiles"; they could take minutes, hours, and in some cases, days. Today the Internet moves not only money, but information of all types, to any location on the globe in milliseconds. In addition to traditional financial and economic groups, local and national governments enable electronic government through Web sites; manufacturers execute just-in-time ordering and delivery; and non-traditional state actors influence international opinion regarding local and national authorities. In addition, political groups discuss international trade, elections, and political candidates; grassroots groups discuss the environment, land mines, and urban protests; and social groups discuss art, literature, and music. The Internet is a thriving real-time communication system for any person or group regarding any topic of interest. And it's free.

The third characteristic of today's global computing landscape is the systemic nature of those network connections. Not only are global digital networks increasingly numerous and pervasive, but those networks are increasingly connected to one another. The "I Love You" virus infected thousands of computer systems within hours by traveling across global network paths, but the inter-dependence of those paths allowed the virus to move significantly more quickly than if the connections had been serial. Global networks also interact with economic, political, and social systems thus creating complex, dynamic socio-technical communications phenomena and events. On the morning of 9/11, cells phones in New York City relayed information to family and friends in other areas of the country who then transferred that information to the Internet for quicker dissemination. That information was then summarized by CNN and broadcast around the world. International political and social events affect global stock markets which, in turn, affect those same political systems. Companies sell goods and services in the global marketplace through the Internet, simultaneously developing new customer profiles that redirect marketing strategies to unexplored market niches. And small, previously unempowered political groups such as the Zapatista movement in Chiapas, Mexico and the International Campaign to Ban Landmines (ICBL) in the United States use the Internet for global reach and building grassroots support to affect international politics.

Thus today's computing environment is one of ubiquitous digital activity communicated globally through technical networks interacting systemically with other technical networks and with human networks. The articles in this book illustrate that new 21st Century computing environment. They are organized into three sections – the first section includes six chapters addressing the management of IT within organizations; the second section includes seven chapters addressing the management of IT across organizations, regions, and countries; and the third and final section includes five chapters addressing the management of global IT. A brief description of each chapter follows:

Chapter 1 examines the applicability of a theoretical model, the theory of entrepreneurship, to research regarding the strategic utilization of information technology in small businesses. The authors argue that small businesses are typically growing and evolving and thus different challenges arise over time, necessitating different approaches to the strategic use of IT. The traditional theoretical models used by researchers and practitioners are more appropriate to large, stable businesses.

Chapter 2 describes a model for systematically assessing the benefits of information technology purchases. The authors propose a modified factor rating approach that separates subjective benefits from the objective cost-benefit analysis. They conclude that the best computer may often be the cheapest computer.

Chapter 3 examines the use of intranets in the United States Federal government, identifying sources of and impediments to intranet development. Six case studies reveal overall trends in intranet use including the importance of upper management support and successful marketing efforts. The authors conclude that intranets offer strong potential for enhancing inter-organizational communications and predict further growth of intranets in the U.S. federal government.

Chapter 4 explores the outsourcing of information technology and its implications for SMEs. The author emphasizes the criticality of up-to-date in-house IT knowledge and its relationship to continuous improvement of business processes; he also stresses the importance of communications between users and in-house software developers. He concludes that outsourcing decisions should be made carefully and with great discrimination.

Chapter 5 describes a model for systematically assessing the monetary and human costs of developing small business Web sites for interacting with customers. The authors illustrate the use of SWOT analysis to build a conceptual model and then describe the process of translating that conceptual model into a spreadsheet to support Web site investment decisions.

Chapter 6 examines a project-oriented undergraduate course at the University of Colorado in the United States. The author describes the processes by which students work with local community service agencies to build and evaluate software for those agencies. He/she concludes that the most important outcome of the course is the relationship building and communication that occurs among the students and with the community service agencies.

Chapter 7 addresses the accelerating development of information resources in China. The authors describe several critical information resources initiatives in China, linking the initiatives to Chinese government information resources policies and their impact. They conclude with a discussion of the challenges of developing information resources in China and suggest potential solutions to these challenges.

Chapter 8 presents an analysis of the factors that influence the ability of small and medium-sized enterprises to effectively utilize Web-based electronic commerce. The authors base their analysis on a qualitative study of thirty-four Australian companies from seven different industries. They identify the internal and external factors that are critical determinants of SMEs success with electronic commerce. They conclude with a discussion of these factors and their implications for maximizing the effectiveness of electronic commerce.

Chapter 9 examines the state of "digital readiness" in the local governments of Japan, consisting of 47 prefectures each divided into several municipalities. The authors conclude that the major uses of technology in local governments are e-mail and local area networks. They further conclude that many prefectures are financially weak and need to redirect financial resources from legacy systems to new IT systems. Other impediments to digital readiness that are identified by the authors are IT security and privacy protections and outdated organizational structures.

Chapter 10 examines the potential of electronic voting systems (EVSs) to enable government reform and renew the democratic and political processes. The authors discuss the advantages of EVS implementation to the citizenry as well as the obstacles of privacy, security, and accessibility. They conclude with recommendations for gaining voters' trust and increasing voters' participation with EVSs.

Chapter 11 reviews the empirical research regarding barriers to electronic commerce adoption and diffusion by SMEs. The authors divide the literature's barriers into those internal to an organization and those imposed by external forces. They conclude that the barriers to e-commerce adoption have not changed over time as newer technologies have entered the market. They further suggest that researchers develop normative models to help SMEs overcome internal barriers and that policy makers develop programs to help SMEs overcome external barriers.

Chapter 12 describes an exploratory study of e-commerce development in the United Kingdom's SMEs. The authors review interview data and documentation from three organizations, each in a different industry, that implemented e-commerce service in the recent past. They conclude that the companies are in the early stages of B2B e-commerce, function on limited financial and educational resources, and would benefit from an increased emphasis on business strategy.

Chapter 13 explores the applicability of game theory and social theory to technology adoption decisions in general, and B2B e-commerce in particular. The authors discuss recent ASEAN public and private e-commerce initiatives in SMEs. They conclude that effective initiatives focus on global reach and the creation of commodity markets and a positive brand image.

Chapter 14 examines the concept of virtualization and its role in society. The author argues that the virtualization process creates enormous opportunity for economic growth for those countries and organizations which have not been competitive in the past. He explores the positive and negative aspects of virtualization in traditional organizations, in small and medium sized organizations, and in educational institutions.

Chapter 15 also examines the concept of virtual organizations using the lens of structuration theory. The authors focus on the relationship between the virtual organization, the real organization, and the human players. Their goal is to initiate theory building for the Internet age and to provide new epistemological frameworks that are more appropriate to the study of virtual organizations than the traditional analytical framework of modern science.

Chapter 16 explores the development of interorganizational communication systems in a rapidly changing environment. The author reviews the concepts of interorganizational relationships, strategic alliances, and interorganizational networks using Barnard's theory of cooperative systems and formal organization as a lens for analysis. He also identifies barriers to creating and maintaining effective interorganizational communication systems and suggests strategies for overcoming these barriers.

Chapter 17 reviews the results of an exploratory study of the internationalization efforts of small Internet retailers. The authors interviewed key personnel in top and middle management in three e-tailers in Singapore, highlighting the issues the companies faced in expanding their operations to service an international customer base. The authors conclude that internationalization strategies must address foreign market accessibility, infrastructure, and localization issues.

Chapter 18 explores the use of the Internet for improving the project management of aid projects in Sub-Sahara Africa (SSA). Based on interviews and supporting observation, the author concludes that effective communication and information openness are critical components of success. He further concludes that the Internet is a potential vehicle for increasing the participation of local people in international issues and improving the effective utilization of aid from the Western world.

REFERENCES

Castells, M. (2001). *The internet galaxy: Reflections on the internet, business, and society: Reflections on the internet, business, and society.* New York: Oxford University Press.

Hunter, R. (2002). *World without secrets: Business, crime, and privacy in the age of ubiquitous computing.* New York: John Wiley.

Kelly, K. (1998). *New rules for the new economy: 10 radical strategies for a connected world.* New York: Penguin.

Tapscott, D. (1996). *The digital economy: Promise and peril in the age of networked intelligence.* New York: McGraw-Hill.

Wilhelm, A.G. (2000). *Democracy in the digital age: Challenges to political life in cyberspace.* New York: Routledge.

Acknowledgments

In closing, I wish to thank all of the authors for their insights and excellent contributions to this book. I also want to thank all of the reviewers, without whose support this book could not have been completed. Special thanks go to Mehdi Khosrow-Pour and Jan Travers at Idea Group, Inc., for their ongoing professional support and encouragement over the years; and to Amanda Appicello also at Idea Group, Inc., for keeping me focused and on schedule. Finally, I want to thank my family and colleagues for their support throughout this project.

Gerry Gingrich
Information Resources Management College, USA

Section I

Managing IT Within Organizations

Chapter I

Adopting the Entrepreneurial Process in the Study of Information Systems and Small Business

M. Gordon Hunter
The University of Lethbridge, Canada

Wayne A. Long
The University of Calgary, Canada

ABSTRACT

This document suggests the adoption of the Theory of Entrepreneurship by researchers who investigate the use of information systems by small businesses. The majority of existing research into this area tends to adopt results determined from investigations of larger businesses. Thus, the uniqueness of small business is not considered. Concepts such as strategic orientation, decision-making, and resource poverty contribute to the unique situation and approach taken by small business managers. The Theory of Entrepreneurship responds to these concepts. The framework suggests that organizations evolve and that entrepreneurs throughout this evolution face various challenges. The components of the Theory of Entrepreneurship are described here, in concert with the challenge to researchers to consider adopting this framework when conducting investigations into how information systems may be employed to support small business.

INTRODUCTION

The adoption of computer-based Information Systems (IS) is creating significant changes in the way individuals perform their duties. Thus, change, facilitated by the implementation of IS, is revolutionizing business processes (Coghlan, 2001). There has been a consequent plethora of research into how businesses can best use IS or adapt to the IS-precipitated change. Researchers, however, have not necessarily recognized those aspects which may differentiate business with regards to how they might respond to the adoption of IS. There has been very little attempt to analyze the differences in how large versus small businesses may respond. Where a differentiation is made, Cragg and King (1993) found that most research regarding IS and small business mainly attempts to confirm the research results determined from investigations of larger firms. They further suggest that the development of a single model for both large and small businesses may be impossible due to the differences in such aspects as objectives, philosophies, size, and proclivity for innovation. Thus, it is incumbent upon IS researchers to explore how the unique aspects of small businesses may impact their use of IS.

There are a number of stakeholder groups who may find the results of these types of investigations important, especially when specifically related to the context of small business. First, small business managers may be able to identify aspects with regards to the use of IS, which may contribute to their organization's competitive advantage. Second, consultants may be able to contribute value-added recommendations regarding the use of IS specifically within the small business context. Third, vendors of both hardware and software may be better able to identify the unique needs of small business and respond appropriately to this new and expanding market. Fourth, government administrators may be able to develop and deliver support programs, which more appropriately address those aspects of small business-related adoption of IS.

The small business sector represents an important segment of most economies. In Canada, for instance, most recent figures indicate that 43% of total economic output is generated by 2.3 million businesses with fewer than 100 employees each (Industry Canada, 1997). In the UK, small businesses employ 65% of all workers and produce 25% of the gross domestic product (Ballantine and Powell, 1998).

The main goal of this chapter is to describe an existing framework, which may address the unique aspects of the adoption and use of IS by small business. To begin, the context of the small business is outlined with respect to its uniqueness. Then, the suggested framework is introduced and described. This discussion presents the Entrepreneurial Process as developed by McMullan and Long (1990) and applies the various challenges depicted by their process to the use of IS by small business. This framework, it is suggested, will provide researchers with the necessary guidance to conduct appropriate investigations into the unique aspects of the adoption and use of IS by small business.

SMALL BUSINESS CONTEXT

Currently, there is not one generally accepted definition for "small business." Some definitions employ a measure of annual revenue, size of investment, or number of employees. This latter definition tends to be employed most often (Longnecker et al., 1997). The European Parliament (2002) has defined micro businesses to include 0 to 10 employees, small businesses to include from 10 to 50 employees, and medium-sized businesses to include 50 to 250 employees. Individual researchers, then, adopt a definition within their respective research projects.

Table 1 presents a dichotomous conceptual interpretation of how managers tend to approach business practice. According to Stevenson (1999), managers in small businesses tend to be oriented toward the "promoter" end of a continuum, whereas managers of large businesses tend to take a "trustee" orientation.

From a strategic orientation, then, managers of small businesses will emphasize responding to opportunities, while managers of large businesses will focus on efficient use of resources. Further, with regards to resources, the small business

Table 1: Approaches to Business Practice

ASPECTS OF BUSINESS PRACTICE	PROMOTER ◄	► TRUSTEE
Strategic orientation	Capitalize on an opportunity	Focus on efficient use of current resources to determine the greatest return
Resource commitment and control decisions	Act in a very short time frame	Long time frame, considering long-term implications
	Multi-staged	One-time, up-front commitment
	Minimum commitment of resources at each stage	Large scale commitment of resources at one stage
	Respond quickly to changes in competition, market, and technology	Formal procedures of analysis, such as capital allocation systems

manager will respond quickly to the environment, with a minimum commitment of resources in a multi-staged approach. The *promoter* conceptually represents these tactics of the small business manager, where resource commitments tend to be multi-staged, with a minimum commitment at each stage. In a rapidly changing environment, this type of stepped commitment enables a firm to respond faster to changes in competition, the market, and technology. Conversely, the manager of a large business will take the time to follow formal procedures to make a one-time decision regarding a long-term commitment. The *trustee*, who tends to engage in a systematic analysis to determine what needs to be done to get the greatest return on the resources currently controlled, conceptually represents this approach. This process ultimately results in a large-scale commitment of resources at one point in time. To some extent, the formal systems adopted by large firms, such as capital allocation systems, tend to encourage up-front resource commitments (Stevenson, 1999).

Another concept, *resource poverty*, (Thong et al., 1994) may also be employed to provide further elaboration of the differences between managers of large and small businesses. Resource poverty refers to the lack of both financial and human resources. Managers of small businesses must continually conduct their affairs with limited amounts of money. This situation tends to increase the manager's focus, as indicated above, on a minimum and multi-staged commitment process. Further, limited human resources may mean either fewer available employees or employees without the appropriate skills. In either case, the manager of a small business will be limited in what activities can be initiated and completed. Hence, there will be a focus on the near term, with an emphasis on allocating these scarce resources only to what is considered top priority activities. Further, as presented later in this document, the scope of activities and the consequent required IS support will evolve as the small business expands.

Unfortunately, the deployment of IS requires the development of a long-term plan and a large one-time commitment of both financial and human resources. As shown above, this is anathema to the manager of a small business. How can this conundrum be addressed? First, the currently available research into this question will be presented. Then, a proposed framework will be presented and discussed.

RELATED RESEARCH

Earlier research (Nickell and Seado, 1986) determined that small business was mainly using IS for accounting and administrative purposes. Research conducted in the 1990s (Lin et al., 1993; Fuller, 1996; Berman, 1997; Canadian Federation of Independent Business, 1999; Timmons, 1999) noted a growing interest by small business in employing IS in daily operations. The impetus for this growing interest originated from various sources. First, small business was becoming concerned about the adoption of IS by competition. The small business manager did not want to be left behind the competition regarding the use of technology. Second, the technology was becoming more affordable, reliable, and powerful. These trends were allowing the small business manager to make decisions about the technology, which fit the general decision-making profile of the small business manager. Third, IS was starting to be recognized as a means for the small business to attempt to compete with larger businesses. Fourth, the wide-spread use of the Internet facilitated the identification and implementation of e-commerce opportunities.

While small businesses have been more than prepared to exploit the use of IS to support daily operations (El Louadi, 1998), there exists little evidence that they are prepared to employ the technology in a strategic manner (Berman, 1997). Bridge and Peel (1999) also determined that small businesses employed computers mainly to support daily operations and tended not to use them to support decision-making or long-term planning.

Recent research has supported the contention that the use of IS by small business represents a unique approach. For instance, Pollard and Hayne (1998) investigated the information systems issues identified by small business managers across Canada. Their results indicate that the issues being faced by small business managers are different than those faced by large business managers. Also, in the area of IS, the issues are in a continual state of change. Also, Belich and Dubinsky (1999) applied information theory to investigate the information processing among a group of small business exporters. They determined that the information processing of the small businesses was not the same as that found in larger firms. Further, Taylor (1999) investigated the implementation of enterprise software in small businesses and found that neither the businesses themselves, nor the software vendors are fully cognizant of the unique problems encountered by small business managers. Finally, Hunter et al. (2002) identified two major themes regarding small business use of IS. These themes are *dependency* and *efficiency*. The authors suggest that the adoption of IS increased the small business' dependency on an internal champion, and a series of external stakeholders, including consultants and suppliers. This increased dependency, Hunter et al. (2002) suggest, results from the approaches to business (Stevenson, 1999) taken by the manager and the concept of resource poverty (Thong, Yap and Raman, 1994). The efficiency theme suggests that IS is primarily used by small business managers as an operational tool to help complete daily activities.

The above reported research, even when the uniqueness of small business use of IS is acknowledged, presents a snapshot view of the small business as though it were spatially and temporally constant. However, the underlying theme of the ideas presented in this document is that the dynamism of the small business, which dictates the ever-changing requirements, must be satisfied from the perspective of the business' on-going development. That is, the needs of the small business change as the process evolves from conceptualisation of the business opportunity through start-up and growth. This idea is supported by the research of McMullan and Long (1990) who suggest that small businesses continue to evolve as they become self-sustaining entities.

USE OF THE INTERNET

Burgess and Trethowan (2002) examined the use of Web sites by small businesses, represented by general practitioners, in Australia. They found that while there was a reasonably high use of computers to improve efficiency and lower costs, there was not much use of computers for Web sites. Those who had Web sites mainly employed them to provide basic information and contact details.

Dandridge and Levenburg (2000) investigated Internet use by small (fewer than 25 employees) businesses. They determined that very few small businesses were moving to this next step in the use of IS. While they found that IS were being employed for daily operations, there was little use of computerization for competitiveness aspects.

A number of research projects have identified that small businesses have not adopted Internet use because of lack of knowledge and experience (Iacovou et al., 1995; Damsgaard and Lyytinen, 1998; Kuan and Chau, 2001). Another set of contributing factors relates to the lack of personnel and time (Bennett et al., 1999). Even when time and personnel are available, there seems to be reluctance by small businesses to investigate the use of the Internet (Chapman et al., 2000).

Actor-Network Theory (ANT), or the innovation translation model, suggests that a network of actors conduct negotiations regarding stances to be taken in relation to the adoption of an innovation. The consideration of the entrepreneurial process allows the ANT theory and translation model to be more appropriately applied in the specific instance of small business. That is, a small business proceeds through a series of development stages, known as the Entrepreneurial Process. Within each of these stages the actors, according to ANT, will bring different inherent characteristics to the innovation translation model within the innovation research paradigm.

To summarize the discussion to this point, it is clear that no single template exists to prescribe the IS needs of a business. Clearly, small and large businesses are different. Stevenson's model (Table 1) suggests differing approaches to business practices between entrepreneurs (promoter) and managers (trustee). They are pursuing different goals and responding to different constraints and strictures – for example, resource poor business owners versus large businesses rich in both financial and human resources. Further, it is generally known that many small business owners initiate IS use in their businesses more to facilitate daily operations and not so much for competitive and strategic reasons.

Articulating the differing IS requirements of small versus large businesses is a useful beginning. A more comprehensive approach is to recognize that a small business is a work in progress. Entrepreneurs are engaged in a creative act of "... impressing their vision on their chosen medium – the venture" (McMullan and Long, 1990, p. 133).

The distinction between big business and small business alone misrepresents the evolving growth dynamics of venture development. The dynamic is inherent in the process of entrepreneurship as put forth by McMullan and Long (1990). Therefore, differing IS requirements will evolve from the dynamics of a developing business. The challenge for the researcher is to recognize the changing context of the small business and its impact on appropriate IS requirements.

A CONCEPTUAL FRAMEWORK – ENTREPRENEURSHIP

Entrepreneurship is a creative process where there is a beginning (vision) and ending (living system) to the entrepreneurial act. Small business and big business are merely points reached during the process that begins with an abstract idea, which the entrepreneur commits to structure as a business venture. Along the way, the entrepreneur makes strategic decisions to meet a series of structural challenges, and in so doing, shapes the venture. For example, an early strategic challenge is identifying, evaluating, and committing to a particular opportunity. Once decided, the venture is delimited to a particular focal environment, i.e., industry/market and all that entails. Successfully meeting each of these challenges brings the venture closer to the entrepreneurial goal of developing a self-sustaining living system with the in-built capacity to innovate and grow. Each structural challenge corresponds to an attribute of a living system (Table 2).

Another component of the process is the need for differing skills, knowledge and information along the way. As the venture takes shape as a small business, it

Table 2: Challenges in Developing an Entrepreneurial Venture

	Entrepreneurial Challenge	Corresponding Living Systems Attribute
1.	Identifying realizable opportunities	All living systems have identifiable environments.
2.	Designing feasible products	All living systems have boundaries, which distinguish them from their environment.
3.	Planning resource requirements	All living systems are composed of interacting parts involving some functional differentiation and specialization.
4.	Negotiating resource and client contracts	All living systems must take in energy and information.
5.	Engineering efficient production	All living systems transform energy and information from one state to another.
6.	Regularizing sales revenue	All living systems export outputs into their environments.
7.	Standardizing operating performance	All living systems have cyclical patterns of changing activities within the system and within the environment.
8.	Expanding strategically and opportunistically	All living systems are characterized by homeostatic balance and government mechanisms, evolving systematically to better fit their environment.
9.	Professionalizing middle management	All living systems become differentiated over time into more and more independent roles.
10.	Institutionalizing innovative capacity	All living systems are characterized by negative entropy.

Adapted from McMullan and Long, 1990, p. 267.

may well be expected that the entrepreneur looks to IS for help with operational matters to help meet the challenge of standardizing operating performance. At another challenge point, IS may play an important role in support of strategic expansion.

The finale, or end, of the entrepreneurship process is a self-sustaining living system, "…no longer needing the entrepreneur's contribution to survive and prosper" (McMullan and Long, 1990, p. 138). At this juncture the entrepreneur has successfully developed the venture with the attributes common to living systems.

Part D (Figure 1) refers to a series of creative entrepreneurial challenges. There are ten of these challenges, each of which corresponds to a structural attribute of a living system (Table 2). The balance of the discussion focuses on these. As

Figure 1: Modelling the Entrepreneurial Process

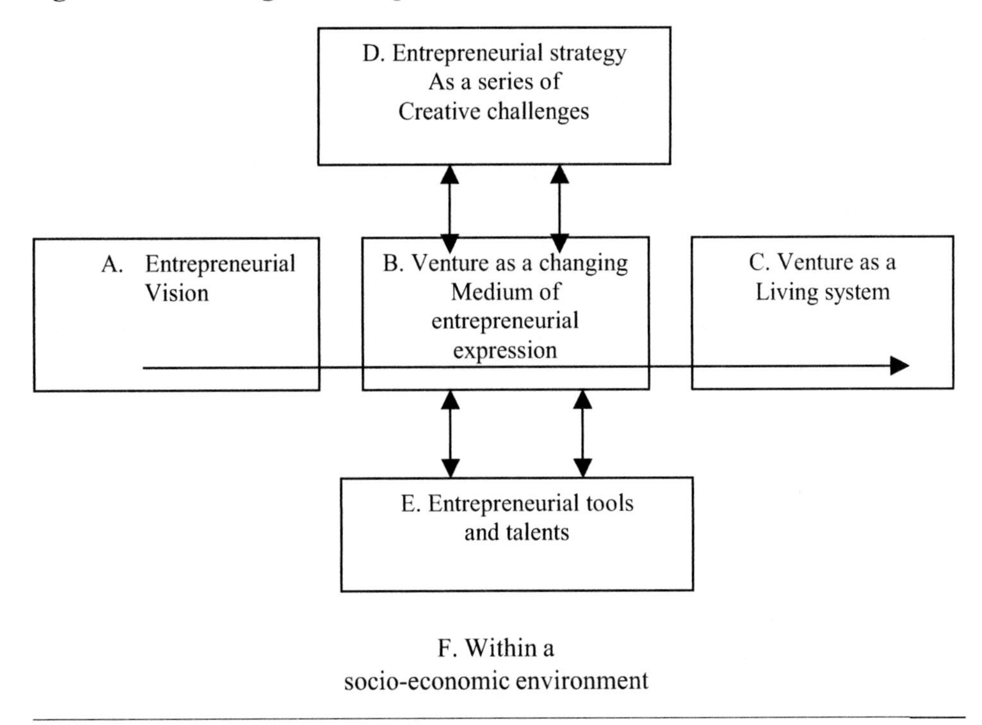

Adapted from McMullan and Long, 1990, p.135.

we review the strategic entrepreneurial challenges, it is important to recognize that (1) their ordering is logically intuitive, (2) each independent strategic decision makes a structural contribution to the business venture, (3) structural components are dynamic and may be revisited, and (4) each decision will build on those made previously and will affect those to come.

To summarize, Figure 1 illustrates the entrepreneurship process, which begins with a vision (A) of a business opportunity. Once a commitment is made to pursue the vision, the entrepreneur undertakes to build a self-sustaining living system (business venture) (C). The venture takes shape (B) as each strategic challenge (D) is addressed. The necessary tools and talents (E) are brought to the venture by the entrepreneur, through the commitment of members, and may in part be acquired from independent consultants, mentors, etc. All of this takes place within and is influenced by a particular socio-economic environment (F).

In Table 3, the ten strategic entrepreneurial challenges are restated in question form, and grouped into four broad categories. The first group of three challenges is preparatory and typically precedes the venture's launch. Second are those challenges that characterize the venture launch and search for market success and operational understanding. Some refer to this phase as the search for survival. Third are the critical challenges facing the venture's successful growth. Finally, the fourth is labelled "exiting," meaning the attributes of a living system are in place, including the capability for ongoing innovation. Exit does not imply the entrepreneur should leave the venture; rather, it suggests the entrepreneurial act is complete and he/she may comfortably leave the venture with reasonable assurance of its continued survival and growth. Each broad grouping of challenges is briefly discussed below. It is important that IS researchers and consultants recognize the context of subject businesses. This discussion presents only abstract direction IS researchers might refer to in developing a contextual map.

It is also important to note that only a small proportion of the multitude of small businesses go beyond being "small to medium-size"; a large proportion of businesses do not survive beyond the first generation entrepreneur.

Preparing the Venture

The first three challenges are preparatory and involve (1) identifying and assessing the opportunity, (2) designing the product service offering, and (3) planning for the resources necessary to actually operate the business. Which markets to serve with what product/service package and with what business competencies and structure are the major issues to be resolved. It behooves the entrepreneur to become fully knowledgeable of the industry: its practices, competitors, and markets. Planning skills are needed to articulate resource requirements and launch strategies. The entrepreneur may take advantage of the available

Table 3: Evolving Entrepreneurial Challenges

Grouping	Entrepreneurial Challenges
Preparing	1. What business will we be in 2. What products/services will we manufacture and sell 3. What is our operating strategy
Launching	4. What resources will we employ 5. How will we produce 6. How will we sell and distribute our products
Growing	7. How will operating efficiencies be improved 8. How will we expand 9. How and when will we professionalize management
Exiting	10. How will we continue to innovate

Adapted from McMullan and Long, 1990, Chapters 5 and 7.

business plan software as well as many archival and real-time sources of market, supply and competitive information.

Launching the Venture

The next three challenges relate to (1) negotiating and acquiring the necessary financial and human resources to implement the launch strategy. It is of course critical to get customer commitment, and (2) to set up production at an appropriate scale, (3) accompanied by effective distribution. Once sales begin generating cash flow it is also critical to establish and implement adequate financial controls and mechanisms to ensure the launch is progressing within plan tolerances. The emerging firm will be faced with monitoring and assuring sufficient cash flow to accommodate growing product/service demand while learning the rudiments of operational activities. The chequebook is no longer adequate financial control and visually scanning inventories will soon require at least a rudimentary inventory control system.

Growing the Venture

In a sense, the venture is now an operating prototype or small business. Whether the entrepreneur intends growth or wishes to remain small will nevertheless require that he/she attend to (1) standardizing operations to achieve certain efficiencies and to facilitate responding to environmental change. If growth is the objective, then these systems should be designed with (2) expansion strategies in mind. Growth will necessitate structuring in (3) additional levels of management, adding complexities to operating and strategic controls. As management is professionalized, information system needs will become increasingly complex. Control will move from face-to-face to performance-based. It will become more difficult to ensure the growing venture retains the entrepreneur's vision without consciously attending to the culture and building communication and feedback mechanisms. The linkages with customers and the distribution network must be tightly aligned and maintained. Formal information systems will be needed to replace what was daily face-to-face contact among members of the small firm team. Management development programs should be integrated with performance controls.

In short, the entrepreneur must be prepared for rapid growth and increasing leadership demands for leadership skills.

Exiting from the Venture

In order to ensure growth potential, the entrepreneur needs to ensure the capacity to innovate is built into the venture. Effective new product development and broader research and development capacity will help to ensure continuance of the firm. The organization now exists as a professionally managed living system and the process of entrepreneurship as such is complete. The organization will now be capable of ongoing entrepreneurial behaviour as a self-sustaining living system, able to continually revisit and address the appropriateness of its structural configuration to profitably satisfy market needs and the goals of the firm. A number of alternatives exist for the founding entrepreneur, from continued active involvement to complete liquidation of the venture. No matter what direction is taken, it is important to develop a succession plan with sufficient lead-time to accommodate a smooth withdrawal of the entrepreneur at the appropriate time.

CONCLUSION

This document has presented the suggestion that IS researchers consider the Theory of Entrepreneurship as a framework to adopt when investigating small businesses. Much of the existing research into the use of IS by small businesses adopts a perspective more appropriate to, and in some cases based upon, large businesses. There is not sufficient consideration for the uniqueness of small business. Where these unique factors are considered, the investigation is conducted as a snapshot of a static situation. The contention of the proposal described in this document is that small business is both unique and continually evolving. Entrepreneurs engage in a creative act of initiating and growing a business and face different challenges as the entity evolves. It is incumbent upon the small business manager to appropriately employ IS to respond, where necessary, to these challenges. The proposed framework responds to this situation. The further challenge, then, is for researchers to adopt this framework and initiate projects that will further elucidate the understanding of how IS may be employed to support small business.

REFERENCES

Ballantine, J. M., Levy and Powell, P. (1998). Evaluating information systems in small and medium-sized enterprises: Issues and evidence. *European Journal of Information Systems, 7*, 241-251.

Belich, T. J. and Dubinsky, A. J. (1999, Fall). Information processing among exporters: An empirical examination of small firms. *Journal of Marketing Theory and Practice, 7* (4), 45-58.

Bennett, J., Polkinghorne, M., Pearce, J., and Hudson, M. (1999, April). Technology transfer for SMEs. *Engineering Management Journal,* 75-80.

Berman, P. (1997). *Small Business and Entrepreneurship*. Scarborough, Ontario, Canada: Prentice Hall.

Bridge, J. and Peel, M. J. (1999, July-September). A study of computer usage and strategic planning in the SME sector. *International Small Business Journal, 17* (4), 82-87.

Burgess, S. and Trethowan, P. (2002). GP's and their Web sites in Australia: doctors as small businesses. *Proceedings of ISOneWorld Conference.* Las Vegas, NV.

Canadian Federation of Independent Business. (1999). Results of members' opinion surveys #37-42. http://www.cfib.ca/research/98internet.asp.

Chapman, P., James-Moore, M., Szczygiel, M., and Thompson, D. (2000). Building Internet capabilities in SMEs. *Logistics Information Management, 13* (6).

Coghlan, D. (2001, Spring). An intervals perspective of OD in IT enabled change. *Organizational Development Journal, 19* (1), 49-56.

Cragg, P. and King, M. (1993). Small-firm computing: Motivators and inhibitors. *MIS Quarterly,* 47-60.

Damsgaard, J. and Lyytinen, K. (1998). Contours of diffusion of electronic data interchange in Finland: Overcoming technological barriers and collaborating to make it happen. *Journal of Strategic Information Systems, 7,* 275-297.

Dandrige, T. and Levenburg, N. M. (2000, January-March). High-tech potential? An exploratory study of very small firms' usage of the Internet. *International Small Business Journal, 18* (2), 81-91.

El Louadi, M. (1998). The relationship among organizational structure, information technology and information processing in small Canadian firms. *Canadian Journal of Administrative Sciences, 15* (2), 180-199.

European Parliament. (2002, July 6). www.europarl.eu.int/dg4/factsheets/en/4_14_0.htm.

Fuller, T. (1996). Fulfilling IT needs in small businesses: A recursive learning model. *International Journal of Small Business, 14* (4), 25-44.

Hunter, Gordon, M., Diochon, M., Pugsley, D., and Wright, B. (2002). Unique challenges for small business adoption of information technology: The case of the Nova Scotia Ten. In S. Burgess, (ed.), *Managing Information Technology in Small Business: Challenges and Solutions,* (ch. 6). Hershey, PA: Idea Group Publishing.

Iacovou, C., Benbasat, I., and Dexter, A. (1995). Electronic data interchange and small organizations: Adoption and impact of technology. *MIS Quarterly, 19* (4), 465-485.

Industry Canada. (1997). *Your guide to government of Canada services and support for small business: Trends and statistics* (Catalogue No. C1-10/ 1997E). Ottawa: Canadian Government Publishing Centre.

Kuan, K. and Chau, P. (2001). A perception-based model for EDI adoption in small businesses using a technology-organized environment framework. *Information and Management, 38,* 507-521.

Lin, B., Vassar, J. and Clack, L. (1993). Information technology strategies for small business. *Journal of Applied Business Research, 9* (2), 25-29.

Long, W. A. (1983, Fall). The meaning of entrepreneurship. *American Journal of Small Business, 8* (2), 47-56.

Long, W. A. and McMullan, W. E. (1984). Mapping the opportunity identification process. In J. A. Hornaday et al. (eds.), *Frontiers of Entrepreneurship Research.* Wellesley, MA: Babson College.

Longnecker, J., Moore, C., and Petty, J. (1997). Small business management. Cincinnati: South-Western College Printing.

McMullan, W. E. and Long, W.A. (1987, Summer). Entrepreneurship education in the nineties. *Journal of Business Venturing,* 261-275.

McMullan, W. E. and Long, W.A. (1990). *Developing New Ventures: The Entrepreneurial Option.* San Diego: Harcourt Brace Jovanovich.

Nickell, G. and Seado, P. (1986). The impact of attitudes and experiences on small business computer use. *American Journal of Small Business, 10* (1), 37-48.

Pollard, C. and Hayne, S. (1998). The changing faces of information systems issues in small firms. *International Small Business Journal, 16* (3), 70-87.

Stevenson, H. H. (1984). A new paradigm for entrepreneurial management. In *Proceedings from the 7th Anniversary Symposium on Entrepreneurship.* Boston, MA: Harvard Business School.

Stevenson, H. H. (1999). A perspective of entrepreneurship. In H. H. Stevenson, H. I. Grousebeck, M. J. Roberts and A. Bhide (eds.), *New Business Ventures and the Entrepreneur* (pp. 3-17). Boston: Irwin McGraw-Hill.

Storey, D. J. (1994). *Understanding the Small Business Sector.* London: Routledge.

Taylor, J. (1999). Fitting enterprise software in smaller companies. *Management Accounting, 80* (8), 36-39.

Thong, J., Yap, C. and Raman, K. (1994). Engagement of external expertise in information systems implementation. *Journal of Management Information Systems, 11* (2), 209-223.

Timmons, J. A. (1999). *New Venture Creation* (5th ed.). Boston, MA: Irwin McGraw-Hill.

Chapter II

Optimal Purchase Decision Criteria for Information Technology

P. Pete Chong
University of Houston-Downtown, USA

Ta-Tao Chuang
Gonzaga University, USA

Ming Chang
University of Houston-Downtown, USA

Jason C. H. Chen
Gonzaga University, USA

ABSTRACT

With the amount of resources dedicated to information technology (IT) expenditure today, we need to have a systematic way for assessing the elusive benefit of all IT purchases. This chapter proposes a modified Factor Rating approach that separates the subjective benefit assessment from objective cost-benefit analysis. Using this method, we often discover that for most users, due to the advancement of computer technology, the cheapest computer may be the optimal computer in the market today.

INTRODUCTION

Knowing the importance of information technology (IT) to productivity, companies and individuals alike have invested heftily in technology, causing IT expenditures in the United States to grow phenomenally. In the fourth quarter of 1999 alone, in the US, PC makers shipped 12.6 million units (Hamilton, 2000). However, the annual comparison shows that the growth of Personal Computer (PC) sales has slowed down to *only* 19%. How were these purchasing decisions made? Even if the process is improved only marginally, the public can realize tremendous gains.

A few years ago, computer trade journals would invariably recommend that consumers purchase the latest technology (Kirkpatrick, 1998; O'Malley, 1999). Even though the state-of-the-art technology demanded a premium price over lesser choices, as a proportion to the cost of the entire system that difference was relatively small at that time. However, the tide has shifted since then. On one hand, hardware technology has advanced so much that consumers begin to realize that they may be buying too much product for what they really need, resulting in wasted resources. On the other hand, prices of hardware have fallen at an increasing rate over the years, which prompts trade journals to recommend delaying purchases for as long as possible. Manufacturers also recognize the need for targeting "general" users. Intel, for example, sees that most PC users do not care how fast their graphics cards are and proceeds to integrate 3D graphics to its 810E chip set instead of using the discrete 3-D chips that have better performance (Gwennap, 1999).

As an example of the premium price attached to "state-of-the-art" technology, Intel's own testing shows that when it comes to running most office-type programs there is little performance difference between the Pentium II and III, but the newer chips command hundreds of dollars more (O'Malley, 1999). Thus, even during the times of pursuing the state-of-the-art technology, acquiring "middle-of-the-road" equipment has been one of the IT manager's purchasing strategies. This approach is based on the reasoning that while at the highest end consumers have to pay dearly for that little additional benefit, at the low end products may not have the quality to meet the consumer needs. Frequently, 80% of the benefit can be achieved with the first 20% of spending in the price spectrum.

One of the difficulties in selecting a computer system is to wade through the sheer number of choices that are available in the market. Besides large PC manufacturers such as IBM, Dell, HP/Compaq, and Gateway, numerous small companies also have a strong presence to the public consumers. Since component technology has allowed PCs to be "assembled" rather than massively "manufactured" (Williams, 1997), each company uses a wide variety of components to assemble their products; and the permutations make product comparisons more difficult. While consumers in general benefit from the increased flexibility, higher quality, and lower cost, the confusing array of available products makes it difficult to determine the product that would give the biggest bang for the buck.

Another problem with this kind of evaluation is the question of proper assessment of cost and benefit. Ignoring all intangible costs for the time being, costs of equipment purchasing can be defined by what the vendor charges. However, benefits are usually in the eyes of beholder. Consumers and IT managers alike often rely on product reviews of trade journals to determine the "best" products for them. Unfortunately, the so-called editor's choices often reflect the editor's personal needs and preferences and may not be the best fit for the purchaser's unique environment. Given the close ties between magazines and their advertisers, consumers also need to be aware of the amount of "plugging" for the advertiser that may take place.

Focused on alleviating these two problems, in this article we will use PC purchasing as an example to illustrate an evaluation process that can help purchasers identify the optimal IT products for their unique needs.

METHODS FOR EVALUATING IT INVESTMENT

Due to the importance and complexity of the decision, many methods have been used to evaluate IT investment alternatives. Some methods place emphasis on the cost-benefit analysis, using mainly return on investment, discounted cash flow, or added economic value as metrics. Typical examples include Expanded Net Present Value (Scarso, 1996) and Economic Value Added (EVA) (Mills, Rowbotham, and Robertson, 1998; Stewart, 1991). More recently, methods based on real option theory have been suggested to take into consideration important features of IT projects, such as flexibility and irreversibility of IT investments (Benaroch and Kauffman, 1999; Kim and Sanders, 2002; Li and Johnson, 2002).

Other methods address the limitations of human information-processing capability in making complex decisions. The underlying strategy is to "divide and conquer" the complexity of the problems – that is, reduce the complexity by dividing problems down to non-confounding characteristics so each characteristic can be tackled individually. This approach can be found in Fisher's separation theorem (Copeland and Weston, 1983; Harvey, 1997; Martin, Cox, and MacMinn, 1988) in Finance. It breaks down an investment decision to that of risk (individuals' subjective preferences) and return (objective market criterion). An important implication here, then, is that the objective part of investment decisions can be delegated to managers, and the investor's individual preferences can still be considered.

Several methods based on the "divide and conquer" strategy have also been used to solve the complex problem of the IT purchasing decision. Examples include the Qualitative Factor Analysis (Brown and Gibson, 1971) and the Analytical Hierarchy Process (AHP) (Saaty, 1994; Arbel and Seidmann, 1984). The AHP is particularly useful in multi-criteria decisions where it is difficult to compare alternatives against multiple criteria and to determine weights for different criteria. The AHP provides a systematic approach to assigning weights to criteria by algorithmically calculating scales resulting from pair-wise comparison, when the decision-maker has distinctive and consistent preference for different criteria of the decision. There are other weighted analysis methods that can be used that are more direct and easier to use by the general public. The one we will focus on in this paper is the Qualitative Factor Analysis.

Qualitative Factor Analysis (Factor Analysis for short) is used in Operations Management for comparing the desirability of multiple locations on an economic basis, particularly focusing on the relevant costs that vary from one location to another (Heizer and Render, 2001; Monks, 1977). Especially when there are no dominant or clear economic criteria available for quick decision, Factor Analysis injects values into a decision-making structure in a relatively formalized manner. Laudon and Laudon (2001) use a similar approach in making IT implementation decisions. Their scoring model gives alternatives a single score based on the extent to which the alternatives meet selected objectives. For example, a firm must decide among three office automation systems: (1) an IBM AS/400 client/server system with proprietary software, (2) a UNIX-based client server system using an Oracle database, and (3) a Windows NT client/server system using Lotus Notes. Using Laudon's scoring model approach, the development of a comparison for these three systems would include the following steps:

(1) Determine the criteria to be applied to the problem. Establishing criteria that is agreeable to those responsible for decision making is often the most difficult aspect of this approach.
(2) Decision makers should then determine the relative weight of each decision criterion.
(3) Using a 1-to-5 scale (lowest to highest), determine the judgments of decision makers on the relative merits of each criterion for each alternative. For example, a score of 1 for the criterion "cost of the initial purchase" for the AS/400 system indicates that this system will be low in meeting that criterion when compared to the other systems being considered.

Table 1: Laudon and Laudon's Example of System Selections

Criterion	Weight	AS/400		UNIX		Windows NT	
		Scale	Score	Scale	Score	Scale	Score
Percentage of user needs met	0.40	2	0.8	3	1.2	4	1.6
Cost of the initial purchase	0.20	1	0.2	3	0.6	4	0.8
Financing	0.10	1	0.1	3	0.3	4	0.4
Ease of maintenance	0.10	2	0.2	3	0.3	4	0.4
Chances of success	0.20	3	0.6	4	0.8	4	0.8
Final score			1.9		3.2		4.0

Scale: 1 = low; 5 = high

Using the above scoring model in Table 1 as an example, in this case the Windows NT option appears to be the preferred office automation system. It may be necessary to cycle through the scoring model several times, changing criteria and weights to determine how sensitive the outcome is to various changes in criteria (Laudon and Laudon, 2001).

This approach can also be applied to evaluate software solutions. Yerxa (1999) evaluated Netscape Enterprise Server 4.0, Microsoft Internet Information Server 4.0, and Apache Software's Apache Server for *Network Computing*. Using performance, development, configuration, management, platform support, and stability as decision criteria, his results are summarized in Table 2.

Recognizing that different environments have their unique needs, Network Computing has developed a customized Java applet, called Interactive Report Card, on its Web site to allow readers to customize the results. For example, for some Web sites the reliability may be more important than performance, and with

Table 2: Network Computing's Evaluation of Web Servers

Feature	Weight	Netscape Enterprise Server 4.0		Microsoft Internet Information Server 4.0		Apache Software Apache Server 1.3.9	
Performance	0.30	4	1.20	5	1.50	3	0.90
Development	0.20	3.8	0.76	4.2	0.84	4.2	0.84
Configuration	0.15	5	0.75	4	0.60	4	0.60
Management	0.15	4	0.60	5	0.75	4	0.60
Platform support	0.10	5	0.50	2	0.20	5	0.50
Stability	0.10	4	0.40	2	0.20	5	0.50
Final score			4.21		4.09		3.94

Scale: 1 = low; 5 = high

this change the conclusion obviously would be different. These managers then may assign higher weight to reliability instead.

While both models illustrated in this section are helpful to decision makers, they either ignore the cost or include the cost of the system as one of the factors to produce one single value. While one single value makes decision making easier, it masks the interactions of cost and benefit that can be better viewed in a two-dimensional chart. In the next section we will introduce a procedure to incorporate a modified factor rating methodology to evaluate PCs.

A FACTOR RATING APPROACH TO THE PC PURCHASING DECISION

Although features do not equate benefit, features (i.e., computer components) do generate different degrees of benefit for users. Dell Computer Corporation, for example, has effectively implemented a "build-to-order" strategy for computer system purchases. On its Web site, a series of Web pages that identify important computer components and their options provide extensive information so the consumers can "build" systems that cater to their unique needs and pocketbooks.

To apply the factor rating approach to PC purchase, it requires that the purchaser is aware of the potential use of the computer system being considered for purchase and that the relative importance of various components has also been assessed. The factor rating process assumes that the purchaser has a basic knowledge of computer components and is aware of the differences between the various options. Without this knowledge, it will be impossible to assign weights and benefit points in any meaningful way. The value of the factor rating process is that the purchaser is able to selectively assemble a set of computer components based upon an individualized benefit value. For example, for a liberal arts student majoring in English, who uses the computer just for e-mail and running standard word processing and spreadsheet software, an entry level PC will be sufficient. On the other hand, an MIS student will require a faster computer to do homework.

Our proposed process includes the following steps:

(1) Assign weight to each component of the system according to the perceived importance by the purchaser. The sum of all the individual weights should be 100(%).

(2) Assign benefit points, ranging from 0 to 100, for each alternative presented in each component category. It is acceptable for multiple alternatives to receive the same benefit points.

(3) Calculate the weighted average for benefit scores.

(4) Use the price of the system as the cost and the result in (3) as the benefit and construct a cost-benefit chart.

Thus, unlike the traditional factor analysis, this approach includes the price as a separate criterion and allows us to create a two-dimensional chart for cost-benefit analysis. We will use a limited system that contains only CPU, RAM, hard drive, and monitor for a simplified demonstration. We will evaluate three computer systems listed below:

- System 1: Athlon 1.2 GHz CPU, 128 MB RAM, 40 GB hard disk, and 19" monitor. Cost: $1,700.
- System 2: Athlon 1 GHz CPU, 128 MB RAM, 30 GB hard disk, and 17" monitor. Cost: $1,200.
- System 3: Athlon 800 MHz CPU, 64 MB RAM, 20 GB hard disk, and 15" monitor. Cost: $900.

Suppose we are purchasing for business school students who live in dorms, we first need to know how these students use their computers. It will be necessary to conduct interviews or surveys to determine the usage patterns and the perceived importance for each component and any alternatives. For example, business students usually do not need a lot of processing power, and the small dorm rooms may render larger monitors a nuisance rather than help. On the other hand, given the fact that many college students today download music and programs from the Internet, a larger hard drive may be desirable. After taking all these observations into consideration, we may assign weight and benefit posts to components and their alternatives. A possible scenario of weight and benefit assignment is shown in Table 3. Once this is done, we can find the weighted benefit scores for all three systems (Table 3).

Note that the most expensive features may not receive the highest benefit scores, and a "lesser" alternative may have equal or even higher benefit to a user. For example, even the best of the soundcards may score a zero if the computer is purchased for a computer lab where no speakers or earphones are allowed.

OPTIMAL PURCHASING DECISION ANALYSIS

The result in Table 3 can be analyzed in many ways. We will only look at the total benefit point, the cost per benefit point, and graphical analysis here. Depending on the level of sophistication needed, decision makers may devise other means that are deemed useful. The importance is that a relatively subjective decision is now quantified, and many quantitative tools may be applied to make the final decision.

Table 3: Prospective PC Systems

Components and Alternatives	Weight	Benefit Points	System 1	System 2	System3
CPU	35%				
Athlon 1.2 GHz		100	35.0		
Athlon 1 GHz		100		35.0	
Athlon 800 MHz		90			27.5
RAM	10%				
256 MB		100	10.0	10.0	
128 MB		80			8.0
Hard Disk	30%				
40 GB		100	30.0		
30 GB		100		30.0	
20 GB		90			27.0
Monitor	25%				
19"		70	17.5		
17"		100		25.0	
15"		80			20.0
Weighted Benefit Points			92.5	100.0	82.5
Price			$1700.00	$1200.00	$950.00
Cost per Benefit Point			$18.38	$12.00	$11.52

These three methods are discussed below, with a special elaboration on the graphical analysis in Section 5.

Total Benefit Points

The result shows that System 1, even with its more advanced features, did not receive the highest benefit points. System 2 will be the choice, with its total of 100 benefit points. Supposing there is a tie in the total benefit score, the less costly one will be the choice. Since this method places emphasis on individual needs, it should not be a surprise that two different individuals will have different results as to what the "best" system is. When money is not the primary concern, this approach should yield the most satisfying result.

Cost Per Benefit Point

This figure is obtained by dividing the cost of the system by the total benefit points. From our example, System 3 actually wins out at $11.52 because of its much lower total cost. We can take one step further and look at the incremental cost per benefit point to improve our decision. For example, a decision maker may decide that the incremental 48 cents per point is worth the moving up to System 2 instead. These data provide a starting point for the decision-making process, and decision makers can always take other attributes into consideration.

From another angle, the inverse of this cost per benefit point measurement is the number of benefit points per dollar, and some may find it more fitting under certain circumstances. However, please note that in our example hidden costs such as training and user comfort to the brand are not taken into consideration. Again, it will be important to note any "overriding factors" when using this method. However, from experience, when these numbers are obtained and consumers are faced with decisions at this point, they tend to notice other factors they previous ignored, thus improve their final purchasing decisions.

Graphical Analysis

If the number of systems to be considered is large, an x-y chart will be extremely useful. By using price for the x-axis and benefit points for the y-axis, we can develop a benefit-cost diagram. Fundamentally, we will be looking at the northwest corner (highest benefit with the lowest cost) for our better choices. A more elaborative analysis of this method will be given in the next section.

PARETO CHART ANALYSIS

A Pareto diagram is a special type of vertical bar chart in which categorized responses are plotted in descending rank order of their frequencies and combined with a cumulative polygon on the same scale. The main principle supporting this graphical device is the ability to separate the "vital few" from the "trivial many," enabling us to focus on the most important responses (Chen, Chong, and Tong, 1994). The Pareto diagram is widely used in the statistical control of process and product quality (Berenson, 1999). Studies on the Pareto Principle (80% of wealth is owned by 20% of people) use a modified Pareto Curve that aggregates items of the same number of usage into subgroups and then shows only the subtotal of that group (Chen, Chong, and Tong, 1994). For example, using the data from http://www.xtechnology.com, it shows the pricing of AMD's Athlon CPU chips, ranging from 800 MHz to 1.1 GHz. Using Excel to generate an x-y-chart based on these data and we can visualize the Pareto curve in Figure 1. It is easy to see that the beginning section of the curve indicates that the benefit rises faster than the cost, supporting the notion that **80% of benefit comes from the first 20% of expenditures**. A similar chart created about two months earlier showed a much shorter linear section, implying that chips with higher speed demanded a premium back then. However, this elongated linear section implies that perhaps due to intensive competition, at present time consumers may choose a faster system without having to pay undue higher prices for performance they may not need.

Cost-benefit analysis includes a systematic categorization of impacts as benefits and costs, valuing in dollars for assigning weights. Of course, the valuation of cost and benefit is only an operational definition in our assessment. Based on the result, we may make a final decision based on the net benefits of each alternative (Boardman, Greenberg, Vining, and Weimer, 1996). We may apply the Pareto Principle to the cost-benefit analysis and state that if the full price reflects the full benefit, then there is a small fraction of expenditure that represents the major portion of benefit. In other words, 80% of the total benefit is realized in the first 20% of cost. The mission then, is to identify this optimal point. Recall that in microeconomics, to maximize total profit, the optimal production level is where marginal revenue equals marginal cost (MR=MC) (Samuelson, 1976). Thus, we should choose the alternative that is at the point where marginal benefit equals marginal cost. From our earlier discussion, if we can construct a cost-benefit curve, that should be the point where slope equals 1.

Unfortunately, with our experience of using this system, the x-y chart never yielded a perfect Pareto diagram, partly because a vendor's pricing strategy does not perfectly match the consumer's perception of benefit. However, invariably some systems would bunch around the general area where the slope = 1. There is also an interesting observation that may have a deep implication. If we construct the x-y chart using (0,0) as the origin, it may surprise us that often the new diagram

Figure 1: Pareto Curve for Athlon Chip Pricing

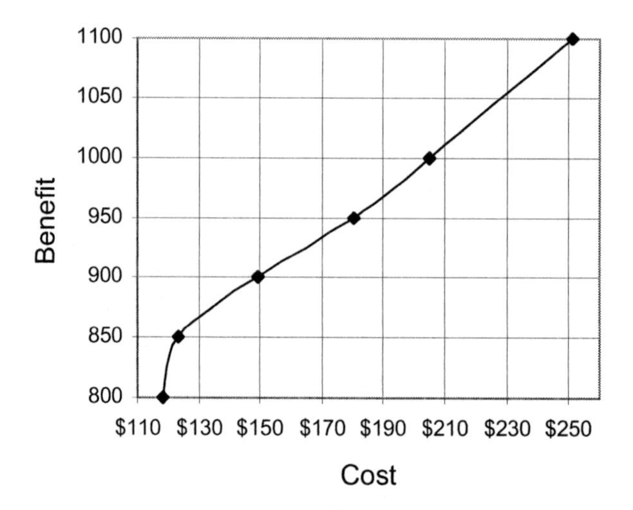

does show a pattern similar to a Pareto chart and indicates that the cheapest computer is the optimal choice today! Intuition tells us that indeed for *most* consumers today, even the cheapest computer has more capability than s/he needs in surfing the Internet and word processing. Given the low cost and the advancement of technology, it may be a good strategy to purchase a cheap computer with the intention of replacing it in two to three years. In other words, treat computer purchasing as an "expense" rather than a "capital investment."

Some may view this conclusion to be a "dangerous" one that may make consumers overlook new features that may improve their productivity. However, this possible conclusion also suggests that in order to fund the rapid IT manufacturers and providers, consumers may have paid (and continue to pay) an exorbitant amount for the excess capacity. In either case, for a variety of reasons, decision makers may feel uncomfortable choosing the "cheapest" computer on the market anyway. This is may be one of the overriding factors we mentioned earlier.

Instead of using the result as a method for finding the "best" or "optimal" product right off the bat, this x-y chart is a very effective tool for eliminating "worst" choices. In other words, the graphical analysis can be effectively used to provide a short list for decision makers. From this short list a purchasing then can apply other methods to come to a decision. However, an enormous amount of time can be saved for the decision maker, since s/he will not have to wade through a myriad of computer choices.

CONCLUSION

Decision makers may further modify this factor-rating approach to IT purchases to fit their special needs. For example, instead of using monitor size as alternatives, we may use three criteria of "best," "good," or "poor," with a collection of brand names and monitor types in each category, thus decreasing the clutter of the table. The advantages of using this optimal purchasing heuristics are described below:

- Separate Subjective from Objective Processes: The assignment of weight and benefit scores is where the expertise and subjective needs of decision makers are captured. Beyond that, the work can be delegated to assistants to calculate measurements described in Section 3.
- Allows Automation: Any structured decision-making process can be automated. The weight and benefit scores can be incorporated into a spreadsheet to simply calculation.
- Simplify Committee Work: Although they are without formal quantitative analysis, our experiments with students show that the weight and benefit

scores assigned by a committee is relatively close to the averages of those assigned by individual committee members. This result implies a more efficient way to generate "consensus" of a group in making IT purchasing decisions.

Operational definition is used to quantify qualitative attributes, and the Qualitative Factor Rating method has been used to quantify site selection decisions for decades. In this paper we proposed improvements that (1) separate cost from benefit quantification to allow a two dimensional graphical analysis, specifically to allow the application of Pareto Principle, and (2) separate the subjective view of "benefit" from a relatively objective "cost" in order to allow at least part of process to be delegated to assistants.

REFERENCES

Arbel, A. and Seidmann, A. (1984). Selecting a microcomputer for process control and data acquisition. *IIE Transactions*, 16 (1), 73-80.

Benaroch, M. and Kauffman, R. J. (1999). A case for using real options pricing analysis to evaluate information technology project investment. *Information Systems Research*, 10 (1), 70-86.

Berenson, M. L. and Levin, D. M. (1999). *Basic Business Statistics: Concepts and Applications* (7th ed.). Englewood, NJ: Prentice Hall.

Boardman, A. E., Greenberg, D. H., Vining, A. R., and Weimer, D. L. (1996). *Cost-Benefit Analysis: Concepts and Practice*. Englewood, NJ: Prentice Hall, 1-2.

Brown and Gibson. (1972). A quantified model for facility site selection: application to a multiplant location problem. *AIIIE Transaction*, 4 (1), 1-10.

Chen, Y.S., Chong, P., and Tong, M. Y. (1994). Mathematical and computer modeling of the Pareto Principle. *Mathematical and Computer Modelling*, 19(9), 61-80.

Copeland, T. E. and Weston, J. F. (1983). *Financial Theory and Corporate Policy*. Reading, MA: Addison-Wesley.

Gwennap, L. (1999). *Intel commoditizes 3D graphics*. Microprocessor Report, 13 (13). url: www.mdronline.com/q/@19942947llcbxn/mpr/editorials/edit13_13.html.

Hamilton, D. (2000, January 24). PC-growth slowed in fourth period. *The Wall Street Journal*, p. B8.

Harvey, C. R., Professor of Finance, Fuqua School of Business at Duke University. (1997). Yahoo Financial Glossary. Retrieved August 10, 1999 from the

World Wide Web: http://www.duke.edu/~charvey/Classes/wpg/bfglosp.htm#portfolio_separation_theorem.

Heizer, J. and Render, B. (2001). *Operations Management* (6th ed.).

Kim, Y.J. and Sanders, G.L. (2002). Strategic actions in information technology investment based on real option theory. *Decision Support Systems*, 33 (1), 1-11.

Kirkpatrick, K. (1998, October). Making sub-$1,000 PCs isn't easy. *ComputerShopper*, 114-115.

Laudon, K. C. & Laudon, J. P. (2001). *Essentials of Management Information Systems: Transforming Business and Management* (3rd ed.). Englewood, NJ: Prentice-Hall.

Li, X. and Johnson, J.D. (2002). Evaluate IT investment opportunities using real options theory. *Information Resource Management Journal*, 15 (3), 32-47.

Martin, J. D., Cox, S. H., and MacMinn, R. D. (1988). *The Theory of Finance: Evidence and Applications.* Dryden.

Mills, R., Rowbotham, S., and Robertson, J. (1998). Using economic profit in assessing business performance. *Management Accounting,* London, 76 (10), 34-38.

Monks, J. G. (1977). *Operations Management: Theory and Problems*. New York: McGraw-Hill.

O'Malley, C. (1999, April). 500 MHz Marvels. *Popular Science*, 64-69.

Saaty, T.L. (1994). How to make a decision: The analytic hierarchy process. *Interface*, 24 (6), 19-43.

Samuelson, P. A. (1976). *Economics* (10th ed.). New York: McGraw-Hill.

Scarso, E. (1996). Timing the adoption of a new technology: An option-based approach. *Management Decision*, 34 (3), 41-48.

Steward, G.B., III. (1991). *The Quest for Value*. New York: Harper Collins.

Williams, J. (1997). *An Introduction to Computing Infrastructure: Hardware and Operating Systems.* Que E&T.

Yerxa, G. (1999, October 4). The Best Bets for Web Development. *Network Computing*, 32-46.

Chapter III

Creating Intranets for Management and Collaboration in Federal Agencies

Julianne G. Mahler
George Mason University, USA

Priscilla M. Regan
George Mason University, USA

ABSTRACT

This chapter briefly examines government interest in intranets, describes the experiences of six federal government agencies in developing agency-wide intranets, and identifies and analyzes trends in intranet use, sources of growth, and impediments to further development. The six agencies are: the Department of Transportation, the Department of Housing and Urban Development, the Environmental Protection Agency, the General Services Administration, the Department of Commerce, and the Department of Justice. The case studies reveal six overall trends in intranet use and development including the importance of upper management support in planning and launching and the importance of marketing in ensuring staff use. The authors conclude that intranets offer more potential for enhancing communication and management and that further development of intranets is likely.

INTRODUCTION

While e-government initiatives have focused on effective linkages between government agencies and their citizens or government agencies and businesses, there is growing interest in intranets connecting government with its employees. Intranets are typically newer applications than Internet Web sites, emerging in the early to mid 1990s in the private sector and, based on our respondents' accounts, mainly after 1997 among federal government agencies. Intranets are Web sites within government agencies that connect the agency administration to its employees and the employees to each other. In large multi-agency departments such as the Department of Transportation, intranets may be nested so that department-wide intranets and program-specific Web sites operate simultaneously.

These intranets make it possible for agency managers to enhance information resources for employees, make opportunities for employees to communicate more freely, and create online work groups through intranet collaboration. Information in bulky and expensive directories and manuals of policies and procedures can be provided in a more convenient, easy-to-find, and timely way in an internal Web network. Intranets make it possible for employers to communicate quickly and efficiently, and to save time and money in the dissemination of news and policy changes. Intranets may principally be portals linking employees to static information resources or they may include interactive elements that provide human resources services, such as the Employee Express payroll contract service. Some offer chat rooms or group works where employees can communicate outside of formal channels, air grievances, and seek solutions.

While the promise of intranets is great, little data has been collected to determine the state of intranet development. The purpose of our research is to describe intranet development in the federal government and to identify and analyze trends in use, sources of growth, and impediments to development. This research was funded by PriceWaterhouseCoopers and further elaboration and discussion of these findings can be found in *Federal Intranet Work Sites: An Interim Assessment* (Mahler & Regan, 2002).

The growing interest in intranets is spurred by their usefulness as management tools to foster productive communication and coordination, manage information, and encourage self-organizing work teams. Business-to-employee (B2E) intranets are developing rapidly because of their advantages in optimizing strategic communications. Allcorn (1997) identifies the "parallel virtual organization" composed of an intranet and organizational databases as the information and knowledge management model for the future. Curry and Stancich (2000) describe the advantages of the intranet for strategic decision-making. Southwest Airlines is cited by GAO as an exemplar of the uses of intranets for informal communication among members at dispersed work sites, which develops a culture of teamwork and pride (GAO/GGD-00-28). Many have noted the use of intranets for speeding and personalizing human resources functions in organizations (Holz, 1997). GAO reports how intranets can be used to foster human capital development in private firms that can serve as models for government (GAO/GGD-00-28). For example, at Federal Express, senior managers apply an automated intranet-based tool to assess leadership skills, potential, and development needs of mid-level managers so that new assignments and promotions can be made quickly and effectively.

Moon (2002) identifies intranets as a central part of e-government efforts in municipal governments, where they have been applied most often to human resources functions. He estimates that over half of the 85% of local governments with Web sites also had employee intranets of varying sophistication. Local governments are using intranets to support direct citizen services, from licenses and tax payments, to providing utility and planning maps (Isaacs, 2001). Intranets enable information sharing and collaboration across structural and geographical boundaries (Sheepers & Rose, 2001), and in doing so support significant government reinvention without massive reorganization (Ho, 2002).

A number of federal agencies have also reported plans to develop intranets, but the extent of the content and the level of actual use in agencies vary widely. For example, intranets are central to the IRS reform efforts by providing a communications strategy for informing staff about changes in tax law and policy and procedures, and for improving agency-wide communication (GAO/GGD-00-85200). The National Resources Center, the IRS's intranet Web site, was created in 1998 to serve as a site for centralized guidance on policy and procedures, to provide a way to disseminate answers to employee questions so that all staff would have the same answers, and to provide training. GAO reports successful strategies by Chief Information Officers (CIO) for enhancing agency information and knowledge management (GAO/GAO-01-376G). One example is the use of the agency intranet to make press clippings available to staff—a significant improvement in speed and cost from traditional methods. In the Veterans Health Administration, intranet access to performance information, such as patient satisfaction data, is used to encourage improvement (GAO/GAO-01-376G).

RESEARCH QUESTIONS AND HYPOTHESES

Based on the development of intranets and e-government solutions in the federal government, we expected to find a range of intranet designs and purposes from simple newscasts to sophisticated portals linking members to sites for human resources needs, travel planning, training, and self-designed collaborative linkages.

We found a narrower range of designs than expected. The reasons for this and other patterns in the development of the intranets emerge from the individual case studies.

We interviewed several individuals in six departments. We began to identify these agencies and the offices and actors within them from leads provided by the Chief Information Officer's Council, its e-Government Committee, and its Intranet Roundtable. Additional contacts were recommended by these actors. Our rationale for case selection was that we wanted to optimize our chances of finding the most advanced examples rather than a representative sample of all stages of intranet development. Case studies of agencies with little intranet experience would not have as much to tell us about its potential or use. The emerging vision of intranets as key management tools is more easily observed in agencies that are more advanced in their exploration of uses and limitations.

We posed questions about the current state of agency intranets, their origins, and major changes to the site. In several cases we were able to document the design of sites at different stages of development. We questioned actors about the original purposes and motivations behind intranet creation. We tried to determine what pressures within the federal setting might encourage intranets. We also probed the sources and level of resources. The composition and mission definition of the intranet development teams were investigated. We also became aware, as research progressed, of the need for agencies to encourage intranet recognition and usage, and so we came to collect stories about how the intranet was marketed to agency staff. Finally, we investigated other factors that appear to have encouraged or impeded intranet development.

CASE STUDIES

Department of Transportation

When the DOT's department-wide intranet was first created in 2000, there were already active intranets in the department's 11 operating divisions, including the Coast Guard, the Federal Aviation Administration and the Federal Highway Administration. In fact, one of the principal reasons for the top-level support of the project was to encourage the development of a more unified organizational culture across the department as a whole. To create appealing and useful functions for the new intranet, designers sought cross-cutting tasks not already included in the divisional intranets. The new intranet offered several communications opportunities including e-mail and chat rooms. Links were available to breaking news, news clippings, sites for information about the organization and its budget, performance measurement databases, the employee directory, the calendar, and human resources information. The intranet linked employees to the agency library and to many other online works and government documents. The newest iteration allows employees to create their own home pages from a selection of administrative tools.

A particularly important innovation in the DOT intranet is the ability of employees to create online work groups around topics of interest or concern to themselves, within or across divisions. The procedures for creating groups are extremely flexible so that open forums or private sessions are possible. Groups that begin as problem-sharing may evolve to problem-solving. These groups may self-organize around current issues. Documents may be simply uploaded and shared. While no evaluation of the groups has been done, many — large and small — continue to be formed.

One characteristic of the intranet identified as critical to its success by designers are that the managers led the design teams. Managers on the design team worked closely with the technology experts, but the managers led the effort and managers offered the suggestions for the functions to be included. The capacities of the intranet were designed around management priorities rather than technological opportunities, and the applications for communications, home page design, and collaborative work were kept simple and transparent with ordinary language terminology. The success of the intranet and its high level of use were attributed to this choic.

Department of Housing and Urban Development

The Department of Housing and Urban Development (HUD) first launched its intranet in November 1996. Since then there have been four subsequent iterations; the first four were named "HUDweb" and the most recent revision in 2001 was renamed hud@work. The genesis for the intranet came from management concerns about communication breakdowns and technical teams that believed online computer functions could facilitate internal communications. The idea was that HUD could "work smarter, not harder, without paper." HUD leadership at the Secretary level supported the intranet as it responded to both internal problems and to the Clinton administration initiative on the information superhighway.

Three factors were critical in spurring the growth of the intranet in HUD. First were a series of external events that challenged HUD's viability. Shortly after the launch of the second HUDweb, Congress proposed abolishing HUD, and Secretary Cisneros used the intranet as a means to communicate with staff. This brought employees to the intranet on a more routine basis. Second were agency decisions to make certain kinds of information available only on the intranet. When the Office of Personnel stopped printing vacancy announcements and posted them only on the intranet, there was a dramatic increase in intranet use. The third factor was marketing of the intranet. The launch of each new intranet was accompanied by a campaign to inform employees about the innovations and to encourage them to use the intranet. Slogans such as "smart HUD employees work online" and the intranet is a "tool, not a toy" were typical of these promotions.

Four items appear on the HUD intranet home page: a daily message from the Secretary, today's feature, employee highlights, including personnel announcements and an employee locator, and a "what's new" feature, which includes personnel rule announcements and policy statements. The current iteration of hud@work has a customization feature by which employees can design the layout and some of the content of their intranet homepage. It also has virtual team technology, which allows staff to exchange files, engage in real-time chat, teleconference, and set up meetings.

Environmental Protection Agency

The Environmental Protection Agency (EPA) introduced its first agency-wide intranet, EPA@work, in 1998. Prior to that, several components of the EPA, including the regional offices, had their own intranets. The goal of the agency-wide intranet was to provide information and functions that were common to all EPA employees. The intranet development team members came from the Office of Information Resources and Management, but had support from upper management in the EPA. The members of the team all had some computer and technical background, but were basically interested in information applications.

EPA employees have consistently used and valued the "EPA intranet locator," by which staff can find contact information for other employees and contractors. Another popular function enables employees to download and print forms and information on travel. Much of the EPA@work content has been facilities-oriented, including activities such as parking, copying, and office cleaning. Links from the EPA@Work front page include organization and locations with charts of headquarters and regional offices, information resources, with calendar and e-mail, and links for comments and help. The EPA intranet offers the capability of work groups, chat rooms, and collaboration, but these have not been used widely because of training requirements, firewalls, and costs.

General Services Administration

The General Service Administration's (GSA) intranet, InSite, was developed in 1996 as a result of an initiative offered by a GSA administrator with private sector dot-com experience. In response to this proposal, the chief information officer worked with a small team to make GSA's computer network Internet and intranet accessible and to develop a vision for a departmental intranet. GSA's intranet was "home-grown," based largely on the experiences of team members in navigating Internet sites.

Key to the success of InSite was having it become a work site, not just a source for documents. The bulletin board feature, "My 2 Cents," was popular and brought employees to the intranet. Travel and human resources links were also well-liked. Basic features, such as a telephone directory, also drew staff to the site. Several links are offered on the InSite home page, including those to the GSA library services, human resources, travel, and the GSA online university. At this time there is no collaborative work space on the intranet, but there are some pilots underway. The GSA agency-wide intranet competes to some extent with subunit intranets that have also developed and draw employees away from the agency-wide intranet.

Department of Commerce

As in the case studies of DOT and the EPA, the intranet at the Department of Commerce (DOC) was created after major divisions within the agency had already established their own intranets. One of those, for the Commercial Service (CS), was created principally to share business process software. This software is used to coordinate business events and make arrangements for trade missions. The integrated intranet was also designed to ease communication and coordination of information among the many CS offices in the U.S. and abroad. One challenge the intranet development has faced has been a lack of funds for the purchase of desired new software. Even when a need is identified, it may not be met. In addition, some of the software that is available requires training, and has not been used as much as had been hoped. As applications become more valued, it is expected that use will increase.

The DOC-wide intranet was created in 1999 by Secretary Daley to enable the DOC to become a "digital department" quickly in response to Clinton administration priorities. The original vision was for interactive functions allowing employees to communicate with each other and to conduct business online. At present, however, the site operates largely as a portal with information links, but few interactive functions. It offers links to a wide variety of departmental documents, policy statements and employee information resources. It was a joint creation by Web technicians and library staff. Resources for the intranet itself, however, lag behind those for the large and relatively well-funded Internet. Synergy between the intranet and the established Internet are seen as a key to good site maintenance and further development.

Department of Justice

The Department of Justice (DOJ) site was created in 1998 in response to the Freedom of Information Act, the Clinger-Cohen Act, and the Clinton administration's requirements for digital government. The new intranet was to provide increased information and communication capability to the department. Like the DOT, the EPA, and the DOC, the DOJ intranet was created well after such well-established divisions as the FBI had developed their own intranets. The site was designed to enhance the communications capacity of the department and to offer news services and policy documents, among other administrative information, but the DOJ intranet partially duplicated the services of the divisional intranets. The department-wide intranet was a spin-off from the DOJ Internet, developed earlier, and is served by the same staff group of Web technicians and library information resource experts —though resources for the intranet are thought to be very limited. The first version of the site was created by outside contractors, but since then the work has been done in-house. Web selections were based on the resources most asked for by clients and on ideas gleaned from the Intranet Roundtable, a meeting of government intranet designers responsible for disseminating many of the innovation ideas described here.

At present, the DOJ intranet site is largely non-interactive and offers links to information on employee resources, news, library links, career development, and technical assistance. Later iterations of the site are expected to be more interactive, enabling actors across the organization to collaborate on litigation, though that will take a major change in system architecture and strain resources. The department hopes the next versions will be more interactive and will attract additional users. Security issues also complicate the development of more sophisticated department-wide sites. There is some reluctance to make the intranet the home page of all department employees because of the very strong identification many have with their divisions.

TRENDS

The case studies reveal six overall trends in intranet use and development.

Within federal agencies, more attention and energy is devoted to the agency's Internet than to its intranet. This is not remarkable given legislative and public support for online government to citizen interactions, the federal government's commitment to digital government, and the number of Internet champions. Despite agencies' focus on the Internet, all agencies are experimenting with transferring Internet technology and software, as well as the knowledge gained from developing and deploying Internet Web sites, to an internal agency intranet.

In the majority of the agencies examined, staff and resources were shared by the Internet and intranet. This was the case in the Departments of Transportation, Justice, and Commerce. Although HUD had a separate staff dedicated to the intranet, the intranet was still considered the Internet's "baby sister." At the EPA the intranet team members were separate from the Internet team, but the EPA intranet's budget was not separate from that of the Internet.

Upper management active support for and interest in the agency's intranet is especially critical in initial planning and launching. In virtually all the agencies examined, support from the Secretary or Deputy Secretary level was essential. An agency-wide intranet would not have developed without this interest and support.

In three of the six agencies examined, support came directly from the Secretary. At HUD, both Secretary Cisneros and Secretary Cuomo were constructive in the development of the intranet and found opportunities to broaden its use. At a GSA information technology meeting in 1996, GSA administrator David Barram proposed that he order GSA to offer employees Internet and intranet access within four months. This proposal resulted in the development of the intranet. Commerce Secretary Daley challenged his department to become a "digital department" within 45 days and he built a consensus for this with a series of town hall meetings.

In two agencies, the Departments of Justice and Transportation, support came from the Deputy Secretary level, primarily from the CIO. At the DOJ, the CIO believed that an agency-wide intranet was needed to provide information and better communication to the department as a whole, as well as to reduce the cost of copying and mailing information throughout the subunits. A subscription to an online news service linked through the agency's intranet replaced the in-house news clipping, copying, and distributing. The CIO in the DOT took the lead in developing an intranet whose goal was to foster a common DOT culture by generating linkages across divisions.

In the EPA, support from the top of the agency was less active and visible than in the other agencies, but was nevertheless vital to the success of the team from the Office of Information Resources and Management, which was delegated to develop the agency-wide intranet.

Marketing of an agency intranet is crucial in encouraging staff use. In some agencies, actual advertising campaigns were developed. In other agencies, events were held to publicize and showcase the intranet. Active promotion was regarded as critical by all agencies.

Three of the six agencies had aggressive marketing campaigns to generate staff interest and use. Marketing of the intranet was important throughout the EPA's developments and deployments. "Intranet Weeks" were held several times and provided the intranet team with an opportunity to do a "dog and pony" show to illustrate the benefits and capabilities of the intranet. In September 2001, with the launch of a new iteration of the intranet, the intranet team designed a "power-up with EPA@Work" campaign using an "Empower Bar" theme to convey the idea that employees can get "vital, up-to-date information" by starting their day with the "new and improved" agency intranet. The campaign involved posters, flyers, and bookmarks with the same slogans and images. HUD also had a concerted marketing campaign to launch each iteration of its intranet. In 1998, HUD held a "Web Awareness Day" in Washington and the regional offices to highlight the message that the intranet was a "tool, not a toy" and to help differentiate HUD's intranet from its Internet site. Again in 2001, when HUD added customization features to the intranet, it was marketed as "HUD's Next Generation Intranet." GSA also aggressively advertised the launching of its intranet on Flag Day in 1996.

Three departments – Transportation, Commerce, and Justice – made more modest attempts at marketing their intranets. For example, the DOC held a town meeting to introduce its intranet in 1999 and followed that with a demonstration in 2000.

In all cases, marketing makes employees aware of the intranet and its possible value for their particular jobs. As employees begin to explore and experiment with the intranet, they tend to rely more on the intranet and to spread the word to other employees.

Agency-wide intranets co-exist with bureau, program and field office intranets. In five of the six agencies examined –DOT, EPA, GSA, DOC, and DOJ– there were smaller bureau, program, or field office intranets that predated the creation of a department-wide intranet. In many cases, employees were routinely using these intranets to conduct their daily work. This was especially true in the Departments of Commerce, Transportation, and Justice. Often, bureau, program, and field office intranets were more sophisticated and better funded and maintained than the agency-wide intranet.

This is evidence of the usefulness of an internal, closed Web site. It may be that there is an optimal size for intranet utility and functionality. In most agencies examined, the agency-wide intranet was eclipsed by sub-agency intranets. It would appear that most of the work of the department occurs in the smaller units and those intranets are more valuable to staff on a day-to-day basis.

These smaller, more focused intranets pose a challenge for the success of an agency-wide intranet. Within all the agencies examined, there was clearly evidence of the usefulness of an internal Web site. To be successful, a department-wide intranet needs to identify a role for itself that will attract employees to the site. The DOT was somewhat successful in doing this by emphasizing the role of the intranet in fostering a common culture within the agency. Similarly, the EPA recognized that it should not duplicate the roles of the divisional and regional intranets but should concentrate on providing information and functions common to all EPA employees. The Department of Justice and GSA appear to be struggling with the role for an agency-wide intranet, especially in light of the strong identity that employees have with their smaller units.

The development of agency-wide intranets is an evolutionary process. Agency personnel responsible for intranets are continually evaluating the effectiveness and use of their intranets and devising ways to improve them. All consider their intranets to be a work in progress and not a finished product. All agencies examined have had several iterations of their intranet. For example, since 1996 HUD has had five different iterations.

To date, intranet applications in some agencies are limited to providing one-way information on fairly mundane agency tasks such as room scheduling and cafeteria menus. But many agencies are adding interactive services such as travel arrangements and personnel record changes. Only a few agencies are developing more interactive managerial uses such as online collaborative work groups and personalized intranet home pages. Security concerns in some cases limit interconnectedness.

As part of this iterative process, several features have been attempted. Chat rooms have been popular in a limited number of agencies. Their use has been more episodic and difficult to sustain. For example, GSA's bulletin board, "My 2 Cents," began as an anonymous, open bulletin board for posting questions and answers, but problems arose as some users did not follow standard conversational norms. Another feature of the evolutionary process has been the customization or personalization of intranets in a few agencies. This feature generally occurs late in the process of intranet development when employees have become used to the intranet and are looking for more innovation. DOT's most recent iteration offers a personalization feature whereby employees can create their own version of the standard home page elements, can establish links to favorite sites, and can include their personal calendar. Development of collaborative or shared work areas is another feature that has evolved in some agencies and is being planned in others. At the DOJ, for example, virtual work groups and collaboration are facilitated through divisional and program intranets where litigation preparation can be shared.

Cost constraints limit the ability of agencies to purchase the applications and the consultant work they would like. In most agencies the development of an agency-wide intranet began as a small-scale pilot project with the active involvement of a few staff. These projects generally had upper-management support and thus received some money, although not a separate budget line that was funded and refunded on a yearly basis. Resources were limited and not predictable. Much of the work of intranet development and refinement was done in-house. This was particularly true in the Departments of Justice, Transportation, and Housing and Urban Development, as well as the Environmental Protection Agency. In all cases, staff experimented with innovations that they had seen on other sites or had heard about through conversations with employees in other agencies or the private sector. Staff reported that they did not always have the funds to purchase new off-the-shelf software or to contract with specialists for development of customized software.

ANALYSIS

Our analysis indicates that there may be several pathways for intranet development, especially at the initial stages. In some agencies, intranets were designed by information technology specialists with little guidance regarding potential management uses. In others, mid-level managers controlled the early formation of intranets. In a few agencies, top-level management supported an intranet because they wanted to appear progressive, but had little understanding of its potential or any particular expectations for its use. In still other agencies, much of the design of an intranet was in the hands of information resource managers. Each of these paths gave rise to different objectives, technologies, and results.

We found that intranet development is most effectively directed by administrative staff and program managers, rather than by technical staff. This ensures that employee desires and organizational needs define intranet functions and applications. When decisions are driven by technical capacity, employees must readjust work habits to suit the new technology, discouraging use. The IRM model creates portal sites with potential for management use, but without the configuration that makes the site useful for coordination and performance feedback — core management concerns. To be utilized and functional, intranet technology should support employee and organizational needs. If management and staff needs drive development, new technical features may be created. Managers can challenge technical people to find appropriate solutions that may spur new technological solutions.

Managers may not always push for innovative uses of intranet technologies, however, especially for the kind of interactive applications that can have the greatest long-term impact on workflow or on collaboration and learning. Several factors may explain such management reluctance. First, managers may first want to gain employee acceptance of the basic intranet and ensure high use rates. Our cases suggest that making highly salient information, such as phone directories and news clippings, available only on the intranet is a good way to do this. Making key announcements on the intranet or using it to make important documents available, such as regulations or agency housekeeping information, all contribute to high use rates. Additionally, these non-interactive uses of the intranet are relatively inexpensive to administer. Interactive functions, on the other hand, may require expensive changes in intranet architecture, another strike against them. The uses and benefits of self-organizing collaborative teams are also harder to imagine.

Another reason behind the absence of interactive features on agency-wide intranets has to do with the federal setting of our study. In most cases department-wide intranets are more recent than and must compete with established divisional or regional intranets. Different solutions are emerging to the problems in communication and culture that these overlapping intranets bring. No one fixed model now appears superior. In some cases the divisional intranets are dominant and host the employee home page with a link to the departmental intranet. In other cases the departmental Web site may dominate. Collaborative work spaces may emerge more naturally at the program or divisional level, where the day-to-day work of the agency takes place than at the departmental level. Our interviews at the DOC, in particular, support this conclusion.

Finally, use of intranets for collaborative work raises issues of workplace surveillance and monitoring. Employees seem to recognize that if they participate in online collaboration and discussion, they will leave behind an electronic trail of comments that managers can monitor and evaluate. Managers thus need to formulate and disseminate clear policies so that employees will know what information will be captured as a result of intranet use, who will have access to that information, for what purposes information will be used, and how long information will be retained.

What prospects are there for removing these roadblocks to fuller use of the intranet's potential for enhancing the information resources in federal agencies? We think they are good. The successful use of intranets to increase workflow and foster collaboration in the private sector and in local governments can serve to model and encourage intranet applications. Institutions such as the CIO Council and its Intranet Roundtable offer a way to spread the news about the potential for more interactive intranet developments in federal agencies. The capacity of intranets to facilitate workflow and encourage collaborative work across organizational boundaries offers real value to agencies struggling to do more.

REFERENCES

Allcorn, S. (1997). Parallel virtual organizations: managing and working in the virtual workplace. *Administration and Society*, 29, 412-439.

Curry, A. and Stancich, L. (2000, August). The intranet—an intrinsic component of strategic information management? *International Journal of Information Management*, 20, 249-268.

GAO. (2000, January 31). *Human Capital: Key Principles From Nine Private Sector Organizations*. (Letter Report, GAO/GGD-00-28).

GAO. (2000, April 21). *Tax Administration: IRS' Implementation of the Restructuring Act's Taxpayer Protection and Rights Provisions*. (Letter Report, GAO/GGD-00-85-00).

GAO. (2001, February 1). *Executive Guide: Maximizing the Success of Chief Information Officers: Learning From Leading Organizations*. (Guidance, GAO/GAO-01-376G).

Ho, A. Tat-Kei. (2002, July/August). Reinventing local governments and the e-government initiative. *Public Administration Review*, 63 (4), 434-444.

Holz, S. (1997, Autumn). Strategizing a human resources presence on the intranet. *Compensation and Benefits Management*, 13, 31-37.

Isaacs, L. (2001, November). The world at your fingertips. *American City and County*, 116 (17), 38- 43.

Letter Report. (2000, April 21). (GAO/GGD-00-85).

Mahler, J. & Regan, P.M. (2002, June). *Federal Intranet Work Sites: An Interim Assessment*. PriceWaterhouseCoopers Endowment for The Business of Government, E-Government Series.

Moon, M. J. (2002, July/August). The evolution of e-government among municipalities: Rhetoric or reality. *Public Administration Review*, 63 (4), 424-433.

Scheepers, R. and Rose, J. (2001). Organizational Internets: cultivating information technology for the people by the people. In Sudhashish Dasgupta (ed.), *Managing Internet and Intranet Technologies in Organizations: Challenges and Opportunities* (pp. 1-20). Hershey, PA: Idea Group Publishing.

Chapter IV

Maintaining the Own Responsibility: Selected Information Systems Architecture, Selective Outsourcing and Organizational Learning as a Base for a Sustainably Positioned Information Technology Service

Ruediger Weissbach
LBS Bausparkasse Hamburg Aktiengesellschaft, Germany

ABSTRACT

This chapter introduces an alternative concept against the dominating trend of a complete outsourcing of IT services, especially in small and medium-sized enterprises (SME). It argues that the undiscriminating adoption of this trend tends to reduce IT on a cost factor and neglects the importance of specific IT knowledge for the continuous improvement of business processes. Also, it neglects the importance of a "communication interface" between the IS users on the one hand and the software development and IT production on the other hand.

In opposition to leading management trends, this chapter will present an approach that bases on an internal competence centre for IS and that demands a steady communication between the IT staff and the various departments. In this approach, only selected IT services are externalized and the continuing growth of specific IS knowledge is essential.

This approach was developed since the end of the 1990s at the building society, with about 100 employees, in which the author is working.

INTRODUCTION

This chapter introduces an alternative concept against the dominating trend of a complete outsourcing of IT services, especially in SMEs. It argues that the undiscriminating adoption of this trend tends to reduce IT on a cost factor and neglects the importance of specific IT knowledge for the continuous improvement of business processes. Also, it neglects the importance of a "communication interface" between the IS users on the one hand and the software development and IT production on the other hand.

In opposition to leading management trends, this chapter will present an approach that bases on an internal competence centre for IS and that demands a steady communication between the IT staff and the various departments. In this approach only selected IT services are externalized and the continuing growth of specific IS knowledge is essential.

This approach was developed since the end of the 1990s at the building society, with about 100 employees, in which the author is working.

THE PROBLEM

In the 1990s the outsourcing of IS services became a dominating trend, especially in SMEs. It is indisputable that outsourcing *can be* a possibility to reduce costs, to participate in new technological developments, to reduce the time to market, to increase the reliability of IS, and so on. But the discussion about outsourcing was guided along the requirements of large enterprises and international companies and along some actual trends just like e-commerce. Also the arguments for outsourcing have been the same for the last decade, while business strategies, organization structures, and techniques have changed.

For this reason it seems to be helpful to discus the problem of outsourcing now again. Only a few publications treat IT outsourcing and SMEs. So, the following concept bases upon the author's own experiences, mainly from financial service companies and discussions with IS managers and consultants from several branches.

BASIC ASSUMPTIONS

Interdependences Between Business Processes and Use of IT

The first and most fundamental aspect of the concept is that there are strong interdependences between the design, the improvement, and the re-engineering of business processes on the one hand and the use of IT on the other hand. The usage of IT changes the working processes simultaneously on a concrete and on a more abstract level. For example, the introduction of e-mail has changed the way of writing business letters in a way of classical rationalization. The process of preparing documents for shipping or of copying became simplified; the costs for delivering e-mails are less than the costs for conventional postage. But on the other side, the introduction of e-mail systems has changed the relations in and between organizations: because communication is accelerated, answers are expected within a shorter time, and more recipients can be involved with a simple copy. So IT is at the same time a tool and an organizational technique (Papadimitrou, 1981).

The impact of the use of IT on business processes seems to make it necessary to keep a certain level of technical and organizational skills inside the organization. This knowledge is needed for rating and for transforming and implementing new ideas and IT products — if necessary with external help.

Figure 1: Interdependences Between Business Processes and Information Systems

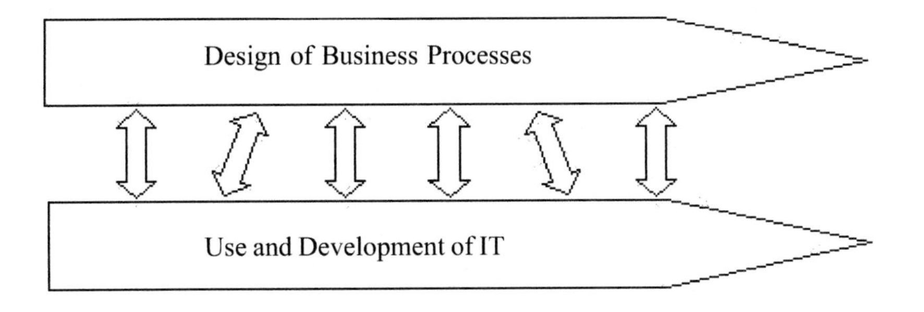

Depending on the organizational strategy, the main action fields for IS services will be defined. But also depending on the knowledge of the (IT) actors, new action fields for IS support of business can be planned. In this sense, Sahraoui (2002) makes a distinction between reactive and proactive roles of the so-called information-enabled leaders. Both types of roles are existing simultaneously.

The Structure of User Support Tasks

The second aspect is the structure of the user support tasks. One of the ideas of outsourcing is to reduce the need for special skills for the maintenance of information systems. But a large part of the user's requieries do not need special technical skills and they are simple to solve, such as forgotten passwords or transaction codes, a simple help for addressing an e-mail, and so on.

Typically, the support cases can be divided into the four following scenarios:

1. A small number of support tasks need specialized, high-level technical support *(2nd and 3rd level support)*. For these support tasks, a support contract with the hard- and software suppliers is possible, and seems to be an adequate way.
2. A larger number of support cases need low level skills *(1st level support)*, such as re-setting forgotten passwords, changing defective mouses and monitors, and so on. These cases can be solved within a few minutes. This

Figure 2: The Structure of User Support Tasks

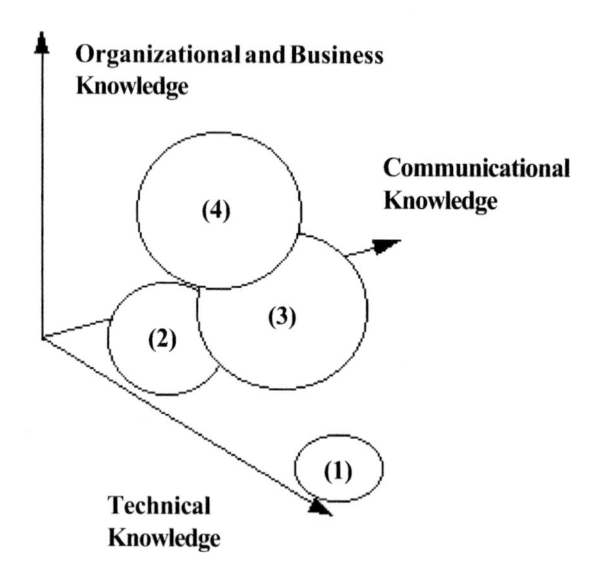

support does not require special technical skills, but the ability to communicate with the users. A benefit of this communication is the early detection of organizational and training deficits.

3. A large number of tasks need a mix of technical, communicational and organizational skills (each on an average level) that can be defined as *business-related user support*. Cases are, for example, the development of spreadsheets, the development of simple database applications, or the organization of e-mail systems.
4. A few tasks – but with high expenditure – need a medium level of technical skills and a high level of organizational knowledge and communicational skills. These tasks are *business project work*.

The business-related support and the project work are the support cases where the importance of internal IT knowledge is emerging.

Development of Costs

The third aspect is the cost reduction for automation and for highly reliable hardware in the recent years. Tape loaders, RAID systems, servers with redundant power supplies and network interfaces, management tools, and other similar products are now affordable for SMEs too. The usage of these products reduces operating costs, administration, and trouble-shooting and allows a grade of automation comparable to large data centers.

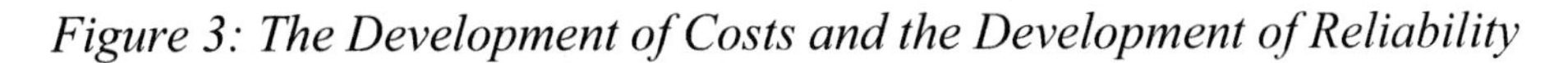

Figure 3: The Development of Costs and the Development of Reliability

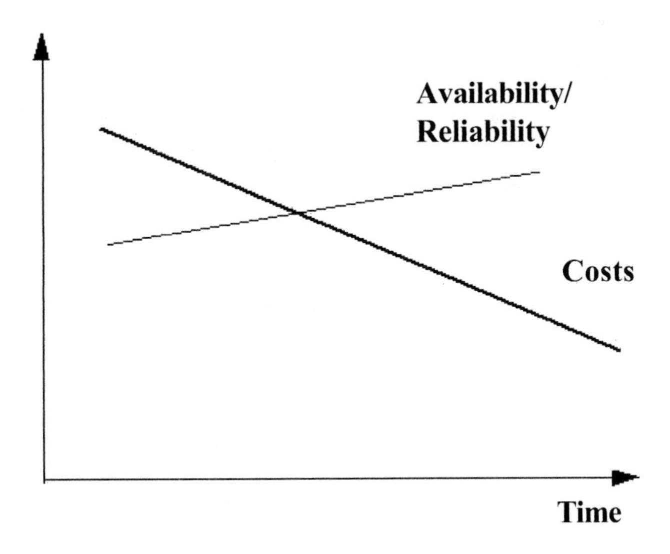

In combination with a simple-structured IT architecture and a restricted use of applications, it is possible to guarantee a high availability at low costs. While the reduction of administration costs and high availability of the systems have been main factors for the outplacement of IT services, these arguments cannot be accepted as valid in every case any more.

Also, the decreasing costs of innovative products reinforce the (well-known, and therefore not additionally listed) argument that the long-lasting outsourcing contracts are potentially not flexible enough regarding the changes in business.

Structure of Working Tasks for the IS Service Group

The working tasks of the IS service groups in SMEs are the same as in larger enterprises. These tasks can be divided into:

1. technical tasks, such as:
   - systems management and operating
   - 1st, 2nd, and 3rd level technical support
   - development of new applications and new releases
   - software maintenance
2. business and organizational tasks, such as:
   - (re-) engineering of business processes
   - tuning or improving business processes
   - strategic planning
   - user support and training.

The management problem is to find an adequate division of these tasks among the different actors, like the IT / IS service group, internal customers, and the top management and external support companies. This is a general problem in enterprises, but with at least two specific qualities of SMEs. One specific quality of SMEs is the difficulty of an exact division of labour, caused by the low number of employees. Another resulting quality is the difficulty of re-engineering business processes on an abstract level, without regarding the concrete staff in the enterprise.

CONCEPT

In many cases the complete outsourcing of IS services will not be cheaper than a combination of internal employees and external suppliers. In this situation, the question turns upside down: What kind of support can be done by the "communication interface?" What knowledge is necessary to support the business processes?

Communication Flow

As a result of the situation described above, we chose an approach of organizing the IT / IS department in the company as a "communication interface" with additional technical functions.

The experiences made in the support tasks are the base for training and for improving business tasks, software, and technical infrastructure. Besides these experiences, the observation of new technological innovations and organizational trends is another source of new ideas.

In this approach the communication with the IS users, with the management, and of course within the internal group, is an essential factor in the design and reengineering of the IS support jobs. To be able to communicate with the users and the management, the IS employees need knowledge about the business to reduce the knowledge gap. But they will need also a more general view than the employees

Figure 4: Working Tasks and Communication Flow

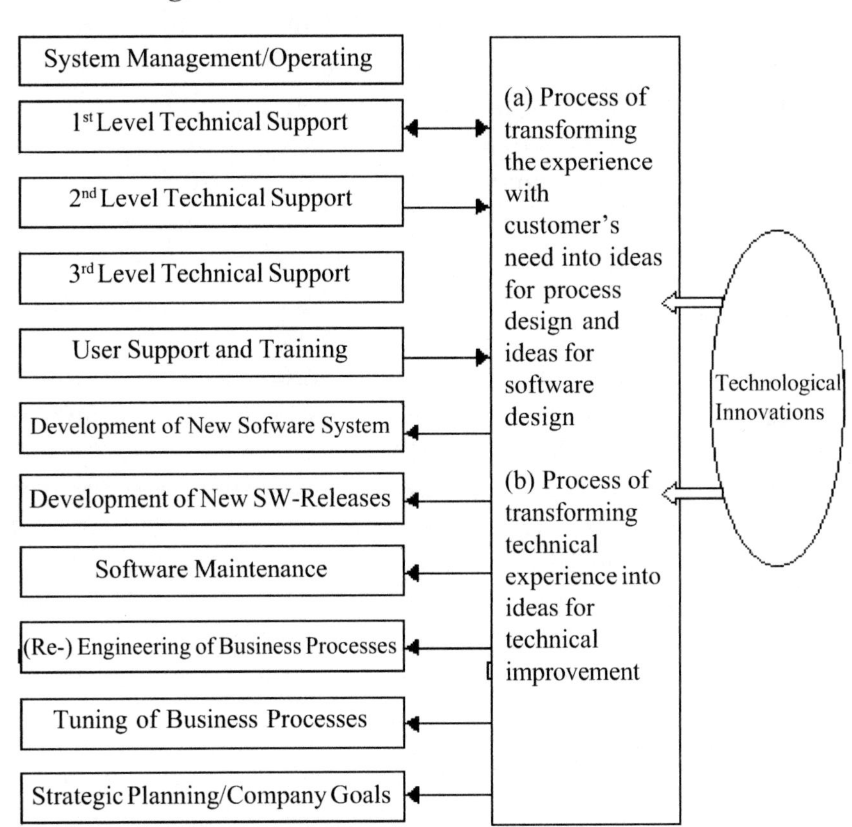

in the business departments. So the culture gap (Leonard, 2002) between IS and business departments will not be bridged. On the contrary, this gap can be a progressing force in re-engineering and changing processes. Even if the business departments have the responsibility for the project management, the IS employees can have the function of a project moderator.

Fundamental Objectives

The fundamental objectives of the IT service group are orientated on the following four aspects, which have individual characteristics regarding the cooperation with the various divisions and with the executive board:

1. Routine support: The normal support (system administration, 1st level support) is done either without any communication with the users or triggered by a direct user call. The 2nd and 3rd level support is done in cooperation with external suppliers.
2. Current projects: Projects focusing only on technical improvements (system integration, security) are settled under the direct responsibility of the IT service group. Projects for business process improvements are done in cooperation with the business divisions. These projects are regularly managed by a project manager of the respective business division, not of the IT group.
3. Acquisition, definition and preparing of new projects: Because of the knowledge about actual users and application problems on the one hand, and the knowledge about the technical developments on the other hand, the IT service group is able to detect potential solutions and to discuss them with the users and the management. Some of these solutions lead to new projects. This linkage between business objectives and IT objectives is the function of the so-called "information-enabled leaders" (Sahraoui, 2002, p. 39).
4. Advancement of sustainability: The sustainability and the "potential to survive" of the IT service group are advanced by a high degree of flexibility. Thus, the group can fulfill new requirements, for example the integration of new applications. Aspects of this concept are:
   - Building up and securing actual and future-needed skills,
   - Securing low support costs,
   - Continuing control and optimization of the costs, and
   - Maintaining accordance to laws, standards, and best practices.

Make or Buy? Make and Buy!

The aim of sustainability influences the make-or-buy decision: Projects which are supporting the business of the company in an organization's specific way demand the development of in-house skills. The less crucial the project, the more the decision tends to buying. But this simple idea has to be modified by the influence of time. Normally, the implementation of a new application cannot be adjourned until the employees have built up their skills.

New applications and technical innovations normally are bought as standard applications or they are developed by externals. They will be introduced in a smooth way: The training of the internal staff is part of almost all contracts with externals. The aim of this training is to enable the internal staff to improve existing applications and develop new applications. This corresponds to an incremental software development processes, in which communication between the users and the developers is crucial — in some aspects similar to the concept of extreme programming (XP).

The typical implementation process can be divided into the following phases:

- Defining a problem,
- Decision about the solution,
- Realisation or implementation of a new application,
- Start of production, and
- Further development.

With the exception of the first phase (defining a problem), external specialists and internal employees are working together. Typically, for each new technology or new application at least two employees will be trained. Ordinarily the training is a combination of on-the-job and off-the-job training. After the start of production, the internal employees will take over an increasing part of all tasks, but with the possibility to refer to the external specialists. The further development will be done by the internal staff if possible. In this sense, the project is the centre piece for the organizational developments of the IS service group.

Technical Infrastructure and Support

The technical infrastrucure is selected with regard to high standardization, high availability and lean administration. New demands from the divisions are analysed concerning to costs and complexity of IT services. If necessary, the demands are modified or refused. Software updates are installed only if absolutely necessary (end of life of older releases, serious bugs).

Hardware, especially servers and storage systems, but also printers, are selected with special regard to guarantee and on-site service. A service contract with suppliers and / or technical specialists for crucial systems is important.

The concentration on standard products simplifies the work and reduces the dependence on manufacturers or specialized service companies. In most cases there is, especially for SMEs, no need to use non-standard products or non-standard installations.

Intentionally and in contrast to some "philosophies of outsourcing" the 1st level support is done by internal employees. In this way, the enterprise maintains the possibility to detect potential for improvements in technology and processes. So the 1st level support has a "seismographic function." The 2nd level support is done both by internal staff and by external service companies; 3rd level support is mostly done by external service companies. In a longer space of time the essential knowledge will diffuse to the internal employees, so that an increasing number of the 2nd and 3rd level problems can be solved by internal staff too.

Skills

The employees need a general *knowledge* (with the ability to further specialization, if needed) which encloses a general IT knowledge, product skills, and knowledge about the processes of the enterprise and project management. People are not hired for some special technical skills, but for their wide experiences and interests. The employees have to handle a lot of complexity in their jobs (Lally and Garbushian, 2002) and have to track several tasks at the same time. The employees will be trained in technical aspects, in communication skills, and in business and organizational skills. The aim is that the employees of the IT department will be able to discuss concepts of business processes with the business departments. Because of the combination of technical and organizational skills, the IT service group is also an internal consultant to the divisions and to the executive board.

Experience shows that younger professionals are less interested in such jobs than older professionals. The younger professionals prefer employments in software companies and / or international companies. This corresponds to the situation that — at least in Germany — the typical career path runs in the direction of specialization. On the other side, there is no typical way in education to get the skills for IT management jobs, especially in SMEs.

Every system can be administrated by two or three employees of the building society. In case of absence, no direct substitution by another employee is necessary. Rather, the organization exploits a certain overlap. Specific knowledge is documented in a Lotus Notes database, which the employees are filling after solving a non-standard problem. With this tool, most of the trouble can be solved by all employees in the IT service group, not only by the specially trained staff.

A Case Study: A Building Society

The stated concept was worked out in a building society with about 100 employees. In Germany about 20 building societies are existing. The products of the building societies are very complex compared to other financial products, but the business processes are relatively stable. A contract normally lives for 7 to 20 years; therefore, long-term planning is important. So on the one side, there exists no standard application for the business processes of a building society on the market; on the other side, the complexity of the product and the amount of legal changes makes it impossible for a small company to develop such a core application on its own.

At the building society an old self-developed mainframe-based application was the core application for the savings contracts and building loan contracts until 1997. Then this application was replaced by another mainframe-based application, which was developed by a cooperation with other building societies and which is externally hosted.

But besides this core application there are a lot of applications with increasing relevance for lean and customer-guided business processes, like a document management system, office software, messaging software (Lotus Notes), software for product simulations, software for cost management, and so on. In the building society, the organizational support for all applications (except for the mainframe application) and the technical responsibility for all the locally-sited systems are concentrated in an IT service group with five full-time and two part-time employees.

The concept has led to the following situation:

The current technical service (operating, system administration, troubleshooting) offers a high quality. It requires about 1.1 employees per 100 users, scattered over five locations in one town. The average availability of the applications is >99% (where scheduled maintenance is rated as "not available"). The typical time to identify and to fix a problem is less than 1 hour; most of the problems are solved immediately (in a few minutes). Nevertheless the costs are less than 75% of the costs calculated by outsourcing service providers for a 10-year-contract.

The other resources (4.9 employees) are engaged in business-related tasks:

- Business-related user support (for example, development of spreadsheets for business applications, user training or the transformation of a paper archive into an electronic archive),
- Planning, development, and implementation of new software products or new releases, and
- Commercial tasks (cost management, supervision of contracts with service providers).

The skills of the employees are increasing permanently. So in the last years five years knowledge about the following items was built up: JAVA programming, shell script programming, development of Lotus Notes applications, administration of NT, UNIX and communication servers, and firewall administration.

The IT service group is highly accepted and integrated within the whole enterprise.

CONDITIONS AND LIMITS

In principle, this concept seems to be transferable to other SMEs. The differences will be in the fraction of the outsourced services. This will mainly be influenced by:

- the absolute number of service staff,
- the complexity of the systems,
- the service times, and
- the geographical extension of the users.

A minimum of resources is necessary for tracking all tasks and for substitution in the case of vacancies or illness. The indispensable number of employees depends on several factors and cannot be rated generally.

The complexity of the systems is a main factor and influences the expenditure and the needed skills. A well-chosen infrastructure and IS architecture allows the reduction of this complexity. A typical problem is the increasing of complexity over the years, caused by the introduction of new applications or the co-existence of different software releases. This can be solved by consolidation projects.

The service times and the geographical extension of the users are influencing the expenditure, especially for the technical and the 1st level support.

Besides these operative aspects, there exists a dominating general management aspect: It is necessary that the top management is convinced of the importance of IS for business processes and business strategy.

RESULTS

- Outsourcing of IT/IS services is still an actual trend. It offers a lot of advantages, such as a short time to the introduction of new technologies or applications, a guaranteed availability, and so on. But the undiscriminating adoption of this trend tends to reduce IT on a cost factor and neglects the importance of specific IT knowledge for the continuous improvement of business processes.
- The establishment and maintenance of internal IT skills is important in any case, at least for assessing the possibilities for supporting business processes.
- The typical structure of SMEs does not fit to the offers of the large part of IT

outsourcing providers. Typically these offers are tailored for large enterprises or international companies.

- A complete outsourcing has some disadvantages, especially for SMEs. The transaction costs will be relatively high and the potential savings will be absolutely low. Instead of a complete outsourcing it seems to be advantageous to externalize permanently only selected technical, non business-specific services.
- A selected technical architecture and the application architecture are laying the foundation for highly available, low cost IT. These factors – low cost and high availability – are more important for an enterprise than the immediate adaption of new technologies or of new products or product releases.
- The combination of general technical knowledge and specific business knowledge allows a focussed development of the IT infrastructure and an efficient support of business- oriented projects by the internal IS employees.
- The management of the IT/IS service group has to regard the sustainability of this department. Aspects of the sustainability are building up and securing actual and future needed skills, securing low support costs, continuing control, and benchmarking with best practices.
- The organization of the internal knowledge diffusion improves the quality of service and flexibility.
- The continuing feedback between user support on the one hand and planning and project work on the other hand enables broad knowledge about the requirements and allows a focused project management.
- The project work is the centre part for the development of the service group.

REFERENCES

Jentzsch, R. (1998, November 7). *Getting the Balance Right.* Canberra: Proceedings of the 1998 Information Industry Outlook Conference. Retrieved January, 3, 2002, from the World Wide Web: http://www.acs.org.au/president/1998/past/io98/rghtbl.htm.

Lally, L. and Garbushian, B. (2002). Hiring in the Post-Reengineering Environment: A Study Using Situationally Conditioned Belief. In: E. Szewczak and C. Snodgrass (eds.), *Human Factors in Information Systems* (pp. 169-179). Hershey, PA: IRM Press.

Leonard, A.C. (2002). The Importance of Having a Multidimensional View of IT End User Relationship for the Successful Restructuring of IT Departments. In: E. Szewczak and C. Snodgrass (eds.), *Human Factors in Information Systems* (pp. 241-252). Hershey, PA: IRM Press.

Papadimitriou, Z. (1981). Entwicklung der kaufmännischen Berufstätigkeit im Gefolge des Einsatzes von EDV-Systemen im Bankenbereich. In Boehm, U. et al. (eds.), *Rationalisierung und kaufmännische Berufsausbildung*. Frankfurt/New York: Campus.

Raymond, L. and Menvielle, W. (2000). *Managing Information Technology and E-Business in SMEs*. Synthesis watch report submitted to Canada Economic Development within the framework of the project. Quebec. Retrieved January, 3, 2002, from the World Wide Web: http://www.dec-ced.gc.ca/en/biblio/observatoire/pdf-obs/expanding.pdf.

Sahraoui, S. (2002). The Social Antecedents of Business Process Planning Effectiveness. In E.J. Szewczak and C.R. Snodgrass (eds.), *Managing the Human Side of Information Technology: Challenges and Solutions* (pp. 35-59). Hershey, PA: Idea Group Publishing.

Weissbach, R. (2000). Supportmanagement einmal anders – Anmerkungen zum Outsourcing bei Anwenderorganisationen. In H. Mayr et al. (eds.), *SWM'2000 – Fachtagung Software-Management 2000* (pp. 181-186). Wien: OCG.

Chapter V

Using Spreadsheets as a Decision Support Tool: An Application for Small Businesses

Stephen Burgess
Victoria University, Australia

Don Schauder
Monash University, Australia

ABSTRACT

This chapter discusses a model that has been set up to assist small businesses in the decision-making processes associated with setting up a Web site by which they can interact with their customers. Specifically, the chapter addresses the use of a spreadsheet to support decision-making processes in relation to the level of capital needed to devote to the Web site and who should be used to develop it. The chapter describes the process followed, from the initial SWOT analysis used to collect information about the business to the decision-making process modelled in the spreadsheet.

INTRODUCTION

Spreadsheets have been used as a decision support tool to assist businesses. This chapter discusses a model that has been set up to assist small businesses in the decision-making processes associated with setting up a Web site by which they can interact with their customers. A particular aspect of the model, the decision processes needed to determine the cost of the Web site and the skills needed to implement it, are described here.

A Model for Small Businesses to Interact with Customers Using the Internet

Burgess and Schauder (2000a) identified a number of steps that are common to models that can be used to assist firms in identifying strategic IT ideas (such as Porter and Millar, 1985; Barton and Peters, 1990; Osterle, 1991) and/or e-commerce opportunities (Marchese, 1998; Al Moumem and Sommerville, 1999). These steps included a need for a thorough business investigation. This is typically the first step in any model and needs to occur to increase the likelihood that decisions to be made later in regards to Web design and content are based upon a sound knowledge of the firm. Typical analysis tools used at this stage are Critical Success Factors (CSFs) and **strengths, weaknesses, opportunities** and **threats** (SWOT) Analysis.

The SWOT analysis has been traditionally used in the marketing or economics areas of the business. An analysis is performed on the various areas of the organisation to identify current or potential strengths and weaknesses when compared with other competitive forces. From this analysis, the organisation identifies actual or potential opportunities to gain strategic advantage or threats to the organisation's well being. Actions taken by the organisation to take advantage of an opportunity are **proactive.** Actions taken by the organisation to combat a threat are **reactive** (Kotler et al., 1989).

E-commerce is seen as a way in which small businesses can compete with large businesses (DIST, 1998; Penhune, 1998), but small businesses have little time or resources to address potential changes to their current activities. Many lack the availability of technical expertise and avoid proper planning techniques to help them take advantage of opportunities that may present themselves (DIST, 1998; Engler, 1999; Conhaim, 1999; Conroy, 1999). A number of attempts have been made to set up models to assist small businesses in the adoption and use of electronic commerce, but many of them lack sufficient detail to explain how they operate and how each step of the model links with the next to provide a complete solution. In fact, small business owners find themselves confronted with information from many sources (books, magazines, newspapers, government, friends, business contacts, and so forth) and can find it extremely difficult to sort out just where to access reliable information (Stiller and Burgess, 2001). In order to address some of these problems, particularly those relating to a lack of proper planning techniques, facing small businesses that wish to use the Internet to interact with customers a conceptual version of a model to guide small businesses was proposed by Burgess and Schauder (2000b). Figure 1 shows the model that was developed.

The model is based upon the major steps in other IT and e-commerce models. It represents an attempt to address the specific needs of small businesses by guiding them through a planning process that is relatively easy to comprehend (Burgess and Schauder, 2000a).

The initial stage of the model, the business investigation, involves a modified SWOT analysis. The firm's internal and (some) external forces are examined. Internally, the firm's resources in relation to time, money and expertise are examined, as well as the characteristics of the firm's goods and services. The firm's overall strategy is also examined, as a firm wishing to grow in size may require a more aggressive Web strategy than a firm that is satisfied with its existing customer base. Externally, the Web sites of competitors are examined, as well as the ability of customers to access the firm's Web site.

Figure 1: A Model to Assist Small Businesses to Interact with Customers on the Internet

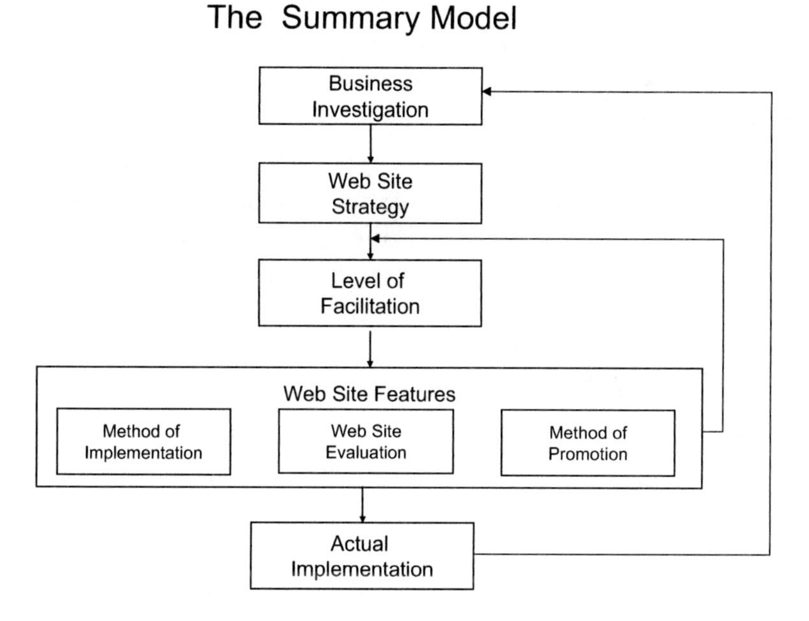

Other steps of the model, after the business investigation, refer to identification of the firm's overall Web site strategy: what Web site features they are going to implement, what method they use to implement these features, how they promote the Web site, and how they evaluate its success.

The next stage is to develop it into a more detailed, usable model. This applied version of the model consists of two major components: a procedures manual (showing the various steps of business investigation, strategy, and so forth) and a spreadsheet program for recording the results of the analysis provision of recommendations. The development of aspects of this model is discussed in this chapter.

THE USE OF SPREADSHEETS FOR DECISION SUPPORT

Spreadsheets have been used as decision support tools in many different ways. For instance, one recent example describes the use of spreadsheets to allocate production resources and combine raw materials in an optimal mix in wood panel manufacturing (Buehlmann, Ragsdale and Gfeller, 2000).

Spreadsheets, Decision Support, and Small Business

Spreadsheets provide users with the capability to alter figures and to see the effects the alterations have on recommendations. Although spreadsheets have been associated with the concept of decision support for a number of decades (Stair and Reynolds, 1999), there are few documented examples of their successful use in small businesses. Much of the limited research into small businesses has investigated the success factors for information technology, based upon the current use of IT/DSS or the design and development of specific DSSs for small and medium-sized enterprises (SME). Little work has been done specifically to identify those areas that have not been adapted to DSS, but show potential for its introduction for the small business (Duan, Kinman and Xu, 2002). In relation to their use of IT, small businesses are often resource-poor – suffering from a lack of appropriate know-how in relation to using IT effectively, and lacking the time, financial resources, and planning ability to improve their situation (Burgess, 2002).

A 2001 study of 133 manufacturing small businesses in the UK revealed limited use of decision support systems (Duan, Kinman and Xu, 2002). A lack of staff time to analyse needs and identify solutions was the primary reason given for the lack of use. Where used effectively, firms with a more strategic outlook implement them. They mainly take the form of previously developed packages and most of them are targeted towards support routine decisions.

Because of these factors, there is an opportunity for effective decision support tools to make a real impact on small businesses (Duan, Kinman and Xu, 2002).

THE CHOICE OF A SPREADSHEET

The major problem faced in this project was how to take the conceptual model and turn it into the applied model. The initial idea was to develop a manual or book that small businesses could work through and use to record the results of the analyses that they carried out along the way. This would then lead to recommendations as to what Web site features they should implement. There were two major concerns with this approach. The first was that if the small business user wished to go back and alter any of the data entered, he or she would have to use an eraser or liquid paper. The second concern was how to lead the person to the eventual recommendation once the analysis was completed. The need to follow the somewhat complex paths that were designed through to the various recommendations might have been enough drive the small business person to distraction and a subsequent decision to abandon the process.

It was finally decided that the spreadsheet package, Microsoft Excel, would provide the solution. Most small businesses that have computers use a spreadsheet package, and the majority of spreadsheet packages in use are Microsoft Excel. The spreadsheet has long been recognised as a tool that can be used to support basic decision-making. It provides users with the capability to alter figures and to see the effects the alterations have on recommendations (Stair and Reynolds, 1999). In this case, it provided a means by which the complex path from analysis to recommendation could be handled automatically by the software.

The programming language that is part of Microsoft Excel, Visual Basic for Applications, provided the flexibility to alter the software and the interface easily.

THE DECISION-MAKING PROCESS

Two of the elements that affected the decisions made by the model in relation to the cost of implementation of the Web site and the skills needed to implement it were the financial outlay that the business was prepared to make and the skill level of employees.

Financial Outlay

In determining the mechanisms for asking small businesses to estimate the capital that they were prepared to commit to the Web site, users were provided with a range of four typical options as the estimated financial outlay for the project, ranging from the inexpensive (a small Web site) to the most expensive (a larger Web site with interactive features). A range of setup and maintenance costs was provided for each option in the accompanying manual. In this way, some guidelines were provided for the small businesses as to what they would get for their money.

The various financial outlay options were given a rating ranging from "1" for the most inexpensive (a small Web site developed with a package or wizard) to "4" for the most expensive (a larger Web site containing a number of interactive features). These are referred to later in the analysis.

Employee Expertise

This section allowed the expertise level of employees who would be associated with the Web site to be entered. Again, a range of choices was provided and

Figure 2: Level of Financial Commitment Screen

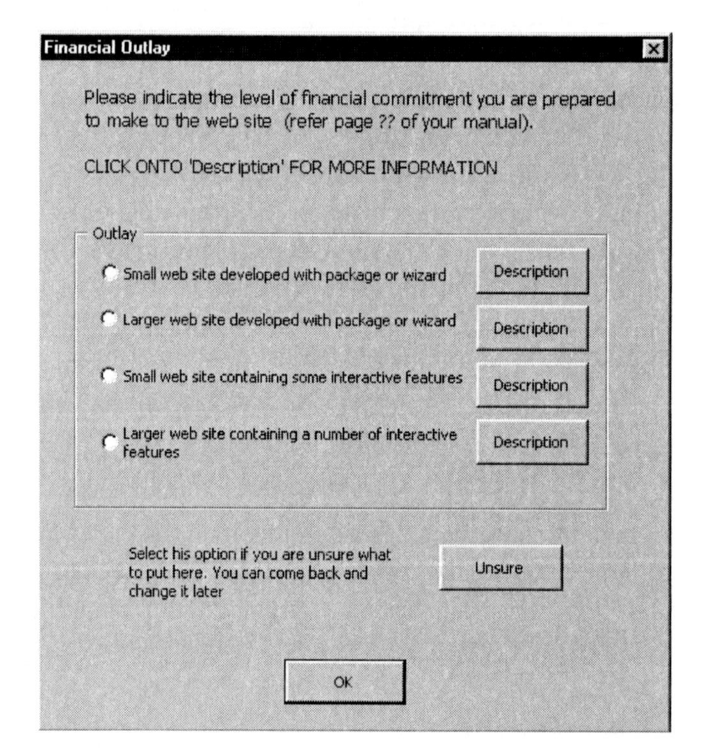

Figure 3: Information Technology Expertise Screen

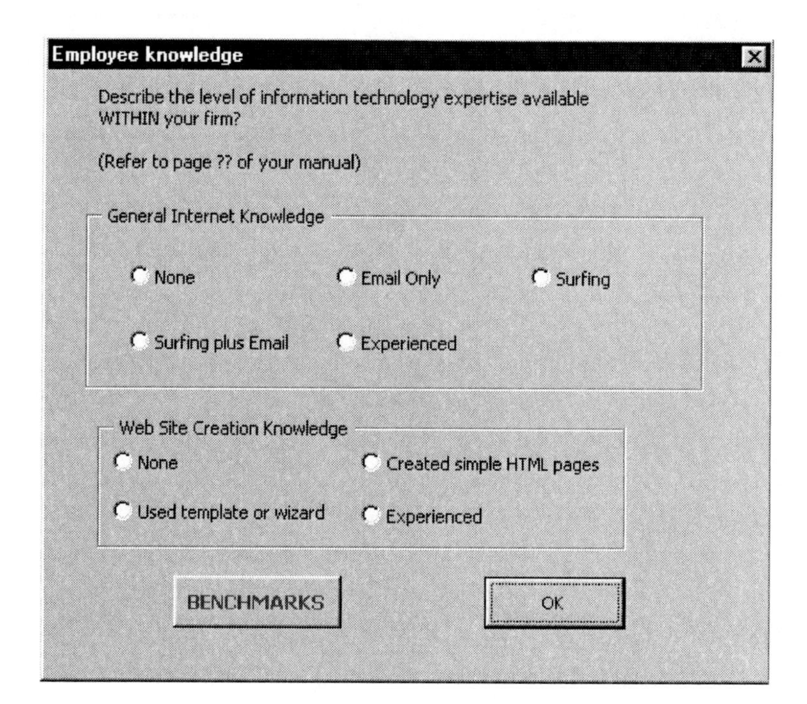

explained in the manual. Users of the model would then select the option related to the most skilled employee that would be working on the Web site.

COST OF IMPLEMENTATION AND SKILLS NEEDED TO IMPLEMENT THE WEB SITE

The Cost of the Web Site

This section allowed the user to accept or reject the recommendations of the previous section for each Web site feature. Upon choosing to implement a feature, a judgement was made by the system as to whether or not it could be implemented within budget. This is based upon the costs of the Web site being affected by the following (Burgess and Schauder, 2001):

- The cost of hosting basic information provision features is relatively small. This statement does not take into account the time taken to transfer the information to the Web site initially and the time needed to update it.

- The ongoing cost of providing product catalogues does tend to rise as the firm increases the number of products listed on the Web site. On average, once the number of products reaches 15, the costs of creating the catalogue increases markedly.
- The ongoing and transaction-based costs increase when online payment features are introduced. They increase markedly once 100 transactions per month have been reached.
- Options that allow some interaction with the Web site (more than just viewing information) require a greater outlay.

The various Web site features were divided into the following categories (these can be viewed as "cost drivers" in the Implementation screen (Figure 4). Each Web site feature was assigned a value from "1" to "7." The ability to implement the feature was based upon the outlay selected in the Financial Outlay section of the Business Investigation.

The Implementation screen allowed users to select particular Web site features for implementation, based upon the recommendation made in the previous section. It then made a judgement as to the ability of the firm to develop the site internally, based upon entries that had been made in the Financial Outlay and Employee Expertise sections of the Business Investigation stage.

Figure 4: The Implementation Screen

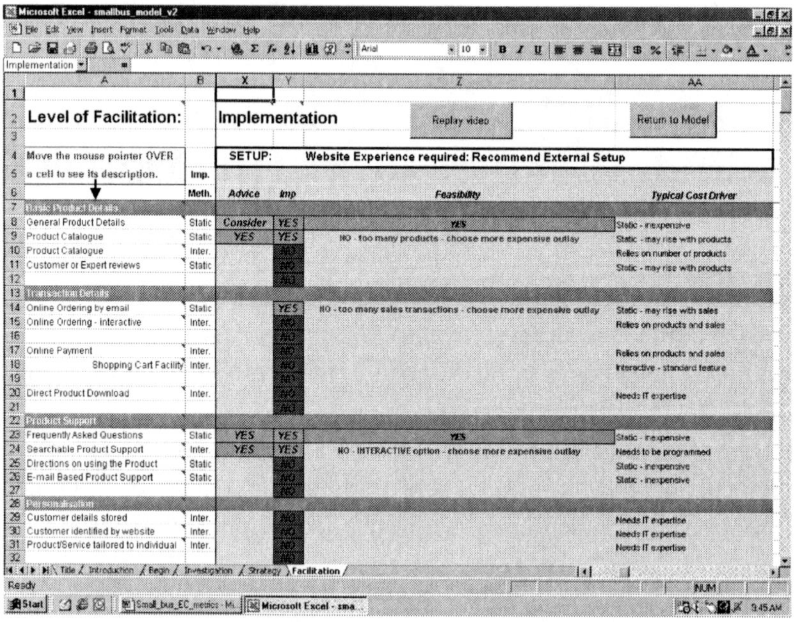

Table 1: Web Site Feature Cost Driver Classifications and Implementation Message Provided, Based Upon Outlay choice

Cost Driver	Rating	Implementation Message Provided
Static – inexpensive	1	**YES**
Static - may rise with products	2	If < 15 products or Outlay Rating > 1 then **YES**, else show **NO - too many products - choose more expensive outlay**
Static - may rise with sales	3	If < 100 online transactions/month or Outlay Rating > 1 then **YES** else show **NO - too many sales transactions – choose more expensive outlay**
Interactive standard feature	4	If Outlay Rating > 2 then **YES**, else show **NO - INTERACTIVE option - choose more expensive outlay**
Interactive – Relies on number of products	5	If < 15 products and Outlay Rating > 2 then **YES** If < 15 products and Outlay Rating = (1 or 2) then show **NO - INTERACTIVE option - choose more expensive outlay**, else If Outlay Rating >3 then **YES**, else show **NO – too many products - choose more expensive outlay**
Interactive - Relies on products and sales	6	If < 100 online transactions/month and Outlay Rating > 2 then **YES** If < 100 online transactions/month and Outlay Rating = (1 or 2) then show **NO - INTERACTIVE option - choose more expensive outlay**, else If Outlay Rating >3 then **YES**, else show **NO – too many online transactions - choose more expensive outlay**
Needs IT expertise	7	If Outlay Rating = 4 then **YES**, else show **NO - INTERACTIVE option - choose more expensive outlay**

The model provided a message to the user, based upon whether or not it was considered possible to implement the Web site. Table 1 shows the logic behind the message provided to the user, based upon the cost-driver rating, the number of products on the Web site, the number of online transactions per month, and the level of outlay selected in Business Investigation.

Note that it is considered that a simple static Web site is regarded as being inexpensive. In the second level of Web site rating, if the users have identified that they are listing 15 or more products on their catalogue, they are informed that they have too many products and that they must go back and allocate more resources to the Web site. At level 3, the same logic is used, but this time for greater than 100 transactions. At level 4, users have started to request some interactive options. As these are more expensive to set up, they will be informed that they need to select a higher outlay for the Web site if they have not already selected outlay level 3. The other levels (5,6 and 7) require an increased outlay for the Web site as the level of sophistication required increases.

Skills Needed to Implement the Web Site

This section also provided a recommendation as to how the Web site could be developed, internally or externally. The recommendation was based upon the employee expertise identified in the Business Investigation stage and the **highest**

rating cost driver (as per Table 1) for the Web site features that were selected by the user.

Table 2 represents the logic used. If there was no internal experience at developing Web sites, the recommendation was that the Web site be developed externally. If there was some internal experience (either by the development of simple HTML pages or the use of a package or wizard), the option was provided to develop the Web site internally, provided that it does not contain any features that require IT expertise. If there was internal IT expertise, the option was provided to develop the Web site internally irrespective of the level of difficulty.

At the basic level, if users indicate that their business has no experience in setting up Web sites, they are recommended to look externally for someone to set up the Web site for them. In the case that they have created simple HTML pages or already used a template or wizard to set up a Web site, the level of sophistication required determines the recommendation that is made. If a simple (static) Web site is required, the recommendation is that it is done internally. If a highly sophisticated Web site (level 7) is required, the recommendation is that it be set up externally. For Web sites somewhere in between, it is suggested that it may be possible to set up the Web site internally using a template or package, but that further investigation is required. In the case that the business has experienced Web site developers in its midst, the recommendation is that it is possible for all levels of Web site to be set

Table 2: Web Site Feature Cost Driver Classifications and Web Site Development Options, Based Upon Level of Employee Expertise

Level of Employee Web site Expertise	Web site Development Message Provided
None	**No Web site Experience: Recommend External Setup**
Created Simple HTML Pages	If Static site (High rating <=3) then show **Static Web Site: Internal Setup Possible,** else If Interactive site (Highest rating >3 and <=6) then show **Interactive Web Site: Possible internal setup: Template/Package,** else show **Website Experience required: Recommend External Setup**
Used Template or Wizard	If Static Web site (High rating <=3) then show **Static Web Site: Internal Setup Possible,** else If Interactive Web site (Highest rating >3 and <=6) then show **Interactive Web Site: Possible internal setup: Template/Package,** else show **Web site Experience required: Recommend External Setup**
Experienced	If Static Web site (High rating <=3) then show **Static Web Site: Internal Setup Possible,** else If Interactive Web site (Highest rating >3 and <=6) then show **Interactive Web Site: Possible internal setup: Template/Package,** else show **Web site Experience required: May be available internally**

up internally. It is still recommended that templates or packages be used for the simpler Web sites.

Note that there is a level of uncertainty incorporated into this part of the application. Where the business has employees with *some* level of Web site implementation expertise and the setup task requires *some* level of expertise, it is not possible for the model to make a sound recommendation. It therefore suggests "possible internal setup" and that the decision needs to be further investigated.

OTHER EXAMPLES

The spreadsheet model contained a number of other decision support modules within its operation. An example of one of these modules is where the model recommended whether a particular Web site feature should be adopted based upon the identification of overall business strategy by the user and the particular cost or differentiation benefits that the feature could offer the business.

Figure 5 shows the screen that users could use to record the overall direction of the business.

Figure 5: Input Form to Select Overall Business Strategy

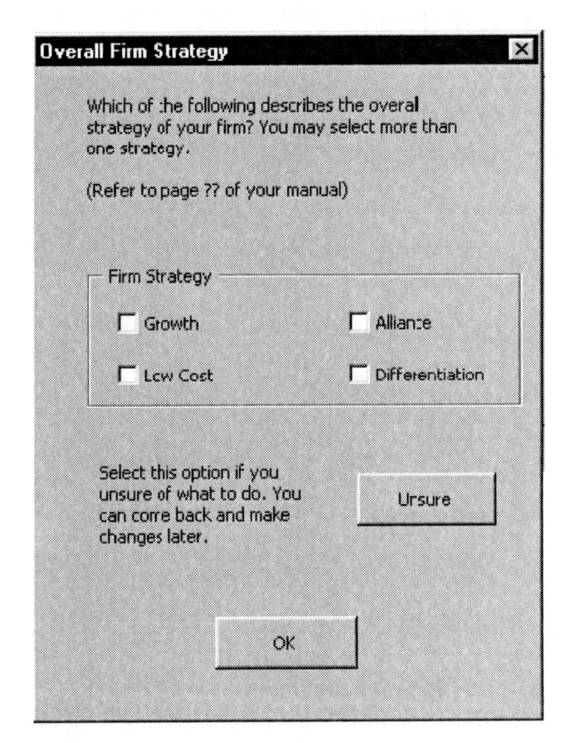

The idea behind this form is to allow the business to make sure that its Web site strategy is in line with its overall business strategy. In this instance, we are interested in whether the user selects that his business has adopted a "cost" (try to lower costs) or "differentiation" (try to differentiate their products and services from their competitors) strategy. The model recommends various Web site features if the user has selected one of these categories. Table 3 shows the Web site features and if they are nominated according to the user's selection.

A description of each of the decision support recommendations follows:

- The small business should consider listing the basic detail of its products on the Web site. If it has adopted a cost strategy, this could be to save costs by not having to print as many catalogues. If differentiation has been recommended, the feature may allow the business to provide more information about the quality of the products versus that of its competitors.
- Online transactions (ordering and purchasing) will be recommended (based upon the suitability of the product or service, which is not covered here) if a differentiation strategy has been selected. The business may be able to differentiate itself on the speed of the transaction, and therefore delivery, of the product or service.
- Provision of product support will be recommended for both cost and differentiation strategies. This is because it may save employee time (and costs) in relation to answering customer queries and allow the business to differentiate itself from competitors by offering superior and faster product support.
- The business may even be able to differentiate itself by the provision of very basic information about the business, like where it is located. If a customer is ready to buy and happy to travel, information about where the business located (or even how to contact it easily) may turn out to be the difference.

Table 3: Web Site Feature Recommendations Based Upon Cost and Differentiation Selections by Model Users

Web site Feature Category	Potential Benefits if Cost Strategy Selected	Potential Benefits if Differentiation Strategy Selected
Basic Product Details	Save catalogue printing costs	May provide information about product quality
Online Transaction	*Feature not recommended*	Faster transactions/ Reduce geographic boundaries
Product Support	Reduction in employee time answering queries	Extra Product Support
Basic Information	*Feature not recommended*	May imply reliability/ Customers find stores faster

FUTURE IMPLICATIONS

The next stage in this project is to trial the decision-making components of the model (via testing of the model itself) with a series of small businesses. If this is successful and small businesses find the model useful and the decision support offered helpful, the model (incorporating the decision support modules) could be modified for other communities of small organisations, such as non-profit enterprises.

CONCLUSION

There are a number of examples of spreadsheets being used to support business decision-making. This paper has shown how a spreadsheet can be used to support small business decision-making in relation to how much it should outlay on a Web site and where it can access the skills to implement the Web site. This is presented within the context of a model designed to assist small businesses in identifying and carrying out the processes that they need to follow to set up a Web site. The particular examples identified, determining the suitability of the level of outlay chosen by the user for the Web site and an assessment of the suitability of internal staff of the business to set up the Web site, have shown how some of these decisions can be quantified and setup to be made by the decision support application. Where there is some uncertainty, the user is informed of such and it is suggested that further investigation needs to occur.

REFERENCES

AlMoumen, S. and Sommerville, I. (1999, May). *Marketing for E-Commerce.* 10th International Conference of the Information Resources Management Association, Hershey, PA.

Barton, P. S. and Peters, D. H. (1991, October). *A Synthetic Framework for Describing the use of Information Technology for Competitive Advantage.* Australian Computer Conference 1991 Proceedings, 47-62.

Buehlmann, U., Ragsdale, C.T., and Gfeller, B. (2000, October). A spreadsheet-based decision support system for wood panel manufacturing. *Decision Support Systems*, Amsterdam, 29 (3), 207-227.

Burgess, S. (2002). Information Technology in Small Business: Issues and Challenges. In Stephen Burgess (ed.), *Managing Information Technology in Small Businesses: Challenges and Solutions*, Hershey, PA: Idea Group Publishing.

Burgess, S. and Schauder, D. (2000a, May). Interacting with Customers on the Internet: Developing a Model for Small Businesses. *Challenges of Information Technology Management in the 21st Century, Proceedings of the 2000 Information Resources Management Association International Conference*, (pp. 517-521), Alaska.

Burgess, S. and Schauder, D. (2000b, November 30-December 1). Refining a Model to Assist Small Businesses to Interact with Customers on the Internet: A Delphi Study. Working for E-Business: Challenges of the New E-conomy, Proceedings of the 1st. *International WE-B Conference*, (pp. 1-11) School of Management Information Systems, Edith Cowan University.

Burgess, S. and Schauder, D. (2001, May). *Web Site Development options for Australian Small* Businesses. 2001 Information Resources Management Association International Conference Proceedings Toronto, Canada.

Conhaim, W. W. (1999, January/February). The Business-To-Business Marketplace. *Link-Up*, 16 (1). 5-12.

Conroy, A. (1999, May). Evolving E-Commerce: Solutions for SMEs. *Australian PC World*, 88-92.

DIST (Department of Industry, Science and Tourism). (1998, April). *Stats: Electronic Commerce in Australia*. Commonwealth of Australia, Canberra.

Duan, Y., Kinman, R. and Xu, M. (2002). Use of Decision Support Systems in Small Businesses. In Stephen Burgess (ed.), *Managing Information Technology in Small Businesses: Challenges and Solutions*, Hershey, PA: Idea Group Publishing.

Engler, N. (1999, January 18). Small but Nimble. *Information Week*, 717, 57-62.

Kotler, P., Chandler, P., Gibbs, R. and McColl, R. (1989). *Marketing in Australia*, (2nd ed.). Victoria: Prentice-Hall.

Marchese, L. (1998). *Brand Recognition*. Internet World 98: Australia Pacific Conference Proceeding on CD-ROM. Kirby Network Services, NSW.

Osterle, H. (1991, October). *Generating Business Ideas Based on Information Technology*. Australian Computer Conference 1991 Proceedings, 153-165.

Penhune, J. (1998, Fall). A Quiet Revolution: Technology Fuels the Entrepreneurial Dream. *Forbes Buyers Guide Supplement*, 12-15.

Porter, M.E. and Millar, Victor, E. (1985, July-August). How Information Gives You Competitive Advantage. *Harvard Business Review*, 63.(4), 149-160.

Stair, R. M. and Reynolds, G. W. (1999). *Principles of Information Systems* (4th ed.) Course Technology – ITP, USA.

Stiller, A. and Burgess, S. (2001). Developing Guidelines for Linking Small Businesses and Customers on the Internet. In Mohini Singh and Thompson Teo (eds.), *E-Commerce Diffusion: Strategies and Challenges*, Australia: Heidelberg Press.

Chapter VI

Teaching Technology for Community

E. R. Jessup
University of Colorado, USA

ABSTRACT

Technology for Community is an undergraduate computer science course taught at the University of Colorado under the auspices of the Institute for Women and Technology's Virtual Development Center. In the course, students use computers to do community service. More specifically, they work with local community service agencies, building computational solutions to problems confronting those agencies. Student projects are developed following the method of task-centered design and are evaluated by the students and the users according to three formal methods. In this chapter, we describe in detail the content of the course and review the design and evaluation methods we use.

INTRODUCTION

Technology for Community is an undergraduate long-term projects course offered by the Department of Computer Science at the University of Colorado at Boulder (UCB). In it, students develop computational products designed to serve the needs of local community service organizations.

BACKGROUND

During the summer of 2000, UCB's Department of Computer Science was selected to participate in the Institute for Women and Technology's (IWT) Virtual Development Center (VDC) (IWT, 2002). The VDC is a network of collaborative educational centers, termed Development Centers that share the dual goals of stimulating the participation of women in technology and increasing the positive impact of technology on the lives of women. Through the Development Centers' educational activities, a diverse community of women is encouraged to participate in the development of technology. In particular, universities participating in the VDC all commit to teaching technical courses in a style thought to be open and appealing to women. Presently, the Development Centers are at Purdue, Santa Clara University, Smith College, Texas A&M, the University of Arizona, the University of California at Berkeley, UCB, the University of Texas at El Paso, and the University of Washington. UCB's Center is unique in its emphasis on computer science; the others all focus on traditional engineering disciplines.

The primary activity of UCB's center is the Technology for Community course offered through the Department of Computer Science. Project ideas for the course are generated in community brainstorming workshops, held annually and facilitated by IWT staff members. Participants in the workshops include technical and non-technical women from the Boulder community at large, representatives of local community service agencies, a few interested academics, and the students enrolled in the course. At the workshop, the attendees identify problems confronting the agencies that can be solved computationally. Over the course of one or more semesters, the students work in groups to bring their solutions to product form, with technical and non-technical faculty members and interested community members all serving as advisors. A particular strength of the workshops is that they encourage participants to think beyond their workaday concerns. The resulting project ideas have been creative, interesting, and broad in scope.

The course has been offered each semester since Spring 2001. Its pilot offering will extend for four semesters, but we expect that it will become a permanent part of the UCB curriculum.

We note that, for the purposes of this course, "community service organization" is quite loosely defined. Clients have included a variety of non-profit and governmental organizations that provide aid or education of some kind to the people of Boulder, Colorado. In particular, the Boulder Valley School District has been an important participant.

CONTENT AND RESULTS

In the course, students learn to use software tools for such computational tasks as composing and editing Web sites, maintaining and manipulating databases, and creating CD-ROMs. The students study the process of turning an idea into a useful software product and methods for evaluating that product in terms of usability.

In the first three weeks of the semester, students put their new computational skills to work by creating "guest books." A guest book is a dynamic Web site where users can enter or retrieve information. That information is stored in a database. Each guest book is developed independently by one student; it may have any purpose and design that the student chooses. This assignment gives all of the students a common experience, a common vocabulary, and a common set of computational tools. The guest book represents a substantial piece of individual work. For students who enter the course with little computational experience, designing a Web site, creating the database, and hooking the two parts together is a major accomplishment.

The remaining weeks then are devoted to completing a computational project in collaboration with a local community service agency. Representatives of the agencies meet with the students in order to refine the project ideas generated at the workshop, and they later work with the students to test and evaluate prototypes. To date, all of the projects have been Web-based although that characteristic is not a requirement of a course project.

While representatives of many agencies have played some role in the course, some of the most important projects to this point include:

- A self-paced introductory tutorial about computers and the Internet for Boulder Senior Services,
- A variety of educational products for Sojourner Charter Middle School,
- A game for fourth graders simulating the ecology of a local marsh for the Boulder Valley School District, and
- An on-line events scheduling calendar for use by local non-profit agencies, developed for the Boulder Community Foundation.

While most of the projects satisfy small-scale needs of the client agencies, a local bank executive who is very active in non-profit work expects the events calendar to save local non-profits $100,000 a year by reducing events-scheduling conflicts. The full set of projects is showcased at http://www.cs.colorado.edu/VDC.

ENROLLMENT

The course is open to all undergraduate students at UCB. About 48% of the students who have enrolled in the first three semesters are female. That is a remarkable percentage in the Department of Computer Science, where females have totaled between 11 and 16% of undergraduate majors during the last 14 years. It demonstrates that UCB's Development Center is achieving its goal of woman-friendly technical education.

The student body is also diverse in terms of majors. In the first three semesters, 40% of the 41 students have come from the College of Engineering and 60% from three other UCB Colleges (Arts and Sciences, Business, and Journalism and Communication). About 28% of the students have been Computer Science majors. Freshmen and sophomores have enrolled, but most (85%) of the students have been juniors or seniors. The course is part of the Technology, Arts, and Media [TAM] certificate curriculum (TAM, 2002), and 35% of the students have come from the TAM program. Enrollment has grown each semester, but teaching facilities will likely limit class size to about 20-25 students.

The heterogeneous student body is suitable. Students work in small, interdisciplinary teams to complete the projects. Students with capabilities in such areas as design, art, writing, and social science find natural roles, as do students with strong computational skills. There is particular need for students with expertise in databases, Web site development, and the writing of educational materials.

There are no formal prerequisites for the course, but, for maximal comfort, participants should be able to write a simple program, compose a Web page, or have some familiarity with at least one commercial software package. Students with more advanced computing knowledge are invited to help with computational instruction.

PHILOSOPHY

The course is a long-term projects course, meaning that projects may be larger than can be completed in a single semester. Students who do not deliver a finished product at the end of the semester are asked to write a continuation plan to guide student teams who take up the project in subsequent semesters. Students may also repeat the course any number of times for credit. Indeed, students are strongly encouraged to participate in the long term. It is hoped that future years will find a varied group of collaborating students enrolled, from beginners to experienced technical leaders.

Because the course is based on new and developing concepts in technology education, students are encouraged to help to drive its direction and content. Students in the course also need to be independent learners, willing to take responsibility for learning new material from sources other than textbooks. Students must also be open to both teaching and learning from a variety of people of very different backgrounds.

METHODOLOGY

In building their projects, students learn and use the process of task-centered user interface design (TCD, 1994). In this process, the users' statements of their own needs and capabilities drive the product design. While developed for user interface design, task-centered design applies to the creation of any product where usability is the key concern.

Task-centered design follows these steps:

- Figure out who will use the system to do what
- Plagiarize!
- Rough out a design
- Think about it
- Prototype
- Test with users
- Iterate
  - Build it
  - Track it
  - Change it

Students begin by interviewing prospective users of their product, learning about their backgrounds, and about what they want the product to do. From the interviews, the students formulate a list of *tasks*. A task is a statement of something that needs to be accomplished that does not include information about implementation. A sample task for the events scheduling calendar might be "Mary, the events coordinator for XYZ organization, wants to change the starting time for an event she posted on the calendar last week." The collection of tasks defines the functionality of the product.

Working from the list of tasks, the students research commercial products and Web sites, looking for existing materials that relate to their projects. From those products, students liberally borrow features and functions (within the constraints of copyrights and patents.) The value of this "plagiarism" step is two-fold: borrowing reduces development time and borrowed features are often already familiar to users. The students then sketch out a detailed design on paper (a "low-fidelity" prototype) and proceed from the sketches to a rough computer implementation (a "high-fidelity" prototype). See, for example, Rudd, Stern, and Isensee (1996) for more information about prototyping.

In practice, evaluation of paper sketches proves too difficult for the students, so students instead "think about" or evaluate the high-fidelity prototypes. Project groups first judge their work using heuristic evaluation (Nielsen, 2002a). Each group member examines the prototype individually, looking for usability problems. The students are guided by Jakob Nielsen's ten usability heuristics, (Nielsen, 2002b) which are crafted to cover most known usability problems. The group members compare the results of their evaluations and determine how to correct the prototype in response to their findings. Each project group then carries out a cognitive walkthrough (Rieman, Franzke, and Redmiles, 1995) of the prototype. The students begin with a task statement and the list of steps needed to accomplish that task using the prototype. They walk through the list of steps, keeping in mind the interests and abilities of the users, and trying to tell a believable story about what the user might think and do at each step. Again, the students correct their prototypes to fix awkward or non-intuitive features. The two different types of evaluation help the students to identify different types of problems with their prototypes.

Carrying out the evaluations is typically difficult for the students as they, as undergraduates, are seldom asked to evaluate their own work. As a result, not all of the students appreciate the importance of the evaluations, and many are not patient enough to do a thorough job. They often believe that they have made only the best design choices and that there is no room for improvement. Their opinions change markedly, however, with the final round of thinking aloud (TA) evaluations (Lewis and Rieman, 1982). In contrast to the other two evaluation types, TA evaluations are done with users. In TA evaluations, the students observe a user trying to accomplish a task with the prototype. The user is asked to speak aloud all of her or his thoughts about the prototype during the process. Almost without exception, most of the user's thoughts and decisions (and stumblings and errors) catch the students completely by surprise. More than one student group has redesigned its prototype completely from scratch following the first round of TA evaluations, but responding to the users' actions and opinions typically gives the students a good sense of accomplishment.

The steps of high-fidelity prototyping, evaluating, and correcting the projects correspond to the last, iterative phase of task-centered design. Students repeat these steps until they and the users are satisfied with the results. Typically, the first round of TA evaluations has a large impact on the projects, while the second and third rounds deliver refinements.

ASSESSMENT OF STUDENTS

Given the experimental nature of the course and the large time commitment of setting it up, assessment of the students' work to date has been quite informal. Grades are assigned as about 85% for work on the project and 15% on preliminary assignments (mainly the guest book). The project grade is determined in part by the instructor (30% of total) and in part by the client (10%), but mainly by the project group members themselves (45%). By means of an evaluation form that poses several questions, group members are asked to evaluate themselves and their teammates with respect to both effort and results. In reality, a well-functioning group with an ecstatically happy client can expect high grades regardless of the other factors. It has not proven necessary to distinguish students according to major, but freshmen and sophomores are graded on a somewhat easier scale than are upperclassmen. We expect more formal evaluation of learning gains and outcomes to be included in future semesters.

WHAT THE STUDENTS SAY

Every semester, the students have reported that the strongest feature of Technology for Community is the multidisciplinary project groups. Engineers rarely have the opportunity to interact with fine arts or journalism majors in their usual coursework. The students come to recognize the diverse strengths of their project teammates and the variety of contributions those teammates are able to make to the project. The students also report that the biggest challenge of the course is learning to deliver a usable technical product to someone with little or no technical background. Not only must the features of the product match the abilities of the users, but also the students must find ways to present those features clearly to the users. Even the liberal arts majors in the course have grown up with some exposure to computers, while not all of their clients and product users have. For most, successfully finding language that allows the students of different majors to communicate with each other and their community service partners represents the biggest accomplishment of the course.

REFERENCES

Institute for Women and Technology (IWT). (2002). Retrieved July 20, 2002 from the World Wide Web: http://www.iwt.org/.

Lewis, C. (1982). *Using the "thinking aloud" method in cognitive interface design* (Research Report RC 9265 (40713)). Yorktown Heights: IBM Thomas J. Watson Research Center.

Lewis, C. and Rieman, J. (1994). *Task-Centered User Interface Design: A Practical Introduction.* Retrieved October 11, 2001 from the World Wide Web: http://www.acm.org/~perlman/uidesign.html.

Nielsen, J. (2002a). *How to Conduct a Heuristic Evaluation.* Retrieved June 10, 2002 from the World Wide Web: http://www.useit.com/papers/heuristic/heuristic_evaluation.html.

Nielsen, J. (2002b). *Ten Usability Heuristics.* Retrieved June 10, 2002 from the World Wide Web: http://www.useit.com/papers/heuristic/heuristic_list.html.

Rieman, J., Franzke, M. and Redmiles, D. (1995). *Usability Evaluation with the Cognitive Walkthrough.* Retrieved June 10, 2002 from the World Wide Web: http://www.acm.org/sigs/sigchi/chi95/Electronic/documnts/tutors/jr_bdy.htm.

Rudd, J., Stern, K. and Isensee, S. (1996, January). Low vs. High-Fidelity Protyping Debate. *Interactions*, 76-85.

Technology, Arts and Media Certificate (TAM) Program, University of Colorado at Boulder. (2002). Retrieved June 11, 2002 from the World Wide Web: http://www.colorado.edu/ATLAS/.

Section II

Managing IT Across Regions and Countries

Chapter VII

Information Resources Development in China: History, Present Situation and Problem Discussion

Lai Maosheng
Peking University, China

Fu Xin
Peking University, China

Zhang Liyang
Peking University, China

ABSTRACT

This chapter introduces the history and current situation of information resources development in China, with emphasis on the introduction of various initiatives underway and the initial impact of some information resources development policies of the Chinese government. It also analyzes problems in China's information resources development and raises possible solutions.

INTRODUCTION

Under the promotion of the international information technology revolution, China has been experiencing an upsurge in information development since the last decade of the 20th century. Information infrastructure construction keeps a rapid pace in development. The ownership of telephones, cellar phones and computers has been increasing steadily. The overall scale of China's information infrastructure now ranks number two in the world. On the other side, however, information resources development is lagging far behind. The lack of information, especially Chinese information, in networks and information systems influences the benefit of investment in information technology, which has become a major obstacle not only to China's informationalization drive but also to the competitiveness of Chinese economy.

This paper intends to introduce the history and current situation of information resources development in China, discuss its problems, and put forward several countermeasures.

BRIEF REVIEW ON THE HISTORY AND PRESENT SITUATION OF CHINA'S INFORMATION RESOURCES DEVELOPMENT

History of Information Resources Development in China

In its several thousand years of social progress, China has put continuous efforts on cultural development. Various ancient Chinese dynasties, such as the Han, Tang, Song, Ming, and Qing, carried out large-scale cultural development movements, which to a certain extent contributed to the exploitation and utilization of information resources.

Since the founding of the People's Republic of China in 1949, the government has been attaching great importance to information resources development. In 1956, the government set "March Towards Science" as the directing principle for the course of information resources management, and made a conscientious plan in information resources development with the emphasis on collecting, rearranging, analyzing, indexing, and reporting scientific and technical documents from home and abroad to serve the needs of professionals in various disciplines. Until 1987, the scientific and technical information sector alone has already possessed 26,000 foreign periodicals, 6,000 domestic periodicals, 120 million patent manuals, and more than 32 million books. There were 236 abstracting and indexing journals published annually, covering more than 1.2 million documents and articles. Besides this, there were 2,038 public libraries at county and higher levels, collecting more than 200 million books; 745 academic libraries, collecting 250 million books; and more than 4,000 libraries in research institutes (collection of these libraries was not revealed, but the 1,400 libraries in the Chinese Academy of Sciences alone collected more than 18 million books) (Guan, 1988).

In the late 1980s and early 1990s, however, information resources development was affected by the readjusting of China's economy. Non-profitable libraries and information service institutions suffered from a severe shortage of money for collection development. As a result, information resources development was captured in a severe logjam or even retrogress. Types of document collections in some libraries dropped by one-half or even two-thirds (Fu, 1996). Many abstracting and indexing journals stopped publication. On the other hand, there emerged some new abstracting and indexing journals as well as bibliographical databases, which catered to market demand.

Since the mid-1990s, under the promotion of the tide of the information superhighway construction in many countries, information resources development in China entered a new phase.

In 1997, the Chinese government constituted the "Draft on China's Informationalization," drawing the outline of China's information infrastructure (Zou, 1997), which includes six elements as follows:

- Information Resource
- National Information Network
- Information Technology (IT) Application
- Information Industry
- Information Professional
- Information Policy, Code and Standard

Information resource was set as the primary element among the six, which showed the state's emphasis on its development. This also indicated that people once again realized the importance of information resources development. Several years later, the proposal was accepted as a part of China's tenth "five-year plan," which marked that information resources development became the central task of China's informationalization drive.

Academic Research on Information Resources Development

Information resources development has consistently been a research hotspot for Chinese librarians and information professionals. In a search conducted in the *Chinese Journal Full-text Database*[1] by limiting the phrase "information resources development" to title, a total of 273 articles were returned. The foci of the articles range from document resources development to the construction of the information superhighway, from scientific and technical information resources development to information resources development for social sciences, from information resources development at the national or international level to information resources development at the regional level. Some articles focus on the development of a specific type of information resource, such as database development or Internet information resources development. Some articles focus on development of information resources in one of the social sectors, such as agricultural information resources development, national defense information resources development, aquatic information resources development, or geological information resources development. Most of the articles of this type appear in journals of respective disciplines. Many articles review the achievement of information resources development in China, analyze its problems, and put forward suggestions for its future development.

The concept "Information Resources Development" used in this paper refers to the collection, processing, organization and dissemination of document resources, as well as their digitalization and networking. Fact and data resources ought to be included in the concept. However, China's progress in these aspects is relatively slow. In recent years, people started to realize the importance of fact and data resources development. The departments concerned have started to work out a plan for constructing a National Data Center.

MAJOR INITIATIVES IN CHINA'S INFORMATION RESOURCES DEVELOPMENT

Under the guidance of the policies introduced in the last section, the Chinese government initiated several major information resources development projects to change the current situation of inconsistency between information resources development and information network construction and to lessen the discrepancy between information resources available and those required by the public.

CALIS (China Academic Library and Information System)

CALIS is an initiative under China's plan to build 100 key universities in the 21st century (named "211 Project" by the Ministry of Education). It aims at constructing a networked information resources-sharing system based on the China Education and Research Network (CERNET) (details of which will be covered later) so as to parallel the development of communication networks and information resources networks — thus providing university staff and students, as well as professionals in research institutions, with easy access to a national information service system characterized by abundant information resources, advanced technologies, and a convenient service system.

The service system consists of a CALIS national management center, four CALIS national information centers (covering sciences and social sciences, engineering, agricultural science, and medical science respectively) and seven CALIS regional information centers (in Beijing, Shanghai, Nanjing, Guangzhou, Xi'an, Chengdu, Wuhan and Changchun respectively). The system will be also linked to major information service systems outside China to form China's Academic Library and Information System. The construction of CALIS will greatly increase the amount of information available to academic libraries and also improve their capability in information services (www.calis.edu.cn).

Digitalization Projects

The China Digital Library Project was carried out under the coordination of the Ministry of Culture. In July 1997, the National Library of China (then Beijing Library), together with the Shanghai Library, Shenzhen Library, Zhongshan Library, Liaoning Library, and Nanjing Library and Cultural and Technological Development Center under the Ministry of Culture, started the Chinese Pilot Digital Library Project (CPDLP). Later in 1998, the Ministry of Culture formally put forward the proposal of constructing the China Digital Library. The project, called the China Digital Library Project, was participated in by a variety of enterprises and organizations such as China Telecom, the National Library of China, the Chinese Academy of Sciences, the China Aerospace Industrial Corporation, Peking University and Tsinghua University.

The project strived to:

- build a cross-region, cross-industry cultural and information network, making it the National Information Infrastructure (NII) in China;
- collect cultural information from nation-wide libraries, museums, memorials, press and publication institutions, art groups, sports institutions, travel agencies, etc., and build a huge knowledge repository represented by digital libraries, digital museums and digital film and TV centers;
- build an integrated information resource network based on existing backbone communication networks, so as to provide user-oriented service to satisfy users' demand for flexible network connection and fast-speed information retrieval to different kinds of resources databases; and
- develop an intellectualized user interface in Chinese and popularize the use of the Internet so that users can have access to resources on the Internet with

such convenience as the easiness they enjoy when they watch TV. This will undoubtedly maximize the utilization of the cultural information resources on the Internet.

As the achievements of the project, it was expected that some twenty resource databases would be made available on the China Cultural Information Network, among which are the China Medical Science Resource Database, China Tourism Resource Database, and China Economic Resource Information Database, etc. The network will become a significant channel of spreading Chinese culture and will strongly support China's project of "rejuvenating the nation through science and education." As a cross-century comprehensive project, the construction of a China Digital Library will be conducive to the development of many related industries, especially the information industry and cultural industry, finally benefiting the national economy as a whole (Xu, 1999, 2000; Sun, 1999).

Besides the China Digital Library Project, various other digital library projects were also carried out. The construction of the China Scientific Digital Library was started in late 2001. The project, as part of the Knowledge Innovation Project of the Chinese Academy of Sciences, aims to build a digital information service system that meets the international developing trends of digital libraries and caters to the development of the Chinese Academy of Sciences. It should be able to serve the needs of researchers and professionals in information accessing and knowledge innovation when it is finished in three to four years' time (Zhang, 2002).

In China's Taiwan Province, eight digital library initiatives are currently underway, including the construction of a Digital Library and Information Center and the building of Haoran Digital Library in Jiaotong University. Objectives of the initiatives are to promote information exchanges among learning and research institutions in Taiwan and coordinate their purchase of information resources, such as databases, from foreign countries. Another object is to promote research on Chinese culture, especially on Chinese history (Lv, 1999).

There are also digitalization projects other than construction of digital libraries. In January 1999, the Geology Department of the Chinese Academy of Sciences raised to the State Council a proposal on strategies of China's "Digital Globe" development, indicating the importance of building a national Global Information Infrastructure and establishing a digital global spatial information-sharing system (*Information Industry Newspaper*, November 22, 1999). During November 29 – December 2, 1999, the first "Digital Globe" International Conference was held in Beijing, showing that the Chinese government attached great importance to international cooperation in this area (*China Computer World*, December 6, 1999.).

Construction of the China National Science and Technology Library (NSTL)

In 1998, the State Council initiated a reform to scientific and technical information institutions. In June 2000, the China National Science and Technology Library (NSTL) was formally established through the cooperation among China's Ministry of Science and Technology, State Committee of Economics and Trade, Ministry of Agriculture, Ministry of Health, and the Chinese Academy of Sciences. As a virtual scientific and technical resource center, it consists of eight library and information institutions, such as Library of the Chinese Academy of Sciences, National Engineering Library of China, Library of the Chinese Academy of Agricultural Science, Library of the Chinese Academy of Medical Science, and Institute of Scientific and Technical Information of China. The center utilizes advanced technologies and methods to collect information from domestic and foreign sources. It also makes standards and criteria in information-sharing. Moreover, the center serves as a bridge of cooperation between Chinese information resources management professionals and their foreign counterparts (Yuan and Meng, 2001).

Regional and Special-Topic Information Resources Development

Practice of Information Resources Development in Shanghai – Co-development and Sharing

In September 1957, the State Council of China released the "National Book Coordination Scheme" and set up two central library committees, respectively in Beijing and Shanghai, to coordinate the nationwide development of library and document resources. This initiative gained marked achievements in its early phase, although its later development was not satisfactory.

On March 25, 1994, the signing of three documents about resources sharing by 19 academic libraries in Shanghai declared the founding of the Document Resources Coordination Network in Shanghai. By the end of May 1998, members of the network had reached 30, including almost all the large and medium-sized academic libraries and public libraries, such as Fudan University Library, Shanghai Jiao Tong University Library, Tongji University Library, East China Normal University Library, Shanghai Document and Information Centre of the Chinese Academy of Sciences, the Institute of Scientific and Technical Information of Shanghai (ISTIS), and Shanghai Library.

Based on the network, libraries and information institutes in Shanghai responded actively to the "Scheme on Nation Document Resources Coordination" released in January 1999. On May 13, 1999, the "Plan on Document Resources Sharing in Shanghai" was passed. Its main aims were to establish express and effective information infrastructure with the collaboration of member libraries, to foster scientifically distributed document collection system, and to develop a quick-responding and well-equipped document providing system. The plan also aimed to recruit and train a pool of library and information professionals, well-known both within China and in the world. The implementation of the plan would establish a new system for document services, which could benefit Shanghai as well as the whole country. In 2000, one year after the start of the plan, member libraries purchased 900 more types of foreign periodicals than in 1999, and a networked interlibrary loan system was put into operation. The plan had won its first success.

Government Information Resources Development – The China Online Government Project

On January 22, 1999, the China Online Government Project Start-Up Conference was held in Beijing, sponsored by China Telecom and the State Economic and Trade Commission, together with the information sectors of more than forty ministries. At the conference, the China Online Government Project was started. Subsequently, the main Web site of the China government portal, www.gov.cn, was established in 1999.

According to the White Paper on the China Online Government Project, the project refers to the practice by the government at all levels to establish their formal Web sites to promote office automation in government work, offer public services via the Internet, and fulfill the roles of management and service in the fields of society, economy, and social life.

The Online Government Project will improve the government's image on the Internet and promote the use of computers in government work. More importantly, it enables the government to provide public services via the Internet, adds to the amount of Chinese information resources on the Internet, and promotes the development of the information industry. The major aspects of the online government project, such as online government information service, B to G e-business (including e-procurement), e-government (the introduction of OA systems in the government), the restructuring of the government, and the citizen's participation in the government's decision making (Huang and Zhu, 1999) all require the development of government information resources. Therefore, the online government project is actually a great impetus to government information resources development.

Patent Information Resources Development

Patent information is an essential part of a country's technical information resources. As a typical kind of intellectual asset, patent information plays the role of both technical information and economic information. The amount of patent application reflects the technical power of an enterprise or a country. Moreover, the content of the patents usually reveals the potential marketing demand. Therefore, patent information resources development is highly valued in all the countries.

To meet the users' requirements of searching and utilizing patent information, China Patent InfoNet was established by the Retrieving and Consulting Center, under the State Intellectual Property Office in May 1998. In January 2002, its new version (http://www.patent.com.cn) was published online and started to offer all-around services to patent users and researchers, such as patent information retrieval, introduction of patent laws and regulations, and guidelines for a patent application.

Education Information Resources Development — China Education and Research Network (CERNET)

Since the 1980s, almost every developed country in the world has set up state-level education and research computer networks, which have been interconnected to constitute the cross-border academic network — the Internet. The advent of the Internet has accelerated information transmission; created a brand new networked computing environment for teachers, students and research and development personnel worldwide; virtually changed and driven interpersonal communication, resource sharing, scientific computation and collaborative research and development; and become the most important infrastructure for education and research in these countries, which has significantly boosted the development of education and research in these areas.

Under such a background, the Chinese government made the decision of constructing the China Education and Research Network (CERNET), and developing it into a nationwide digital platform for sharing educational and research information.

As the first nationwide education and research computer network in China, CERNET would allow teachers, researchers, and students in most universities and colleges around the country to study and do research in a networked environment. It would link every part of the country and every corner of the world, which would significantly improve education quality and research abilities and provide Chinese universities and colleges with an easy access to the world's science and technology arena.

Funded by the Chinese government and directly managed by the Ministry of Education of China, the construction of CERNET involves the establishment of a nationwide backbone network, which connects eight regional networks, and links to the global Internet. The CERNET has a four-layer hierarchy: the national backbone network, regional networks, provincial networks, and campus networks. CERNET National Center is located in Tsinghua University, which is responsible for operation and management of the CERNET backbone network. The ten regional network centers and main nodes are distributed among Tsinghua University, Peking University, Beijing University of Post and Telecommunications, Shanghai Jiaotong University, Xi'an Jiaotong University, Central China University of Science and Technology, South China Institute of Technology, China University of Electronic Science, Southeast University, and Northeast University, which are responsible for operation, management, planning and construction of the CERNET regional networks.

A large-scale China Education Information System has been built on the CERNET. Mirroring systems for discipline-specific information of famous overseas universities and a full-text searching system for higher education information and information on key projects will soon be finished. The construction of CERNET greatly facilitates the information resources sharing among Chinese universities, adding considerable impetus to the development of higher education in China as a whole.

Construction of National Research Centers for Information Resources Management (IRM)

Three national research centers for information resources management have recently been set up in Beijing, Nanjing, and Wuhan to promote research on theories, policies, and technologies in IRM. Based on the cooperation with the Department of Information Management of Peking University, Department of Information Management of Nanjing University, and School of Information Management of Wuhan University, the centers will focus on establishing information resources management policies, mechanisms, and technologies that not only accord with the current situation in China, but also help to strengthen international cooperation in the field of IRM.

INITIAL IMPACT OF THE POLICIES

CALIS System

Started in November 1998, CALIS completed its first phase of construction by the end of 2001. Currently, the system can provide an online public access catalog, interlibrary loan (ILL), Internet navigation, online cataloging, cooperative literature purchasing, and various other functions through digitalization of information resources, networking of information services, and cooperation among participating academic libraries. As a result, universities and colleges in China now possess information resources greatly more than ever before. The variety of foreign periodicals increased by one-third, 95% of the Chinese literature and 80% of foreign literature are now available, and more than 100 academic libraries offer 24-hour online information services. In addition, 25 distinctive databases and 194 disciplinary navigation databases have been built.

In its second phase of construction, starting in 2002, CALIS aims to further strengthen the document supporting ability of academic libraries. It plans to realize the automation and networking of about 1,000 academic libraries, among which 100 will be fully automated and networked, becoming the backbones in information resource-sharing. Some 20 academic libraries will be developed into digital library bases, acting as the kernels of information service systems and distributing centers of information resources. Besides this, digitalized information resources imported from foreign countries are expected to cover all subject areas, while domestic information resources will be as much as several terabytes (Zhu, 2001).

China Digital Library Project and NSTL Construction

Construction of the China Digital Library and the National Science and Technology Library have been advancing smoothly. In April 1999, the China Cultural Information Net started operation as the top level of the China Digital Library. In November 1999 and February 2000 respectively, the Capital Library and China Radio International (CRI) became experimental units of the China Digital Library project. Experts from various fields of study are doing extensive research on technological, operational, and legal issues involved in the construction of the digital library. Recently, the directing committee of the China Digital Library project proclaimed that construction of the China Digital Library must be expanded to include digital resource development. The China Digital Library should be more than a digital library; it should be constructed into a digital resource center. It should include information resources not only from libraries, but also from the government, and even from international channels. The ultimate goal of the project is to build a "Digital China."

The initiative of building the National Science and Technology Library is near conclusion. Through two years of construction, participating libraries now collect more than 16,000 types of foreign scientific and technical literatures (including periodicals, conference proceedings, technical reports, etc.), as compared to no more than 4,000 types in 1996. Some 6.5 million bibliographical records were put online by the end of March 2002, and this number is expected to increase at a rate of 2 million per year. The network service system provides 24-hour, free, secondary literature retrieval service to Internet users. In March 2002 alone, 1.37 million users visited the system, as compared to 150,000 when the system was started in January 2001. More than 60,000 users have received full-text document service.

Development of Commercial Information Products

Information resource development in a market-oriented approach achieves great effect. Many database and information service providers (such as ICP and ISP) come into operation, including the China Academic Journals CD-ROM database, ChinaInfo Group, Chongqing Weipu Information Consulting Corporation, Ltd. (www.vipinfo.com.cn), Beijing Scholar Sci-Tech Co., Ltd., and China Infobank, etc., and enjoy nation-wide reputation. The Chinese Journal Full-text Database includes more than 6.1 million articles from 6,600 major periodicals published in mainland China since 1994, as well as more than 15 million bibliographical records. The database is available both online and in CD-ROM form.

In a broader context, Internet-based information resources have also undergone rapid development. According to statistics from the "Survey on Information Resources in China," which was released by the China Internet Network Information Center (CNNIC) in September 2001 (http://www.cnnic.net.cn/tj/rep2001.shtml), there were 692,490 registered domain names, 238,249 Web sites, 159,460,056 Web pages, and 45,598 online databases within China. A recently released report shows that the number of Web sites increased to 293,213 by June 2002 (http://www.cnnic.net.cn/develst/2002-7e/index.shtml).

With the further improvement of information infrastructure and the intensifying of international communication brought by its entry into the World Trade Organization (WTO), China will surely embrace a boom in information resource development in the 21st century.

PROBLEMS IN INFORMATION RESOURCES DEVELOPMENT IN CHINA AND COUNTERMEASURES

The aforementioned projects and their achievements lead to our discussion and analysis of some problems that hindered information resources development in China from faster advancement.

Information Need is the Decisive Factor of Information Resources Development

The stalemate of China's information resources development between the late 1980s and early 1990s was heavily due to the reformation of the country's economy. With the change of the society's information needs, products and services of information agents could no longer meet social demands. The key issue in information resources development, therefore, was understanding and satisfying new information needs of society. A project, even if supported by state finance, would very probably lead to unsatisfactory or tragic results if it were not directed to market demand. Satisfying social and market demand is a principle that should always be carefully observed in China's information resources development.

Role of the Government

The emphasis on demand-orientation does not mean the neglect of the government's roles in information resources development. Information resources development requires both the driving forces from the market and the participation by the government. The government's participation includes: (1) It should make guidelines and policies for information resources development, such as the overall layout of information resources development, the arrangement of key projects and their preferences, policies on investment, financing and taxation, and mechanism of coordination, etc. (2) The country's legislative body must set legal standards and provide judicial guarantee for information resources development projects, such as protection of intellectual property. (3) The government should take the lead in opening its information to the public and providing high-quality, non-profitable information services to organizations and citizens.

Choice of Information Resources Development Strategies

Information resources development involves huge investment and a long duration of time. Therefore, it is extremely important to choose appropriate development strategies. From past experience, we feel that the following two issues are worthy of greater attention. The first is that the government should carefully lay out the emphasis of their interference in information resources development. The state should mainly be responsible for information resources development projects for public welfare, while leaving non-public welfare projects for the market and regulating through policies. The second issue is cooperation in information resources development, including both the cooperation between different industries within the country and cooperation between China and other countries in the world. An additional issue is the protection of the state sovereign and national culture. The tendency of undue reliance on foreign information resources should be attended to.

Attention Should be Paid to Construction of Infrastructure in Information Resources Development

Collection, construction, cataloging, indexing, and abstracting work and database construction are fundamental work in information resources development. Nothing could be done without abundant high-quality information resources, and no information resource can play its role without high-quality catalogs, indexes and abstracts. Cataloging, indexing, and abstracting, as the infrastructure in information resources development, are effective tools for information users to make use of the huge pool of information resources; however, it is also an often-neglected aspect in information resources development. Therefore, we must pay special attention to it.

Digitalization and Networking are Inevitable Trends in Information Resources Development

Developing countries such as China are exploring methods of managing information resources with advanced information technologies and spreading them with digitalized and Internet technologies. Digital library and distributive information resources on the Internet are the directions of information resources development. What should be emphasized here is the correct understanding of the connotation of digital library. The construction of digital libraries not only contains the digitalization of current document resources in the libraries, but also involves digitalized management and dissemination of social information resources and cultural resources at a wider context. In the process of digitalization and networking, great attention must be paid to the protection of intellectual property and privacy. Any action eager for quick success and instant benefit may finally hinder the healthy advancement of information resources development work.

Promoting the Development of Information Service Sector to Boost Better Information Resources Development

With the development of the information service industry, more and more information resources will be needed to satisfy users' needs, which will in turn promote information resources development, opening the market for information resources, and reclaiming some capital for consistent development of information resources. On the other hand, however, the development of the information service industry requires a certain amount of information resources as its base. How to properly handle their relationship and coordinate their development is an issue worth our attention. The construction of an academic CD-ROM by Tsinghua Tongfang Co., the ChinaInfo Group's practice of "serving while constructing," and successful experiences of other information agents on information resources development and information services prove that information resources development must take the path of industrialization. Information resources development is no longer solely a public welfare course. Instead, it is an important component of the information industry. The well-known example of the competition between the Human Genome Project and Celera Company can also serve as a proof.

CONCLUSION AND FUTURE TRENDS

The projects that we have introduced above lay a solid foundation for the further development of information resources in China. Although the restructuring of China's economy poses some negative influence on the information resources development practice, it meanwhile creates plenty of new opportunities. Looking into the future, we can feel the long way ahead for China to improve its information resources. The digital library projects will be further expanded and the information resources development projects are expected to receive continuous support from the government; in addition, as one of the most important problems of information resources development, the issue of nationwide cooperation across industries is expected to come out soon.

With the development of China's economy and the recognition of the importance of information resources to social and economic development, there is reason to believe that China's information resources development will reach a new high in the near future.

ENDNOTES

1 Chinese Journal Full-text Database covers more than 6,000,000 academic papers that appear in more than 6,600 major Chinese academic journals.

REFERENCES

Chen, S. and Fu, Q. (1998). Development of the Internet and the Construction of Information Resources in China. *Journal of the China Society for Science and Technology Information*, 17(1), 4-7.

Fu, L. (1996). Some Thinking on the Strategies of China's Sci-Tech Information Resources Construction. *Journal of the China Society for Scientific and Technical Information*, 15(5), 374-377.

Guan, J. (1988). *Information Work and Information Science Development Strategy*. Beijing: Sci-Tech Document Publishing House.

Huang, C. and Zhu, H. (1999). Preliminary Approach to the Strategy for Information Resources Construction in China. *Journal of the Chinese Society for Scientific and Technical Information*, 18(9), 47-51.

Lv, Y. (1999, May). Digital Library in Taiwan. *China Computer World*, pp. D2-D3.

Shao, B. and Yuan, Q. (2000). Construction of CERNET North Eastern Regional Network: Situation and Problem. *Modern Information*, 1, 23-28.

Shao, B., Yuan, Q., and Wang, W. (2000). Information Resources Construction of CERNET Central China Regional Network: Situation and Problem. *Academic Library Work*, 20(1), 29-33.

Sun, C. (1999). *Towards Digital Library in Collected Thesis on Digital Library*. Shenyang: NEU Press.

Xu, W. (1999, May 7). Constructing China Digital Library Project. *Guangming Daily*, 8.

Xu, W. (2000, March 8). Great Significance in Building China Digital Library. *Guangming Daily*, C1.

Yuan, H. and Meng, L. (2001). A Practice on Information Resource Sharing in Web-based environment – Construction and Development of National Research Centers for Information Resources Management. *Proceedings to Academic Seminar Commemorating 45th Anniversary of China's Scientific and Technical Information Cause*. Beijing.

Yuan, M., Liu, S., and Lai, M. (2002). *Social Science Information Resources Network Construction*. Beijing: Nation Library of China Press.

Yuan, Q. and Shao, B. (1999). Information Resources Construction of CERNET Beijing Regional Network: Situation and Problem. *Information Theory and Application*, 22(3), 201-202,182.

Zhang, X. (2002). China Scientific Digital Library: User-Oriented Digital Information Service System. *Sci-Tech International*, 4, 21-23.

Zhu, Q. (2001). A Rewarding Practice on Information Resource Sharing Oriented towards the 21st Century—Advances in the Construction of China Academic Library & Information System. *Proceedings to 2001 Annual Meeting of China Society for Library Science*. Chengdu.

Zou, J. (1997, September 16). Promoting National Informationalization. *China Electronics Daily*, 1.

Chapter VIII

An Analysis of Factors that Influence the Ability of SMEs to Derive Benefit in Four Phases of Electronic Commerce: 34 Australian Case Studies

Stephen B. Chau
University of Tasmania, Australia

Paul Turner
University of Tasmania, Australia

ABSTRACT

This paper builds on research presented by the authors at IRMA 2001. Previous research by Chau and Turner (2001b) adapted the work of Venkatraman (1994) to explore the relationship between the degree of SME organisational transformation and potential benefits derived from e-commerce. The qualitative data explored reveals various factors that influence SME's ability to derive benefit from conducting Web-based e-commerce. A preliminary review suggests that these factors can be distinguished into internal factors (organisational and technological) and external factors (nature of supply chain, level of service provided by third party organisations, industry influence, and government assistance). This paper discusses these factors and their implications for modelling e-business organisational transformation.

INTRODUCTION

Inhibitors to the adoption of e-commerce (EC) by small to medium-sized enterprises (SMEs) have been well researched (Freel, 2000; Lawrence and Keen, 1997; MacGregor, Waugh, and Bunker, 1996; Poon, Swatman, and Vitale, 1996; Poon and Swatman, 1998). More recently it has emerged that even where e-commerce technology adoption occurs, this has often not translated directly into the active utilisation and conduct of e-commerce (NOIE, 2000a; Wong and Turner, 2001). Amongst those SMEs who do actively utilise e-commerce, previous research has highlighted that the level and extent of Web-based e-commerce can be usefully categorised into four phases (Chau, 2001). These phases emerge as transitional states in the use of e-commerce that SMEs may establish themselves at directly or migrate to from other phases.

Preliminary case study analysis suggests that the potential to derive benefit from e-commerce activities increases where SMEs have been able to re-align business processes and structures (Chau and Turner, 2001). The ability of SMEs to re-align business processes depends upon a number of factors. To date however, there has been little detailed investigation into the factors that impact on SMEs' ability to derive e-commerce benefits within any particular phase of e-commerce activity.

This research paper identifies and explores the range of factors that impact on SMEs' potential to derive benefit from e-commerce activities in each of the four phases. The paper develops a framework for exploring these factors that emerge as either internal or external to the SMEs analysed. Preliminary analysis highlights the utility of the framework for revealing the distinct characteristics of these factors within each phase.

An interpretative epistemology was deployed as the most logical and appropriate approach to capture information about the beliefs, actions, and experiences of SME participants in relation to their use of e-commerce. Data collection consisted of a series of interviews conducted with senior management. Using a semi-structured interview question frame, managers were asked a series of questions investigating the reasons for adopting e-commerce and the current use of e-commerce within the business. Questions also addressed any problems faced during or subsequent to e-commerce adoption and utilisation, any organisational changes that occurred as a result of e-commerce, benefits and problems received from adopting e-commerce and the direct impact of e-commerce on business performance. Each of the interviews was transcribed for further analysis. Data analysis was conducted through a set of coding procedures. The coding procedures revealed distinct characteristics of factors (internal/external) to each phase of e-commerce utilisation.

THE 34 CASE STUDIES

This research paper is part of an on-going study investigating the utilisation of e-commerce by Australian SMEs. These 34 case studies investigate the uptake and use of e-commerce amongst SMEs across a broad range of businesses from seven different industries including agriculture, retail trade, hospitality, education, communications, and manufacturing. These businesses vary in age from start-ups to well-established businesses. The SMEs that participated in this research were drawn from two states in Australia (Tasmania and Western Australia).

THE FOUR-PHASE MODEL OF E-COMMERCE UTILISATION AMONG SMES

A preliminary analysis of the 34 case studies suggests that SME Web-based e-commerce can be categorised into four phases. The phases can be described as a static Web presence, an adjunct to traditional business, substantial reengineering of business processes, and a virtual enterprise (Chau, 2001). SMEs engaged in no Web-based e-commerce are considered to be located in position *Po*. The term *phase* is used to highlight that SMEs did not necessarily undertake a staged approach to using e-commerce but embarked on the use of e-commerce at any one of the phases. A SME can migrate between phases or jump phases depending on the level of organisational transformation applied.

Position P0: Conventional SME utilising no Web based EC

SMEs in this phase do not incorporate any Web-based e-commerce; however, they may adopt basic e-commerce banking functions such as electronic funds transfer (EFT), EFT point of sale (EFTPOS), phone banking, and electronic bill payment (BPAY).

Phase P1: SMEs incorporate a static Web presence

Phase one SMEs consider e-commerce will influence their organisation in their industry in the future and are keen to experiment or gain a presence for little cost or ongoing maintenance. These SMEs incorporate basic e-commerce initiatives, typically a Web site providing information on organisational background, e-mail contacts, and information on product and services. These Web sites tend to be static and require little maintenance.

Phase P2: SMEs add dynamic and interactive functionality to their use of e-commerce

In phase two SMEs demonstrate an interactive utilisation of e-commerce on their Web site. The use of e-commerce is not integrated directly into existing information systems and their core business processes are unlikely to change as a result of the e-commerce activity. The organisation's use of e-commerce is considered to be experimental and is not highlighted as a strategic move. By not incorporating e-commerce applications directly with back-end systems, the organisation can insulate it self from potential security threats; however, the potential benefits derived from e-commerce are limited due to minimal integration of e-commerce into existing business processes. SMEs consider their e-commerce activities to benefit in the long term and do not anticipate substantial short-term gains.

Phase P3: SMEs engage in substantial re-engineering of business processes to accommodate e-commerce initiatives

SMEs located at phase three engage in advanced use of e-commerce utilisation. The SMEs have an in-depth understanding of their business and what benefits e-commerce technologies can provide. Management has a clear e-commerce strategy that links directly to their broader implicit or explicit business strategy. The e-commerce applications require substantial capital/resource expenditure and involve significant organisational transformation in core business processes. Traditional business processes and existing information systems are altered to accommodate the e-commerce systems. The degree of organisational transformation is markedly higher than cases found in phase two.

Phase P4: Virtual business enterprises

The use of e-commerce is central to business operations for SMEs located in phase four. The organisation uses e-commerce as a trading platform and communication medium for all transactions. The development of e-commerce applications is designed to harness the most benefit from e-commerce. Virtual SMEs may be operating from home or other non-commercial settings, substantially reducing the overheads incurred in traditional business operations. Virtual organisations by nature readily embrace new technologies for computer-mediated communications (Barnatt, 1997).

This study has identified two groups of SMEs that may be located in phase four. One group of SMEs consists of established businesses that evolved from a traditional business model to a virtual trading model, where a new business entity is created to trading exclusively online. These types of virtual SMEs may not have resided at any of the previous phases. The second group of phase four SMEs can consist of SMEs that were previously located in another phase (1,2 or 3) and have migrated to phase four.

SMEs that trade in information-related products are highly suited to operating in this virtual enterprise located in phase four.

New start-up e-commerce businesses (dot.coms) with no prior trading history may potentially acquire the same benefits received by phase four SMEs without undergoing the extensive organisational transformations encountered by phase four organisations. These dot.com SMEs have the advantage of designing their business to fully embrace e-commerce technologies; however, they are disadvantaged by not having an establish client base.

THE FOUR-PHASE MODEL OF E-COMMERCE BUSINESS TRANSFORMATION

Subsequent data analysis reveals a link between the degree of SME organisational transformation and the potential to derive benefits from e-commerce activities. This led to the development of an extended four-phase model (Chau and Turner, 2001). The four phases e-commerce business transformation model acknowledges Venkatraman's (1994) work identifying an association between the range of potential benefits enabled by investment in information technology and levels of organisational transformation. It also acknowledges the research on SMEs by Poon and Swatman (1998) that identified a relationship between organisational

Diagram 1: Four Phases of E-Commerce Business Transformation Among SMEs

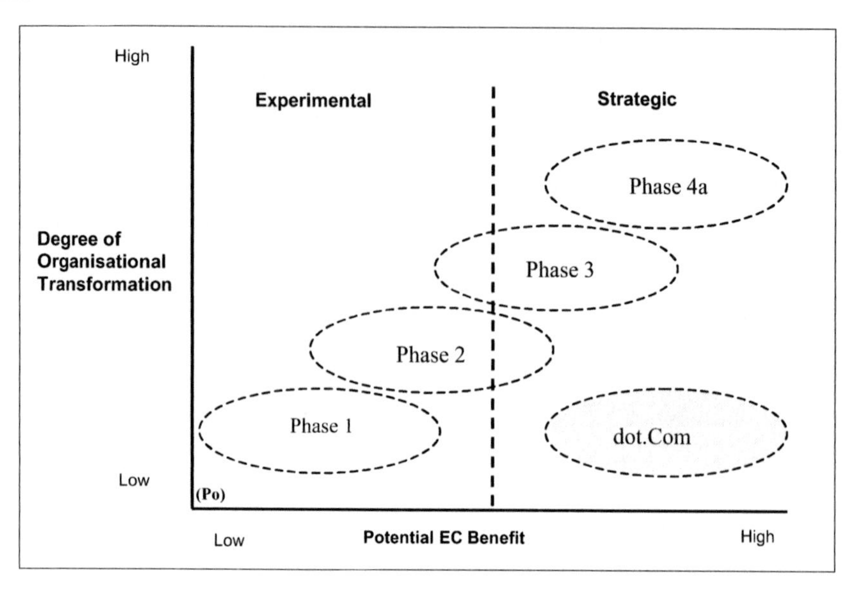

process adjustment and potential benefits from the Internet for internal application systems integration.

The model suggests that the potential benefit from e-commerce can increase if businesses are willing to transform their organisations to facilitate the use of e-commerce within their inherent business processes. The exceptions to this phenomenon exist for dot.com organisations, which design their business to embrace the full potential of e-commerce . The model highlights three major points in the data analysis. First, the potential benefits derived from e-commerce activities increase where enterprises engage in a process of organisational transformation. When an investment in e-commerce technologies increase optimal benefits can only be obtained by suitable changes in organisational structure and processes. Second, the phases depicted do not prescribe an evolutionary path for e-commerce utilisation. The position of a particular SME relies on strategic choices made by management. Subject to business directions and strategic goals, it is possible through investment for an SME to migrate or establish themselves directly at any one of the four phases. Third, there are two distinct perspectives adopted by SMEs in relation to the use of e-commerce. The initial stage comprises a period of experimentation with e-commerce that delivers limited e-commerce benefits and requires limited organisational change. The second stage involves a clear strategic direction requiring greater resources and organisational transformation to acquire increased potential to derive e-commerce benefit.

FACTORS THAT INFLUENCE AN SME'S ABILITY TO UTILISE E-COMMERCE

The four-phase e-commerce Business Transformation Model categorises the utilisation of e-commerce by SMEs into four possible phases. The relative position of SMEs within each phase is influenced by a number of factors. This research presents a range of factors that are apparent from the data analysis. The factors can be broadly distinguished by two main sets. Those factors that are internal to the

Table 1: Internal Factors Influencing the Potential to Derive E-Commerce Benefit

Organisational	Technological
Management • MIS skills • Leadership Qualities • Enthusiasm and Support for EC **E-Commerce Driver** • Client driven • Management • Customer Service • Communications • Access New Markets • Sales • Business Efficiency **E-Commerce Strategy** • Experimental Use of E-Commerce • Strategic Use of E-Commerce • Incremental Approach **Resources** • Capital to Invest in Technology • Support for IT/ E-Commerce Investment	**Technical Infrastructure** • EC Support/Development • IT Experience • IT Infrastructure **E-Commerce Application** • Independent • Integrated • Internet Platform • Communication Oriented

organisation, in which the organisation retains some control, and external factors that are external to the organisation, where the organisation has little control.

The internal factors can be divided into two categories relating to issues that are of an organisational nature and issues that are technologically-related. From an organisational perspective, the role of management, the reason why e-commerce is used, and the manner in which e-commerce is applied all influence the potential to derive benefit from e-commerce. These issues are further governed by the ability of the organisation to implement and support an e-commerce application, such as the amount of resources and technical expertise available.

INTERNAL FACTORS

Organisational Factors

The Role of Management

Management plays a pivotal role in the e-commerce decision-making process. The role of management plays an important role in the implementation and utilisation of e-commerce. Management skills, leadership qualities and strategic direction directly impact on the ability of a SME to engage in e-commerce. Management skills relate to the attributes of the managers of each business. The level of enthusiasm for e-commerce and interest in technology and e-commerce were characteristics that reflect on the level of e-commerce knowledge and understanding possessed by management in the case studies. In all phases management believes that e-commerce can provide benefit to the business; however, the sophistication of e-commerce implementation varies across phases. Phase one businesses use e-commerce in a minimal manner; managers view e-commerce as a support tool as opposed to a mechanism to enhance and extend business processes. In contrast, management support for e-commerce differs substantially in phases two, three, and four. Managers in these phases were found to be more pro-active and enthusiastic with their use of e-commerce. The lack of technical experience and knowledge of e-commerce did not dictate the actual use of e-commerce within the organisations.

The E-Commerce Driver (Why is E-Commerce Used by SMEs?)

The reasons for using e-commerce directly influence the potential gains from e-commerce. The driver for e-commerce varied considerably across all cases. Access to global markets, which can potentially increase sales, was a consistent driver, particularly for SMEs located in phases one and two. The use of e-commerce to enhance customer service was another common theme, by providing an alternative and convenient trading and communication methods. Sophisticated users of e-commerce found in phases three and four considered e-commerce as a strategic tool aimed at reducing operational costs and minimising transaction inefficiencies.

The E-Commerce Strategy (How is E-Commerce Used by SMEs?)

How e-commerce is applied within the organisation will affect the possible benefits form e-commerce. Analysis of the case studies revealed two distinct strategic orientations with the organisational use of e-commerce. Businesses located in phase one and phase two predominantly view e-commerce with an experimental approach, investigating and exploring how e-commerce could be used within the business. E-commerce is used to complement marketing and sales functions; it is applied independently of existing IS systems with no formal integration between existing back office systems and their e-commerce applications.

Alternatively, managers in phase three and phase four businesses consider e-commerce as a strategic device to extend implicit business strategies to reduce costs, promote greater efficiencies, and enhance customer services. Businesses positioned in phase four rely totally on the Internet to facilitate not only their e-commerce applications, but also their whole business infrastructure. E-commerce is used as a strategic platform central to their business operations. Without the Internet these businesses would not exist in their current state.

Internal Resources Available to Conduct E-Commerce

The amount of internal resources available for e-commerce activities varied substantially across all phases. The ability of SMEs to allocate resources for e-commerce initiatives closely correlates to the business size. In terms of available resources, medium-sized businesses possess a greater capacity to conduct e-commerce than micro and small businesses. However, analysis of the cases shows that the capacity to conduct comprehensive e-commerce activities is not a reflection on actual e-commerce activities executed.

Small and micro businesses that employ few staff find it particularly hard to allocate capital, time, and personnel to any venture outside core business activities (CEC, 1996). Some business owners/mangers that could not justify the costs associated with hiring external developers resorted to experimenting with e-commerce development (e.g., Microsoft Frontpage©) themselves.

Technological Factors

The Technological Infrastructure

The technological infrastructure and support is an integral element of e-commerce utilisation. The analysis revealed three types of e-commerce support and development skills amongst the 34 cases. The first type includes those businesses that designed, developed, and maintained their e-commerce applications in-house, which for many this meant after hours at home. Small businesses employing less than twenty employees and micro businesses employing less than five employees typify this scenario. A second group of businesses emerge that predominantly develop their e-commerce application internally and only seek external assistance when required. The third type of businesses employs the skills of professional e-commerce consultants and developers to design, implement, and host the e-commerce initiatives.

The financial constraint of employing external consultants and developers to build e-commerce applications can be a major deterrent for the vast majority of SMEs with little or no IT experience or knowledge. In these cases the decision to embark on e-commerce initiatives is large, financially. The SMEs in the study displayed a vast array of IT experience. In micro and small businesses the owner/manager is often the first contact for IT support. As a result the owner/manger inevitably gains hands-on IT experience by necessity. Medium-sized businesses either possessed in-house IT experts or contracted IT expertise when required.

A SME is not required to own an elaborate IT infrastructure to conduct e-commerce. A computer with Internet access is all that is required for basic e-commerce activities. In four cases, SMEs used their home computer to develop and maintain their e-commerce applications. The ability to host the e-commerce application has not been a hurdle for the SMEs included in the case studies. Interviewees indicated that hosting costs were relatively minor in comparison to the costs of developing the initial e-commerce application.

The E-Commerce Application

The nature of the e-commerce application correlates closely with the driver and motivation to use e-commerce. Phase one and phase two businesses do not significantly alter their core business structure. Their use of e-commerce is reflected by their applications, which include electronic brochures, online stores, and product and service information. Phase three businesses exhibit a more comprehensive array of e-commerce applications, such as customer information systems, electronic procurement systems, and enhanced communication facilities. In phase four, e-commerce is paramount to the business' existence. Without the Internet and e-commerce, the business would not exist. These businesses rely on global and national markets to justify their business strategy. Their e-commerce strategy is their business strategy; without the Internet the business would not survive.

Table 2: External Factors Affecting SME Ability to Acquire E-Commerce Benefits

Clients/Customer • The Ability of Clients to Conduct E-Commerce • Public or Niche Market • Size and Number of Clients (Critical Mass)	Industry • Level of Industry Support for Change • Information and Education • Business Champions
Supply Chain • Level of Automation in Supply Chain • Size and Number of Participants (Critical Mass) • Other Participants Internal Factors	Government • Policy and E-Commerce Framework • Type of Sector Strategy • Level of Financial Aid
External Service Providers • ISP • Web Developers • E-commerce Consultants	

EXTERNAL FACTORS

The external factors embody those factors that affect the environment in which a business operates. The external factors do not directly affect the ability to conduct organisational change; however, the external factors can influence the potential to derive e-commerce benefit from e-commerce utilisation. The three external factors that have been identified in the case analysis are the nature of the supply chain, the industry in which the SME operates, and the level of government assistance.

Clients/Customers

The nature of the clients or customers targeted by the organisation affects the potential benefits derived from e-commerce. Organisations that pursue increased sales revenue from the Internet need to acquire a critical mass of customers to gain the inherent benefits of e-commerce. This is particularly important for start-up e-commerce businesses that have no prior trading background. Alternatively, established businesses that have existing client bases can reap potential e-commerce benefits earlier by improving their client relationships and transaction methods. In each scenario it is important that new or existing clients have the facilities and the desire to trade electronically with the organisation. If a core customer market is unlikely to embrace e-commerce and the focus of the e-commerce activity is customer-centric, the possible benefits derived from e-commerce can be limited.

However, those SMEs that have developed their e-commerce systems in consultations with major clients can expect to receive earlier success and associated rewards from their e-commerce systems.

Supply Chain

The ability to derive e-commerce benefits is influenced not only by the customers, but also by the businesses and individuals that form the organisation's supply chain. In this research, the use of phone and facsimile dominated the communication method between suppliers and SMEs included in the case study. Some of the case study participants were distributors and wholesalers, and were keen to push the use of e-commerce onto their respective resellers; however, many resellers lacked the capacity or desire to be on-line. Until a critical mass of e-commerce customers and suppliers is evident, the draconian nature of the many supply chains remains a significant hurdle in procuring the full potential benefits of e-commerce.

Industry

Industry can assist SMEs in gaining critical mass by supporting and encouraging e-commerce initiatives. None of the cases indicated that they received or sought help from the industry when developing their e-commerce application. One problem identified by a business owner suggested that when large business enterprises dominate the industry, SMEs have very little power, individually, to change the supply arrangements. However, if a SME is a large customer, they can influence to some degree their supply arrangements.

Government

The government can provide e-commerce assistance in a number of ways. E-commerce education and awareness programs are beneficial to break down the barriers of misinformation and e-commerce adoption fears. Direct injection of capital to help subsidise initial e-commerce efforts would help many of the smaller businesses. The development of role models or e-commerce champions would also prove beneficial.

External Support Services

The SMEs included in this research have reported a mixed array of services provided by Internet service providers (ISP), Web developers and e-commerce consultants. Problems with experience and service levels by ISPs were highlighted as the largest external issue by many case studies, particularly those SMEs in the small and micro sectors where IT skills and experience of management were marginal. The businesses that developed the majority of their e-commerce applications in-house had the least amount of problems.

CONCLUSIONS

This paper has developed a framework that identifies and critically analyses the range of factors impacting on SMEs' ability to derive benefit from e-commerce. This framework has examined factors both internal and external to the organisation, and has identified enabling and inhibiting forces generated by their interaction. Significantly, this framework has highlighted that, for SMEs, the ability to derive benefit from e-commerce relies on internal forces where they have some control and external forces over which they have little control. This exploratory study provides an explanation for why many SMEs who are relatively sophisticated users of e-commerce have often found it difficult to derive significant benefit from e-commerce.

This paper has outlined a range of factors internal and external to the organisation, which can potentially provide e-commerce benefit and contribute to e-commerce business transformation. The range of internal factors that emerged from the data mirrors some of the elements of Venkatraman's (1994) work on organisational transformation. Detailed analysis of these internal factors indicates that the mix of internal resources, attributes of management, and technical ability of SMEs are important to the utilisation of e-commerce by organisations included in this study. Factors that are external to the organisation, over which these SMEs had little control, can directly affect the capacity to acquire other potential e-commerce benefits. These factors include the nature of the supply chain, external service providers, influence of the industry, and level of government support. The combination of internal and external factors directly and indirectly influences the ability of SMEs to implement, utilise, and maintain an e-commerce operation.

REFERENCES

Barnatt, C. (1997). Virtual organisation in the small business sector: The case of Cavendish Management resources. *International Small Business Journal,* 15(4), 36-47.

Centre for Electronic Commerce (CEC). (1996). *Electronic Commerce for Small to Medium Sized Enterprises (SMEs).* Report prepared for the Information Industries Board, Department of Tourism, Small Business and Industry. Monash University.

Chau, S. B. (2001). Four Phases of E-commerce a Small Business Perspective: An

Exploratory Study of 23 Australian Small Businesses. *Proceedings of the Information Resource and Management Association Conference.* Toronto, Canada.

Chau, S.B. and Turner, P. (2001, December 5-7). A Four Phase Model of EC Business Transformation amongst Small to Medium Sized Enterprises: Preliminary Findings from 34 Australian Case Studies. *Proceedings of the 12th Australasian Conference on Information Systems*. Coffs Habour, Australia.

Freel, M. (2000, March). Barriers to Product Innovation in Small Manufacturing Firms. *International Small Business Journal*, 18 (2), 60-65.

Lawrence, K. and Keen, C.D. (1997). *A survey of factors inhibiting the adoption of electronic commerce by small and medium sized enterprises in Tasmania.* Working paper 97-01. Hobart, Tasmania: School of Information Systems, University of Tasmania.

MacGregor, R.C., Waugh, P., and Bunker, D. (1996). *Attitudes of Small Business to the Implementation and Use of IT: Are we basing EDI Design Initiatives for Small Business on Myths?* Ninth International Conference on EDI-IOS. Bled, Slovenia.

National Office for the Information Economy (NOIE). (2000a). *Current State of Play-July 2000: Australia and the Information Economy*. Retrieved from World Wide Web: http://www.noie.gov.au/publications/index.htm.

National Office for the Information Economy (NOIE). (2000b). *Taking the Plunge - Sink or Swim: Attitudes and Experiences of SMEs to E-commerce*. Retrieved from the World Wide Web: http://www.noie.gov.au/publications/index. htm.

Poon, S. and Swatman, P. (1998). *Small Business Internet Commerce Experiences: A Longitudinal Study.* Electronic Commerce in the Information Society, 11th International Bled Electronic Commerce Conference. Bled, Slovenia.

Poon, S., Swatman, P. and Vitale, M. (1996). *Electronic Networking Among Small Business in Australia – An Exploratory Study*. Ninth International Conference on EDI-IOS. Bled, Slovenia.

Venkatraman, N. (1994, Winter). IT-enabled business transformation: from automation to business scope redefinition. *Sloan Management Review*, 35(2), 73-88.

Wong, M. and Turner, P. (2001, September 5-7). *An Investigation of Drivers/ Activators for the Adoption and utilisation of B2B Electronic Commerce amongst Small to Medium Sized Suppliers to the Tasmanian Pyrethrum Industry*, (2001), 3rd Information Technology in Regional Areas Conference. Central Queensland University, Rockhampton, Qld.

Chapter IX

Electronic Government in Japan: IT Utilization Status of Local Governments

Tatsumi Shimada
Setsunan University, Japan

Kiyoshi Ushida
Tokyo Metropolitan Government, Japan

ABSTRACT

This paper reveals the actual status of local governments' digital readiness in Japan, and describes the stage of achievement in digitalization and related issues. Items requiring analysis are plans for digitalization of governmental administration, organizations, services for residents, information disclosure, and a driving body, as well as impediments to the realization of electronic local governments. The present IT infrastructure in local governments is not yet sufficient, in that the major uses are limited to local area networks (LANs) and e-mail. Prefectures and large cities have relatively advanced governments; however, they are facing financial difficulties. Therefore, it is essential to reduce legacy systems and redirect funds for new IT systems. Security, privacy protection, and organizational conservatism are more important problems to address than equipment shortages.

INTRODUCTION

Information Technology is ubiquitous in many public and nonprofit organizations. Nearly all public and nonprofit organizations have computers that are routinely used by administrative staff, managers, and others. IT enables managers and employees to accomplish more and increase their effectiveness by using more – and frequently better – information (Berman, 1998). In 1992, David and Ted argued for a customer-driven government in their book, *Reinventing Government*. In their book they hardly gave IT a mention, but governments now are shifting away from traditional bureaucratic functions to include interactive services that encourage active involvement on the part of the citizens (Stratford and Stratford, 2000; Holmes, 2001).

Electronic government is usually presented as using IT:

- To provide easy access to government information and services to citizens and business.
- To increase the quality of services, by increased speed, completeness, process efficiency and other.
- To give citizens opportunities to participate in democratic processes of different kinds.
- Focus is typically on external services, but one important idea is to use these to make internal operations more efficient, for instance by relying on self-service (Åke, 2002).

In Japan, various measures to introduce digital technology to public administration, citizens, and businesses are being implemented in the early part of this century to create an evolution towards an "electronic government."

This paper reveals the actual status of local governments' digital readiness in Japan, and describes the stage of achievement in digitalization and related issues. Local governments in Japan consist of two layers: 47 prefectures and 3,250 other municipalities under the central government. Under the two-layer system, all districts of the country belong to one of the 3,250 municipalities and at the same time fall within the boundaries of one of the 47 prefectures. In addition, within the prefectures and municipalities, there exist many special local authorities, such as special wards and designated cities. Tokyo is the only prefecture called a metropolis and differs from the rest of the prefectures in that it has a system of special wards. Designated cities having populations exceeding 500,000 are designated by cabinet order, and are authorized to administrate with the same level of governmental jurisdiction as prefectures in many policy areas.

Items requiring analysis are plans for digitalization of governmental administration, organizations, services for residents, information disclosure, and a driving body, as well as impediments to the realization of electronic local governments.

FRAMEWORK OF ANALYSIS AND RECOGNITION OF ISSUES

To realize electronic local governments with high organizational performance, it is necessary to draw up plans for the digitalization of governmental administration based on clear strategies of the local governments, and to digitalize internal organizations and services for residents. At the same time, to promote digitalization, information disclosure and a driving body are indispensable. Furthermore, overcoming various impediments to the realization of electronic local governments is another important issue (see Figure 1).

We would like to address the following five issues. First, it seems necessary to draw up plans for digitalization, but is it really necessary? Does the formulation and revision of plans significantly affect the movement of the national electronic government? Second, digitalization can be roughly separated into the digitalization of organizations to improve their internal efficiency and digitalization to improve services for residents. What is the status of progress for each? Third, what is the present state of progress on information disclosure to improve residents' democracy and to facilitate residents' participation? Fourth, has the driving body to support digitalization been prepared? And last, what are the impediments to the promotion of digitalization?

RESEARCH DESIGN

To conduct empirical research to answer the above questions, we conducted a survey of local governments, and interviewed officials at eight of the local governments that responded to the questionnaire. The methods of the questionnaire survey are as follows:

Figure 1: System of Analysis

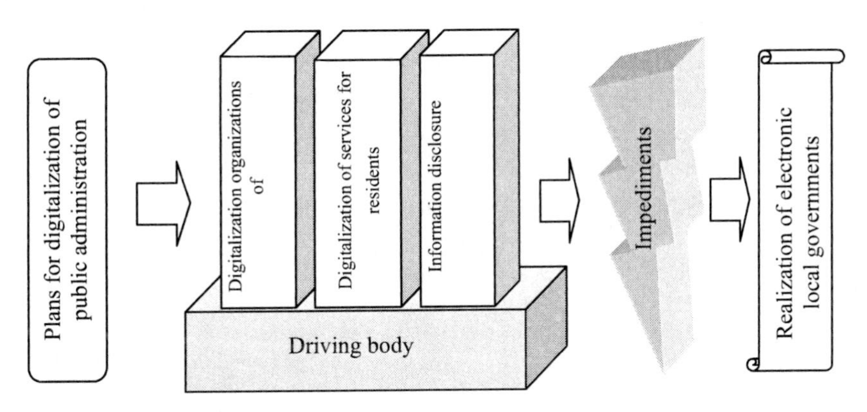

- Period of survey: July 2000 (the questionnaire was issued on April 1, 2000)
- Targets: 203 local governments in Japan (prefectural governments, cities with a population of 200,000 or more, and prefectural capitals, and wards and cities in the Tokyo Metropolitan Area)
- Total number of respondents: 140 local governments (ratio of respondents: 69.0 percent)

The following survey results are given by type of local government. The results are stated below, and compared with the results of a similar survey in 1996 when needed (Shimada, 1999). By chance, two similar surveys about electronic government were conducted in America in the same year. One was prepared by Norris, Fletcher and Holden for ICMA and PTI (2001)[1], and another was prepared by Hart-Teeter for the Council for Excellence in Government (2000)[2]. We used parts of their survey results for a comparison of the results from our survey.

OUTLINE OF SURVEY RESULTS

Information Infrastructure

PC Diffusion Rate

The PC diffusion rate (the number of PCs per employee) is 36 percent (one PC per about three employees: the average of local governments). The information infrastructure is not sufficient yet on the prefectural level, even though the rate sharply increased from 45 percent in 1998 to 73 percent in 2000. This rate of increase is still low when compared with that of local governments, which had an approximately five-fold increase in four years from the diffusion rate in the 1996 survey of 7.1 percent (one PC per 14 employees).

PC Diffusion Rate at Government Head Offices

The PC diffusion rate at central government offices has increased to 51 percent (one PC per two employees). In particular, prefectural governments achieved a rate of 92 percent (about one PC per employee).

Internet Connection Rate

The Internet connection rate is still at a low level of 20 percent, but the rate for prefectural governments is higher at 39 percent.

Digitalization of Public Administration

Status of Plan Formulation for the Digitalization of Public Administration

Seventy-one percent of local governments answered that they have already formulated plans for the digitalization of their administration and 13 percent answered that they are in the planning stage. As a whole, formulation of plans for digitalization is proceeding well.

The Revision Ratio of Plans for Digitalization of Public Administration in Line With the National Electronic Government

Of the local governments that have already formulated plans for the digitalization of public administration, 9 percent have finished revision of their plans and 48 percent have planned revision in line with the national electronic government. In November 1999 the Millennium Project, aimed at the establishment of an electronic government infrastructure by 2003, was announced. The government is requested to realize an electronic government, which handles electronic information in the same manner as paper-based information, by fiscal year 2003, and even expedite the digitization of citizens and businesses widely. Public administration should be intensively reformed to digitize documents, promote a paperless environment, and share and utilize information through information networks. Moreover, local governments will be encouraged to share information systems, depending upon the level of prefectures and other municipalities, so that all the local governments will be connected to the Local Government-Wide Area Network by fiscal year 2003. In 2000, the IT Strategy Headquarters was established within the Cabinet in order to promote comprehensive measures for the creation of an internationally competitive IT nation, in which benefits of the IT revolution are shared by all Japanese[3]. Because the survey was conducted only three months after the announcement, revision was an issue to be addressed in the future. However, a majority (58 percent) of local governments have already conducted or planned revision, and showed enthusiasm for the establishment of electronic local governments.

Important Items in Formulating Plans for the Digitalization of Public Administration

In formulating plans for digitalization of public administration, the following items are considered to be important by local governments: development of information infrastructure (66 percent); delivery of information using the Internet (53 percent); one-stop services and non-stop services (40 percent); digitalization and simplification of handling of various applications and notifications (39 percent); consistency with administrative reforms (27 percent); and security (23 percent). The fact that the development of an information infrastructure is regarded as the most important implies its backwardness. The top four major items are considered the basic backbone of e-government, which the government should implement as soon as possible.

Digitalization of Organizations

The introduction rates at prefectural governments for LAN (90 percent[4]) and e-mail (74 percent) are high. These are followed by facility management (39 percent) and electronic bulletin boards (35 percent). The introduction rates of schedule management (18 percent), creation of database of official documents (15 percent), delivery of bid information through the Internet (12 percent), and electronic approval (7 percent) are still low. The utilization rate of e-mail at local governments expanded approximately 3.2 times in four years compared to the 20.2 percent rate in 1996. Local governments should introduce facility management, electronic bulletin boards, and schedule management soon; this will promote the use of groupware easily.

Utilization Status of E-Mail by Position

For the local governments already using e-mail, regular employees use it more frequently than top management and managerial-level staff. Utilization from the top and middle management seems low in local governments when compared to private enterprises. Managers suspect that e-government is just a legacy office automation to transact standard mass work. It is important to note that the use of this technology by only general employees does not lead to the digitalization of the whole organization. It is necessary to increase the e-mail utilization rate of top and middle management as soon as possible.

As contrasted with private enterprise data (Shimada, 1999), there are rises in all positions in four years, but still a large gap in the top and middle management. If they do not catch up, it will be an impediment to whole organization's digitalization.

Creation of Database of Official Documents

Only 8 percent of prefectural governments have created a database of official documents on an organizational level. Of the local governments who created a database, only 25 percent created a database of all official documents, and 45

Table 1: Utilization Status of E-Mail by Position (Introduced Governments)

	Prefectures	Government -designated cities	Special wards	Cities inside Tokyo	Cities outside Tokyo
Top management	32%	48%	20%	27%	29%
Middle management	50%	43%	30%	27%	25%
Regular employees	82%	86%	40%	64%	68%

Figure 2: Utilization Status of E-Mail by Position

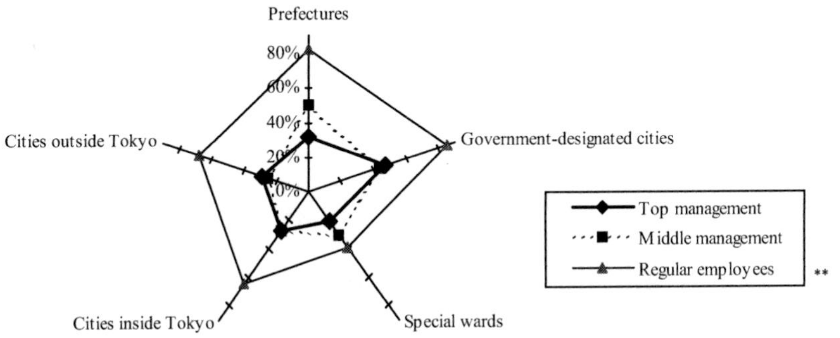

Chi-Square Test about Difference Between Governments: 1% Significance

Figure 3: Change in Utilization Status of E-Mail

Utilization status	points	Top management	Middle management	Regular employees
Very often	1	3.3 ◆2.3 4.1	3.0 ◆2.0 4.1	2.1 ◆1.9 2.8
Fairly often	2			
Average	3			
Not very much	4			
Not at all	5			

Top of the Arrow: Local Government in this Research as of 2000. Bottom of the Arrow: Shimada, 1999 as of 1996.

◆*: Utilization Status of Private Enterprises in Shimada, 1999 as of 1996*

percent of them created a database of only lists and similar documents. To cope with information disclosure in the future, database creation must be implemented without delay.

Electronic Procurement

The following are not conducted using procurement: tendering and bidding via the Internet and applications for participation in qualification examinations. Only 12 percent of local governments provide order placement information using the electronic procurement system. On the other hand, according to the survey conducted in America, almost 53 percent make purchases online. In addition, although one-third of the reporting local governments post requests for bids or proposals (RFPs) on their Web sites, of those that do not, about 70 percent plan to do so (Norris, Fletcher, and Holden, 2001). As a result of the introduction of electronic procurement, combined with the revision of the contract method, some local governments succeeded in dramatically reducing contract prices. Electronic procurement should be introduced for cost reduction reasons as well.

Electronic Approval

Only 1 percent of local governments introduced electronic approval for all operations on an organizational basis. However, 52 percent are examining the issue and introduction in the future is expected. In some local governments, electronic approval is used only for specific operations (1 percent) or by specific divisions (5 percent), such as those related to simple official documents, overtime payment, travel orders, holidays, financial accounting, and utility bill payments.

Digitalization of Services for Residents

Almost all local governments (93 percent) provide services for residents via the Internet; however, other operations are not so digitalized. Following the above are electronic libraries (28 percent[5]), electronic galleries and museums (24 percent[5]), electronic applications (18 percent), and integrated GIS (Geographical Information System) (16 percent). Local governments, prefectures, and government-designated cities have introduced electronic libraries and electronic galleries and museums. The reason seems to be that they can provide service to a wide area and reach a great number of their citizens.

Services for Residents Via the Internet

The rate of introduction for provision of services for residents via the Internet is 100 percent for both prefectures and government-designated cities.

Electronic Applications

Local governments who introduced electronic application mainly use it for the following operations: confirmation related to construction (41 percent), utilization of public facilities (41 percent), port management (18 percent), and drugs, medicines and medical services (9 percent). The scope of utilization will expand in line with the movement of the national government, and operations suitable for

Table 2: Introduction Status of Digitalization of Services for Residents

	Prefectures	Government -designated cities	Special wards	Cities inside Tokyo	Cities outside Tokyo	Average
Services for residents via the Internet **	100%	100%	81%	71%	98%	93%
Electronic libraries *	48%	14%	14%	17%	24%	28%
Electronic galleries and museums **	48%	43%	12%	0%	18%	24%
Electronic applications	23%	43%	13%	5%	20%	18%
Integrated GIS	9%	14%	19%	5%	23%	16%

*(Chi-Square Test: 1% Significance**, 5% Significance*)*

online processing may in principle be digitalized. With regard to the form of application, 35 percent are filed using floppy disks, 32 percent are filed through dedicated terminals, and only 32 percent are through the Internet. An increase of Internet application is needed.

Integrated GIS

Local governments who introduced integrated GIS (Geographical Information System) mainly use it for the following operations: city planning projects (59 percent), valuation of fixed assets (35 percent), geographical information systems (35 percent), sewage systems (35 percent), building construction administration (29 percent), road ledger systems (24 percent), disaster prevention systems (18 percent), and geographical environment systems (12 percent).

Contents of Homepage

The major contents of homepages of local governments are information on upcoming events (96 percent), utilization status of public facilities (89 percent), various business conditions (88 percent), sightseeing and products information (82 percent), health and medical information (82 percent), lifestyle information (80 percent), statistical information (79 percent), public hearings and surveys (71 percent), and regional industrial information (55 percent). The utilization rates of electronic bulletin boards (15 percent) and electronic conference rooms (8 percent) are still low. This shows that many of their homepages provide only one-way communication, so it is necessary to make interactive services such as electronic bulletin boards.

Reflection of Residents' Opinions on Policy

Thirty-nine percent of the opinions provided through e-mail, electronic conference rooms, and electronic bulletin boards are reflected in policies; however, this figure differs depending on the type of local government.

Opinions of residents provided through e-mail are reflected mainly in town building measures such as resident-centered town buildings (30 percent), long-term plans (27 percent), and comprehensive city planning projects (25 percent). These are followed by basic environmental plans (16 percent) and city planning projects (14 percent).

Services for Residents other than Homepages

Twenty-seven percent of local governments provide services for residents other than homepages. These include continuing education services (46 percent), corporate support services (31 percent), medical services (23 percent), social work services (23 percent), library lending services (23 percent), and agricultural support services (23 percent) to name a few.

Information Disclosure Status

As many as 95 percent of local governments have already established an information disclosure ordinance, and 43 percent have issued regulations on disclosure of a request for electronic documents. However, the information disclosure rate through the Internet is very low, and only 3 percent answered, "Only application is possible," and 1 percent answered, "only application and answer are possible." Twenty-five percent are under examination.

Eighty-four percent of local governments established a personal information protection ordinance. Sixty-six percent of local governments prohibit online connection with external parties other than enumerated specific partners (basically prohibited) and 20 percent prohibit online connection with external parties without exception. It is urgent to re-examine this restrictive policy for the construction of e-government.

Driving Bodies

The chief information officers (CIO) are deputy governors and deputy mayors (13 percent), general managers and bureau directors (22 percent), and directors (31 percent). Thus, digitalization projects are mainly driven by director-level officers. Thirty-two percent answered that they have no driving body, which is urgently required to be established first of all.

As for addressing attitude on digitalization, prefectures and government-designated cities got high scores on all positions, and other governments should raise IT consciousness. Among positions, regular employees are generally highly motivated.

Business Process Reengineering by Utilizing IT

Fifty-five percent of local governments implement business process reengineering (BPR) by utilizing IT. Government-designated cities (100 percent) and prefectures (70 percent), in particular, are eager to use it. They are followed by cities outside

Table 3: Addressing Attitude on Digitalization

	Prefectures	Government -designated cities	Special wards	Cities inside Tokyo	Cities outside Tokyo
Top management	66%	86%	44%	35%	45%
Middle management	71%	71%	50%	45%	38%
Regular employees	69%	86%	38%	60%	60%

Tokyo (55 percent), cities inside Tokyo (35 percent), and special wards (31 percent), which have to be encouraged to increase implementation.

Impediments to Realization of Electronic Local Governments

Major factors listed as impediments are financial difficulty (68 percent), assurance of security (55 percent), protection of personal information (44 percent), and old organization structure (30 percent). These are followed by lack of communications equipment and facilities (21 percent), understanding of top management (17 percent), national laws and regulations (15 percent), ordinances and regulations of local governments (13 percent), and understanding of managerial-level staff (10 percent).

On the other hand, according to one American survey, for local governments that engage in e-government and those that plan to, the biggest obstacles are the lack of IT or Web staff (66.6 percent) and the lack of financial resources (54.3 percent), followed by the lack of Web expertise (46.7 percent). Other barriers include security issues (42.1 percent), the need to upgrade current technology (33.9 percent), privacy issues (27.7 percent), and issues relating to convenience fees for online transactions (Norris, Fletcher, and Holden, 2001).

According to the other survey, government officials selected security issues (37 percent) most often, followed by lack of financial resources (26 percent) and the inability to find qualified personnel (23 percent) (Hart-Teeter, 2000).

When comparing the survey results between Japan and America, there is a point in common and one difference. The lack of financial resources and security issues are high barriers in both countries. On the other hand, in America, the lack of human resources is a high barrier, but it is low in Japan.

Figure 4: Addressing Attitude on Digitalization

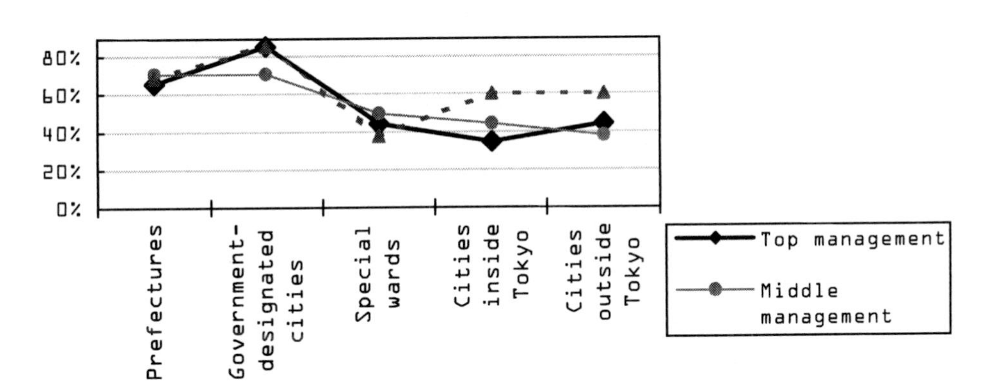

In Japan, the impediment listed first is financial difficulty. To cope with this problem, when introducing information technology, it is necessary to fully revise and streamline operations in order to take advantage of information technology at a lower cost; streamline the existing information systems and improve obsolete systems to reap the benefits of cost reduction from digitalization.

Judging from the fact that the lack of communications equipment and facilities is listed fifth, software-related issues such as security, protection of personal information, and old organization structure are more serious than simple hardware-related factors. Thus, comprehensive measures including reforms related to operations, safety, organizations, and consciousness are considered to be necessary.

Looking into the data by the type of local government, municipal governments recognize protection of security and personal information as a more serious impediment than prefectural governments. Municipal governments put more emphasis on the prevention of personal information leakage because they are in a closer position to residents. Before advancing digitalization of local governments, it is necessary to draw up an information security policy to assure security in all aspects. Many prefectural governments listed the issue of old organization structure. This may be because their structures are older than municipal governments due

Table 4: Impediments to Realization of Electronic Local Governments

	Financial difficulty	Assurance of security	Protection of personal information	Old organization structure	Lack of communications equipment and facilities	Understanding of top management	National laws and regulations	Difficulty in finding suitable personnel	Ordinances and regulations	Understanding of managerial-level staff	Other	Understanding of labor unions	Understanding of the assembly
Prefectures	69%	47%	25%	44%	25%	22%	11%	14%	19%	11%	6%	0%	3%
Government-designated cities	57%	71%	43%	29%	14%	14%	29%	14%	14%	0%	14%	0%	0%
Special wards	88%	63%	50%	13%	31%	19%	0%	6%	6%	19%	0%	6%	0%
Cities inside Tokyo	60%	45%	60%	35%	15%	15%	15%	15%	15%	5%	5%	5%	0%
Cities outside Tokyo	67%	60%	48%	25%	18%	13%	20%	15%	10%	10%	3%	3%	3%
Average	68%	55%	44%	30%	21%	17%	15%	14%	13%	10%	4%	3%	2%

to the larger size of their organizations. Thus, stronger leadership by top management and managerial-level staff is required.

RANKING BASED ON MULTIPLE ATTRIBUTE DECISION-MAKING[6]

According to the evaluation using the Multiple Attribute Decision Making (MADM) method, the top 10 are Kouchi Prefecture, Yamanashi Prefecture, Akita Prefecture, Okayama City, Okayama Prefecture, Yamato City, Yokosuka City, Iwate Prefecture, Hyogo Prefecture, and Shimane Prefecture. They are considered to be the governments do not have a large population, but are eagerly working on digitalization.

TYPES OF E-GOVERNMENT ON CLUSTER ANALYSIS

Local governments are classified by cluster analysis based on the answers for this questionnaire. The types classified are as follows:

Developing Group

This is the largest group consisting of 17 percent. Most IT items are behind others among that includes a low attitude towards digitalization. This group is ranked last out of the 10 in MADM analysis, so this group is considered to be most-developing.

Partially Addressing Group

This group accounts for 16 percent. Many staff have the opinion of "partially addressing digitalization." As for reflection of residents' opinions on the policy, it is also only partially committed. This group includes comparatively large governments, and a total of five government-designated cities in this group out of seven responded accordingly.

Noncommittal Addressing Group

This group accounts for 14 percent. Many staff have the opinion of "noncommittal addressing to digitalization." They seem to step forward at an average pace, watching other governments' performance.

Top Group

This group accounts for 14 percent. The introduction rate of electronic galleries, museums, and libraries is very high and the attitude toward e-procurement is positive. The staff's addressing attitude and PC diffusion rate are also very high. As prefectural capitals account for 74 percent of the eight governments, out of the governments ranked in the top 10 in the MADM analysis, this group is considered to be the most advanced group.

Group Which Attaches Importance to Services for Residents

This group accounts for 11 percent. The rate of introduction of e-libraries, considering information disclosure, on the Internet and planning of e-application are high. The rate of introduction of e-mail is 100 percent. This group is considered to be the one which attaches importance to services for residents.

Positive Attitude Group

This group accounts for 9 percent. The rate of introduction of e-mail, office LAN, e-galleries, museums and libraries are not high, but the staff's addressing attitude is fairly high. This group seems to have a potential to become advanced e-governments in the future.

Developing Group Which is Behind Others Except for LAN

This group accounts for 9 percent. All governments in this group have office LAN, but the rate of introduction for Internet service provision for residents, introduction of BPR utilizing IT, and introduction of e-reference of libraries are the lowest. The introduction rate of e-mail (42 percent) is second lowest beside the Internet connection rate, and the addressing attitude of middle management and ordinary employees is also low.

Preparing Digital Museum Group

This group accounts for 8 percent. It has the highest rate of experimenting with digital galleries, the second highest rate of implementing it, a comparably high introduction rate of digital libraries, and a high rate of introduction in public facilities utilization. But the rate of Internet application of information disclosure, reflection of residents' opinion, and addressing attitude of middle management are not so high.

Group Which has an Average Rate of PC Diffusion, but Advanced in Utilizing IT

This group is the smallest and accounts for only 4 percent, but it has the highest rate of Internet connection, electronic bulletin board introduction, public facilities utilization systems, document databases, electronic approval, electronic applications, GIS, reflection of residents' opinion, and BPR utilizing IT. All the governments have formulated digitalization plans and introduced office LAN and e-mail. The staff's addressing rate is very high and they are going to examine the system's operation completely. However, PC diffusion rate is average and they are not so interested in digital galleries and museums.

As for these groups classified by cluster analysis, the top three groups, Developing Group, Partially Addressing Group, and Noncommittal Addressing Group, account for 47 percent combined, and so it is considered that there are not so many advanced local governments in IT utilization as yet. But there are some which have started utilizing IT, such as the Top Group, Group which Attaches Importance to Services for Residents, Preparing Digital Museum Group, and Group which has an Average Rate of PC Diffusion but Advanced in Utilizing IT.

Judging from the results of this classification, the factor of the staff's attitude is very important. An advanced government is one whose staff's attitude is positive, and a backward government is one whose staff's attitude is negative.

CONCLUSION

Although as a whole, prefectures and government-designated cities are working to digitalize internal organizations and services for residents, fewer local governments have started to work on digitalization.

However, some of them have started advanced digitalization measures. These advanced groups will blaze a path for other local governments. Attitudes of corporate members from top management to general employees are influential factors in the digitalization of local governments. Therefore, it is necessary to raise consciousness and increase the staff's motivation.

In realizing the goal of electronic local governments in the future, financial difficulty is the biggest impediment. It will be necessary to reduce the costs of existing information systems and shift funds to IT investment. Many local governments said that software-related issues are more serious than simple hardware-related issues, such as lack of communications equipment. It will be necessary to induce the top-level management, such as the CIOs, as well as individual division managers, to take organization-wide measures towards digitalization.

ENDNOTES

1. http://www.umbc.edu/mpar/
2. http://www.excelgov.org/
3. http://www.kantei.go.jp/foreign/it/network/
4. Internet connection rate is 52 percent.
5. Rate of introduction of internet delivery services (including experimental stage)
6. Multiple Attribute Decision Making: Evaluation method based on multiple standard. We used the simple additive weighting method in this survey.

REFERENCES

Berman, E.M. (1998). *Productivity in Public and Nonprofit Organizations: Strategies and Techniques*. CA: Sage Publications.

Grönlund, Å. (ed.) (2001). Electronic Government – Efficiency, Service Quality and Democracy. *Electronic Government: Design, Applications & Management*, 23-46. Hershey, PA: Idea Group Publishing.

Hart-Teeter. (2000). *E-Government: The Next American Revolution. The Council for Excellence in Government*. Retrieved from the WWW at : http://www.excelgov.org/egovpoll/report/contents.htm.

Holmes, D. (2001). *EGov: eBusiness Strategies for Government*. IL: Nicholas Brealey Publishing.

Norris, D.F., Fletcher, P.D., and Holden, S. H. (2001). *Is Your Local Government Plugged In? Highlights of the 2000 : Electronic Government Survey*. Retrieved from the WWW at: http://www.umbc.edu/mpar/.

Osborne, D. and Gaebler, T. (1992). *Reinventing Government*. MA: Addison-Wesley.

Shimada, T. (1999). *The Study of IT Utilization in Local Government*. Tokyo: Bunshindo Ltd. (In Japanese).

Stratford, J.S. and Stratford, J. (2000). Computerized and Networked Government Information. *Journal of Government Information*, 27, 385-389.

Chapter X

Concerns and Solutions on Electronic Voting Systems Adoption

Yurong Yao
Louisiana State University, USA

Edward Watson
Louisiana State Universtiy, USA

ABSTRACT

Electronic voting has become a viable form of e-government due to the rapid advances in technologies and communication networks. The United States and most European and Asian Countries, like Japan, have taken the first step towards electronic elections. The unique features of electronic voting systems bring advantages to the public as well as resulting in concerns about electronic voting system (EVS) implementation. In this chapter, we examine those advantages of EVS and the principal obstacles in its implementation: privacy, security and accessibility. By investigating the current technology and government efforts to overcome these problems, some recommendations are proposed to gain voters' trust on EVS and further increase their participation by using EVS.

INTRODUCTION

Within a few short years, rapid advanced in technology developments, particularly the Internet, lead to profound implications for government operations and services. Electronic government (e-government), defined as the utilization of technologies to process governmental operations and to provide political services to the public (Watson and Mundy, 2000), became a popular term quickly. Gartner Group (2001) predicted, "By 2003, more than 60 percent of government agencies in developed countries will allow citizens to conduct some forms of electronic remote transaction" (p. 4). Taking advantage of superior technology, the U.S. has had an early start in this revolution. Nearly every state has set up an information portal and has partially instituted certain electronic services, such as posting of government policies, tax payments, and citizen polling.

As a central component to "digital democracy," voting has attracted the attention of academics and practitioners around the globe. The voting controversy surrounding the Florida vote tabulation for the 2000 U.S. presidential election provides a rich stimulus for research into electronic voting. KPMG, the principal organizer for the United State's first online Democratic presidential primary election at Arizona, is actively exploring the impact of online voting on society (Done 2002; Hiller and Bélanger, 2002). They argue that electronic voting systems (EVS) would make current voting procedures efficient and increase participation. A recent poll indicates that 32 percent of Americans expressed that, if given the option, they would vote online in governmental elections (Westen, 2000). However, some debates concern whether those changes with EVS can guarantee voters' political rights, such as privacy, equality, and security. These issues are certainly to be taken seriously in order to provide a smooth transition to electronic voting.

The objective of this chapter is to investigate the advantages of electronic voting systems and the concerns of voters about their use of this technology. By identifying these concerns, we can help the voters to objectively examine the utility of this approach to voting. Only in this way, can EVS gain the critical mass necessary to make it a viable solution. Also, we offer practical recommendations to guide practitioners in replacing old voting machines with electronic voting systems and, in particular, remote voting devices. The major contribution of this chapter is the holistic examination of the advantages and concerns associated with EVS adoption in practical elections. This chapter has significant implications for both practitioners and researches. Practitioners can gain from the discussions knowledge about voters' concerns, as well as the recommendations for EVS implementation. For researchers, a recommendation is made to steer researchers into the critical areas.

This chapter is organized as follows. First, we will define EVS and discuss its advantages. Then, concerns regarding a transition to electronic voting systems, such as security, privacy, and accessibility, are discussed. The chapter will conclude with recommendations to overcome these problems in practice.

DEFINITION AND ADVANTAGES OF ELECTRONIC VOTING SYSTEMS

In a traditional on-site election, voters must register and identify their qualification before voting in the desired elections. During the election time, voters are required to cast their ballots in specific booths. The most commonly used voting device is the punch card machine (Posner, 2001). Each ballot is processed through this machine. A card is put on a tray, and the voter punches a hole next to the candidate's name to select this candidate. Then this card is dislodged and the "chad" falls to the bottom of the tray (Posner, 2001). The card is placed in a machine that counts votes by beaming light through the holes. If the light cannot go through the hole, this vote will not be counted.

Obviously, this method has many problems, though it has been in use for a long time. The 2000 presidential election in Florida State provides strong evidence. Many voters complained that they were misled by the "butterfly" ballot, i.e., the name of the candidates are listed on the both sides of the ballot rather than on only one side (Posner, 2001). In many cases, a chad from a punched hole may accidentally remain dangling from the ballot so that this particularly vote is not counted correctly by the tabulating machine. That is the main reason that, although many voters participate in the elections, their ballots are not accurately counted. Booth location is another problem. Ideal booth location would provide convenient access to all voters, but this is not the case in practice. The inconvenience of accessing voting booths results in low participation during political elections. In addition, mechanical machines do not guarantee ballot-counting accuracy. To correct the situation through manual recounting introduces more problems. Americans will not forget the confusing, complex, and resource intense recount that took place in Florida. This event lead to numerous other investigations and accounts detailing other instances of improper election procedures.

In an attempt to remedy this problem, governments have begun to utilize information technology to provide more convenience to voters and greater integrity to the voting process. According to the Ney-Hoyer bill (H.R. 3295, "Help America Vote Act of 2001," passed by the House of Representatives in December 2001), jurisdiction is supplied $2.65 billion over three years to improve voting services, such as about $400 million of this to fund the replacement of punch card machines nationally, and poll worker training (Done, 2002). The distinguishing features of EVS are developed to solve the problems integral to the current voting mechanism.

Table 1: Principal EVS Products

Vendor	Product	Function
Diebold	Diebold voting system	Used in Brazil government for voting
Election.com	Elecpro	Used in 2000 Arizona Democratic Presidential Election, which is the first online voting
Hart InterCivic	eSlate electronic voting system	A Direct Record Electronic (DRE) system
VoteHere.net	Non-binding online voting system	Used in Arizona and California governmental voting, friendly new user interface
American Arbitration Association	Telephone voting system and online voting system	Use advanced telephone voting system
Elex Voting Systems	Touch screen voting system	Manufacture the touch screen voting system

An EVS is defined as a voting system based on electronic technology, which enables remote voting and facilitates official administration and counting processes. In response to the increasing demand for electronic voting, a number of companies have successfully developed EVSs and have put them into practice. Table 1 lists some example products (Electronic Voting Hot List, 2001). Currently, there are several mechanisms of EVS: telephone-based, Internet-based, and touch screen based.

By utilizing advanced networking and information technology, different mechanisms of EVS provide many common advantages to the public and to the government. These advantages are presented in the remainder of this section.

Efficiency

Voter registration information is valuable for governments to track participation statistics among the population. According to the National Voter Registration Act of 1993 (NVRA), voting procedures should be arranged to ensure the accuracy and currency of voter registration rolls and assist governments in increasing voter registration and participation (Done, 2002). EVS can meet these requirements perfectly by significantly improving the speed and accuracy of voter registration transactions. Traditionally, all voter information is recorded manually. Each year, this information may change significantly due to change-of-address, death, birth, etc. These changes result in time-consuming manual work. Even so, mistakes and duplicate records commonly occur. By using EVS, especially online registration, data input and maintenance work can be radically reduced. Once the information has been input into a central system, it is a simple matter to make required demographic changes in the system.

High accuracy and efficiency in registration brought about by high technology will not only reduce manual work, but may also encourage voters in the 18-to-20-year age bracket to participate, by simplifying the process and eliminating tedious registration work. In the first online Arizona Democratic presidential preference election at Arizona, roughly 62 percent of currently unregistered voters expressed their intention to register online (Done, 2002).

Efficiency is also impacted by revisions to the ballot casting process. As ballots are cast electronically, they could be quickly and automatically transferred from each remote machine to a central storage repository. Time and labor spent in allocating ballots and investigating and supervising the voting process will be greatly reduced, if not eliminated. Meanwhile, by using EVS, officials can accurately count electronic ballots and report the results to the public right after checking and confirmation. Thus, Americans will not suffer for months anxiously waiting for the final result of their election, and the integrity of this democratic process will be restored.

With well-designed user interfaces, voters could clearly understand those functions and follow the instructions. A good EVS would provide several opportunities for voters to change their minds until they finally confirm their selection visually or audibly. Thus, an EVS provides a reliable way to prevent possible misunderstandings and selection errors.

Moreover, efficiency can further enhance communications between citizens and selected officials. By using EVS, elections can be held more frequently. Increasing communications between government officials and citizens make the officials aware of citizens' requirements better. Thus, those officials can well-represent the opinions of their constituency. Effective elections also monitor officials' performance. Periodic polling could easily be facilitated and public officials could be held more accountable for their actions.

Cost-Saving

Usually, several booths are opened in each county to serve an election. The expenses incurred from running these booths, including labor costs to maintain machines and assist registration, costs of reserving booths and parking spaces, and other utilities, are significant.

When voting goes electronic, these figures quickly go down. Because an EVS supports remote voting, the government need not choose specific locations for citizens to cast their ballot. After remote voting is implemented, automobile emissions could be significantly reduced. The Web site administrator for each state's Internet portal could accommodate an additional voter/polling function relatively easily (Symonds, 2000).

Though the initial investment for replacing all the old voting machines with hardware, software, and other devices is not marginal, a long-term perspective suggests that regular election costs will be much lower. As the two major mechanisms, telephone-based and computer-based EVS, could serve as basic EVS devices, it is realistic to suggest that most voters could make full use of these widely available systems without incurring additional expenses. A report says about 88 percent of adults 18 or older access the Internet at home to send email (Associated Press, 2001). The continuous drop in the price of computers further makes online voting practical. Some newly developed internet-ready devices can be purchased at around $300 (Symonds, 2000). As telecommunications infrastructure has been quickly established in the U.S. and most European countries, the Internet transmission fee through cable or telephone is relatively cheap (Symonds, 2000). Hence, it would be sensible for government to make necessary investments to move to electronic voting in order to save more money in the long run.

Convenience

As remote voting can be effectively supported by EVS via telephone, computer or other electronic device, voters can cast their ballots at any time and any place. The wealth of well-organized, policy-related information available on the Internet may lead to a greater citizen awareness of the activities of government and background information on candidates. An EVS can provide 24-hour voting service via the Web during the election period. Without the restriction on location, the physically challenged have perhaps the greatest to gain from convenience. These conveniences will increase the enthusiasm and, subsequently, the participation of the citizens in political activities. Also, there is considerable evidence that political knowledge is positively related to political participation. About 72 percent of adults, including two in three who do not use the Internet, believe that e-government will make a valuable contribution to participatory democracy (The Council for Excellence in Government, 2000).

In particular, the simple matter of voter convenience will tend to increase participation. Statistics show that since the late 1980s very few young people (ranging between 18 and 20 years of age) are likely to vote. The number in this age group is about half of the number of over-60 voters. However, the younger generation is generally the most technology capable and will experience the greatest success on any Internet-related endeavor. Voting by EVS, especially online voting, can notably attract the younger generation for its simplicity and convenience. The younger generation is able to search for its own answers (via Internet) instead of having a prepared message thrown at them through organized broadcasting. More young voters registering in the Arizona online election provide good evidence to support this statement (Done, 2002). Youth are empowered and do not rely as much on the older generation to learn and acquire information and knowledge. While more and more people participate in the election, the foundation of the democratic political system is strengthened.

CONCERNS OVER THE MOVE TO ELECTRONIC VOTING

In practice, as early as 1996, electronic voting was initiated in the Reform Party primary election (Cranor and Cytron, 1997). In 2000, the first online voting was held in the Arizona Democratic primary election (Solop, 2000a). The overall positive results in these elections reflect the advantages of EVS and imply wide acceptance of EVS by the majority of citizens.

However, critics of EVS draw attention to a number of concerns associated with the shift away from conventional voting. Only after these concerns can be addressed to the satisfaction of the public can a transition to electronic voting smoothly proceed. In this section, three major concerns over the usage of an EVS —privacy, security and accessibility—are discussed further.

Privacy

Under the context of electronic voting, privacy is an essential consideration when voters decide whether to vote by EVS. In this chapter, privacy refers to confidentiality of personal information, which must be maintained, preserved, and protected from outside use. It also refers to their election choices. Privacy in elections, to a great extent, depends on secure information transfer and storage.

A hallmark of the voting process in democratic political systems is that ballot choices are confidential. The ballot should not be able to be traced to the voter by any public authority or private organization. This concern about privacy is echoed in the Clinton administration's "Framework For Global Electronic Commerce" (2000), which emphasizes that security is to be a pillar of *Fair Information Practices*. Fair Information Practices have addressed the process of online information gathering including notice, choice, access, security, and legislation. Especially to some voters, voting privacy is extremely important. For example, in an electronic voting situation held by Pennsylvania's Montgomery County, one voter even held an open umbrella behind him when he was voting in a public area

(Larsen, 1999). Obviously, he was suspicious of the integrity of the protection of privacy in an EVS environment. Undoubtedly, privacy in an EVS environment is an important acceptance factor to consider in any study.

Security

Security is a consideration closely associated with privacy. Here, we define security as the safety of data transfer and data storage. When one considers the consequences of network and database failures that occur on the national or international level, it is not surprising that public confidence in EVS may be a concern. For instance, in February 2001, the Internet linkage between the US and China was disconnected because of a broken undersea cable. Moreover, the Internet is also a host to a number of clever and creative computer hackers. In 2000, hackers invaded the Bibliofind Web site of Amazon.com and stole about 98,000 customer credit card records (SinaNews, 2001). Though it is not certain if hackers could develop effective programs and break into electronic voting systems without detection, this potential threat can dampen EVS acceptance, particularly for online voting systems. Coupling this with the presence of unpredictable and damaging computer viruses that are relayed via the Internet, it is reasonable for people to be skeptical about the reliability of new information systems. It is such distrust that will impede public acceptance of EVS.

In addition, one principal advantage of EVS is that it enables citizens to vote virtually anywhere. This advantage, however, may increase the likelihood of voter fraud. In conventionally held elections (i.e., paper ballots), the voter must be present at the booth and provide documentation of their eligibility to vote. While this process is not immune to fraud, the requirement that the voter appear in person mitigates the risk of widespread vote manipulation. However, in a virtual election environment, there is no poll watcher to ensure proper voter conformance to election law. It is not hard to imagine voting campaign vans equipped with laptops offering money or other incentives in return for votes.

Meanwhile, as it is a highly technical approach, only professionals could operate and maintain systems in local or central databases. Then electronic process and data storage procedures are transparent to ordinary people. Thus, without an effective observation and security system, system administrators or other professionals can easily manipulate vote data under the lure of money, for instance.

Accessibility

Another important concern about EVS is equal accessibility. A serious accusation that has been leveled against EVS and Internet technology in general is the notion of a "digital divide." "Digital divide" means that technology is not equally available to everyone (Turner, 2001). The appearance of Internet-based technology and its increasing utilization represents, some argue, a new form of discrimination against certain groups in the population. Furthermore, this discrimination, if it becomes apparent in the voting process, threatens the cornerstone of democratic government: equal representation. The U.S. Department of Commerce Study, *Falling Through the Net: Defining the Digital Divide*, (National Telecommunications and Information Administration, 1999) states, "the digital divide has turned into a 'racial ravine' when one looks at access among households of different racial and ethnic origins" (p. 8). Other studies find that the factors of income and education have a more significant impact on EVS accessibility than race does (Hoffmann, Tomas, and Venkatesh, 1997; Hoffmann and Tomas, 1999). Considering the diversity of race, income, and education in the U.S., access to EVS, especially an Internet voting system, will likely influence turnout rates among various population groups. Minority and low-income voters are disadvantaged when using EVS. The 2000 Arizona Democratic primary online election was nearly cancelled as the Voting Integrity Project (a nonprofit organization that monitors the voting process) thought online voting discriminated against minority groups from Internet access and filed a suit in a federal district court (Solop, 2000b; Done, 2002).

This concern with accessibility and the disparate impact of EVS in the voting population have led to the criticism that widespread use of such systems may work to the advantage of some political parties and candidates at the expense of others. Will parties and candidates representing more affluent voters reap political advantage as EVS participation increases? On the other hand, will EVS encourage the participation of some groups in important elections more than other groups? The novelty of EVS may appeal to certain segments of the population and spur greater political participation, which in turn may strengthen the power of these parties. Research on this aspect is ongoing; however, one recent analysis suggests that EVS may lead to an increased presence of liberal voters (Hill and John, 1998).

RECOMMENDATIONS

When the practical experimentations with EVS continue on, researchers keep on studying EVS in their attempt to improve the process, address the consequences, and determine its impact on our political system. In this section, we will examine solutions emerging from this effort and give our recommendations for a smooth evolution to EVS. We believe the rapid development of technology will eventually lead to wide acceptance and adoption of EVS.

Security and Privacy

Privacy is perhaps the foremost reason for security. In this section, we will provide the recommendations for privacy and security following a voting procedure, including registration, ballot casting, and tallying.

Recommendation A: Enhance privacy in voter's identification check, such as using biometric systems combined with password or credit card. Research is required to determine which method would be most effective for improving privacy and security.

Verification of voter identification is critical to ensure that only eligible persons vote, and that each only has a single vote. Thus for EVS usage, before election, randomly created passwords would be assigned to each eligible voter and sent out by mail. Password coupled with biometric security systems, such as thumbprint or eye scanner, could be the effective combination necessary to enhance voter identification for EVS. Thus, some special devices, such as a laser-reader or thumb-scanner, would be required in order to process registration checks. Currently, technology companies are collaborating closely with biological institutions to produce biometric identification systems, some of which have already been used as safeguard management systems in residential buildings.

MasterCard is also taken as an effective alternative to improve security in electronic voting. European countries walk of the rest of the world in this respect, especially Northern European countries with established advanced telecommunication infrastructures. In 2001, Finland conducted a joint project titled *Electronic Identification in Finnish Higher Education* to investigate possibilities for implementing a smart card-based electronic identification system in institutions of higher education (Linden, Linna, Kivilompolo and Kanner, 2002). The satisfied results boosted the national implementation of this system. All Finnish citizens and foreign permanent residents with reliable identification are qualified to get an electronic identification card containing the holder's photograph, issued by a local police department. With a unique e-number embedded in the microchip, it is a secure network key for all government and many private sector on-line services. This e-card can assist the government in reliably identifying the user before voting. This verification process significantly reduces the possibility of fraud. In addition, the card can be used as an official travel document for Finnish citizens in 19 European countries (Population Registration Center, 2002). In the future, the government even believes that identification checks can be processed from a mobile device such as a cellular phone installed with a special chip (Fineid, 2002). This successful example from the EU may be a good reference for EVS implementation in the U.S.

Recommendation B: Enhance the security during the election process at three key levels: physical infrastructure, network infrastructure, and data protections.

During the election process, between ballot transfer and storage, and between system operation and maintenance, security still constitutes the most important EVS concern. Computer scientists have focused on developing security protocols for the voting process. In this respect, it is thought that security can be enhanced at three levels: physical, network, and database (EzGov, 2000). Physical security involves optimal server infrastructure design and maintenance for reliable data storage service. At this level, hardware malfunction, power loss, and backup plans should be carefully thought out to best prepare for unexpected emergencies (EzGov, 2000). Also, strict system auditing should be institutionalized internally to ensure hardware security. In particular, access to central computers should be guarded by rigid personal identification validation and biometrical systems.

At the network level, a firewall is the first level of protection from external intrusion. Usually, skillful computer hackers can access the server, damage the system, and change data just via IP address. Especially in voting, a robust firewall is essential to protect the rights of voters and prevent possible fraud. Network companies, such as Nortel Network, TriNet, and HP, are actively producing reliable network products. In addition to protecting central voting systems in the government, special security software and anti-virus software would need to be provided by the government Web site for citizens to download onto their own computer before online elections.

In the context of voting, privacy safeguards are intended to ensure that there is no way to link a vote to the voter who created it, and EVS security ensures that only eligible people can vote and that they vote only once. Currently, encryption is perhaps the best choice in this respect.

Computer scientists, in recent years, have continuously developed and improved security protocol. As early as 1981, public key cryptography was created as the first cryptographic voting protocol (Chaum, 1981). In 1991, the "one agency protocol" was published, which guarantees the secure process of ID tag distribution for voter eligibility (Nurmi, Salomaa, and Santean, 1991; Riera, Rifa, and Borrell, 2000). One year later, the more complicated "two agency protocol" was developed and widely utilized, which separates validation and tally processes to enhance security (Fujioka, Okamoto, and Ohta, 1993). In addition, other protocols related to vote-tags are also in development to improve the accuracy and verifiability of the tally (Riera, Rifa, and Borrell, 2000). In past EVS pilot experiments, no security-related problems occurred. So it is conceivable that EVS based on present security protocols would effectively guarantee the security.

The third level is referred to as data security and has associated with it two categories: transmission and storage. As to data transmission, personal and sensitive information, like candidate selection, need encryption processes. Data can be divided into several packages and encrypted before exchange (EzGov, 2000). At the time of this writing, a 128-bit Secure Socket Layer (SSL) is the highest level of security standard over the Web. Until now, it still plays a satisfactory role in protecting data transmission.

With respect to data storage, in order to prevent potential fraud, data should be separated and stored in different files, even on several servers (EzGov, 2000). "Sand Boxing" is a frequently used encryption approach, which separates user name, password and other data into various files. The powerful database system itself can also provide effective defense, such as central/distributed storage, authenticity approval, and multi-authority allocation. Presently, large database vendors actively provide reliable and secure databases. Especially the database software giant, Oracle, never misses a beat to enhance its database management systems. Complex management mechanism and special operating language strengthen the security of their products. Figure 1 illustrates the network connection for Internet-based voting systems.

In order to ensure that EVS is reliable enough to provide voting services, it is necessary to conduct open testing in practice. In particular, federal and local governments should test consistency in a small-scope and non-critical election. Only after extensive testing and monitoring can the vulnerability of EVS be detected and valuable improvements be made. Also, during these pilot studies, voters would have more knowledge about electronic voting, and be better prepared for later usage in formal, larger elections.

Recommendation C: Develop and issue standard and effective laws and policies to protect privacy and security regulations.

Not only should security and privacy be enhanced from the technology side, but also through policy development. Legal preparation is always the initial step before taking any dramatic change, especially in political environments. In general, government policy on voting security guarantees will enhance people's confidence in electronic voting. As a critical political activity that represents the liberty of the whole of society, elections have gained significant attention from the government. For traditional on-site voting, federal and local governments have issued numerous laws to regulate voting activities with severe restrictions, especially for privacy and

Figure 1: Network Frame on Internet-based EVS

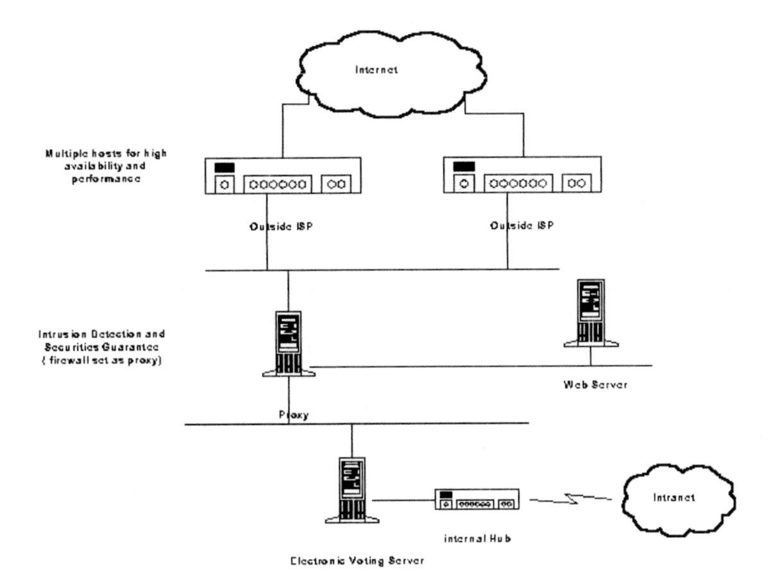

security issues (Done, 2002). Similarly, in order to create a safe and ordered environment for electronic voting, it is the right time for government to publish corresponding laws about privacy and security in the digital context.

As early as 1999, the Clinton administration has required agencies to put forms online for the top 500 government services, as well as keep privacy policies updated on all the federal agents' Web sites (Hiller and Bélagner, 2002). Actually, when the Clinton administration recommended electronic communications and passed the Government Paperwork Elimination Act (GPEA) (Hiller and Bélanger, 2002), an impending problem became how to effectively protect information processing in online transactions. By referencing certain laws and policies for online security management in the private sector, government can enhance the Computer Matching Act, as well as develop associated standard, precise, and clear privacy statements specific for electronic voting procedures.

Recommendation D: Provide an extended education for citizens to gain trust in governmental policies on privacy and security protection.

Finally, education would play a critical role to help citizens gain more knowledge about online elections. Hiller and Bélagner (2002) argue that education on privacy protection and security technology can enhance individual belief in technology effectiveness during electronic voting. In Arizona's online election, an extensive educational outreach program was launched two months before the election (Done, 2002). Detailed information about candidates and the whole voting processes, including when, where, and how to vote online or on-site, were announced repeatedly to the public. These efforts were found to have contributed greatly to the increase in voter participation. As a result, roughly 45 percent of all voters chose to vote online. It proves that effective education on mechanisms and operating processes of EVS can assist the government in gaining voters' trust in this voting revolution, in turn increasing voters' participation by using EVS.

Accessibility

Recommendation A: Research is needed to investigate the real impact of EVS accessibility on election results, as well as the factors associated with accessibility, such as race, income, education and age.

As to the concern about "digital divide," some evidence indicates that demographic differences in technology know-how may be more apparent than real. An alternative perspective is that the racial and ethnic divide may be a transitory phenomenon that will vanish as computer prices continue to drop (Westen, 2000). According to a recent Forrester Research Survey, the percentage of Asian and Latino Americans using computers at home, school, and work is more than that of white Americans (Irvine, 2000). Indeed, race, income, and education are factors in predicting turnout in conventionally held elections as well (Powell and Bingham, 1986; Verba and Nie, 1972; Verba, Sclozman, Brady, and Nie, 1993; Squire, Wolfinger, and Glass, 1987). Therefore, the problem is to determine whether such impact on elections really exists when EVSs are put into practice. In one empirical study on EVS implementation, Solop (2000a) investigated the Democratic primary election in Arizona and found that "racial ravine" did not significantly impact election outcome in an Internet voting environment. Recently, the authors conducted a survey to investigate the factors impacting EVS adoption among hundreds of part-time M.B.A. students in a southern state. The findings confirm the above arguments. This particular group of co-eds from the younger generation, comfortable with computers, did not regard accessibility as a problem for them when using EVS. So more research is needed to examine the true implications of EVS accessibility according to different demographic factors.

Recommendation B: State and local government should continue to experiment and implement multiple EVS channels simultaneously, as well as develop modern and inexpensive devices to alleviate any accessibility concerns. The kiosk voting and on-site voting can be adopted at the same time to reduce accessibility imbalances.

Moreover, an EVS is not confined solely to an Internet-based voting platform. It also includes telephone and touch screen systems as well. In the case of telephone-based voting systems, voter turnout should be greater than with Internet-based voting systems as the percentage of households with telephones is vastly greater than the percentage with computers. Compared with Internet voting systems, telephone-based systems do not require special skills or additional investment. Thus, telephone-based voting systems might be a good option for those lacking exposure to or experience with computers. In most states, such as Louisiana and Pennsylvania, touch screen EVS has already been widely implemented. Though most of them still stay at the level of on-site voting, at least voters are familiar with this mechanism of EVS, which is a good preparation for future remote voting.

Moreover, it is necessary to try the different mechanisms of EVS to see which ones are most effective in increasing participation. In Liverpool, England, Sheffield City Council tried many sorts of odd voting methods in various locations to improve the participation in upcoming national elections (The Economist, 2002). Such methods included the option to vote by mobile phone or the Internet and installing an electronic voting kiosk in close proximity to the World Snooker Championships to assist local fans in voting when they watch sports. It is believed that remote electronic voting could motivate voters' interest and increase voting turnout back from 30 percent (The Economist, 2002).

Besides, more and more new electronic devices are increasingly invented to make the election more convenient. For example, now small mobile devices are developed to facilitate online voting and mobile commerce. University of Wisconsin-Madison has developed EZ access, a trace technology, to apply to various mechanisms of EVS and facilitate the aged and disabled voters in voting (Law and Vanderheiden, 2000). This technology has been practically used in voting services.

The transition to EVS is not an overnight endeavor and requires the support of all voters. It will take years to achieve the final goal. During this slow but smooth transition, in addition to remote voting by different mechanisms of EVS, kiosk and traditional poll-site voting can also be taken as voting access alternatives. Voters need time to know EVS and gain accessibility to it, while they still hold the voting rights by adopting traditional voting methods.

Recommendation C: The government should develop special laws in response to voting process changes in order to prevent possible accessibility discrimination.

As EVS has changed the voting process, special laws are also needed to manage and guarantee citizens' voting rights. The Voting Rights Act, first published in 1965 and amended in 1970 and 1982, prohibits changes in voting procedures to result in racial discrimination. It should be further amended to prevent discrimination related to race, income and education due to accessibility of EVS. The Department of Justice would be responsible for this legal enhancement. Similar to the laws for privacy and security, legal protection for equal accessibility is an essential promise for all the citizens to use EVS. Only after addressing these legal issues can individuals put more trust in EVS.

Recommendation D: Organizations and all levels of government should provide training courses for citizens, especially minority and low-income residents, to increase their ability to use EVS.

A fundamental way to minimize the differences in computer access and skill is through training and education. In April 2000, President Clinton visited several communities that lacked Internet connectivity, which illustrated the willingness of the U.S. government and industry to get low-income communities connected to the Internet (Hunt, 2000; The Council for Excellence in Government, 2000). Funding for educational technology has increased by over 3,000 percent from $23 million in 1994 to $766 million in 2000 (The Council for Excellence in Government, 2000). During Arizona's 2000 online election, a government-sponsored group took laptops equipped with Internet connections to those who lacked Web access during that period (Done, 2002). Moreover, some simple training courses before an election in "technology-poor" communities could effectively increase voter participation. The Florida state government took the necessary steps to implement electronic voting systems (Washington Post, 2002). The government set aside enough money for efforts to teach voters how to use EVS. Besides, if possible, during the move to EVS government could consider providing mobile voting booths or installing computers at certain communities to offer voters with EVS options.

In fact, it is to be expected that with the passage of time, personal computer and Web-based technology will become more and more common. And it turns out to be true. According to a Census Bureau report released on September 6, 2001, (Associated Press, 2001), there has been a dramatic increase in the number of homes connected to the Internet in the U.S. within the past three years. Now over half of the 105 million people over the country have a computer at home (Associated Press, 2001. The differences among the persons with different incomes and races will significantly narrow down. More importantly, among the school-age kids (6-17), almost 90 percent have access to a computer. Those future voters have fewer problems in this aspect. Generally, citizen comfort levels with technology-based voting processes should rise as the role of computers in their daily lives increases. So we can optimistically predict the wide hold and usage of computers and advanced technology. Concerns about accessibility may subside in the near future.

CONCLUSION AND FURTHER RESEARCH

As an emerging technology, EVS brings remarkable promise to enable government reform and to renew the democratic and political systems. Though some challenges still remain to educate the public on the usage of EVS and to enhance the technology advantages of EVS, a January 2000 poll revealed that the majority of people examined (51 percent) regarded electronic voting as an effective way to make local government work efficiently (Westen, 2000). Moreover, about a third of American households would be more likely to vote if EVS were available (Benschoten, 2000). It is clear that the public has the desire to accept EVS.

The main contribution of this chapter is to examine the advantages of EVS, which can boost the interests and confidences of voters. Another contribution is to analyze the major concerns about EVS: security, privacy, and accessibility. Valuable recommendations for practical implementation are provided from technical, legal, and social perspectives. These suggestions provide beneficial guidelines for government. The Gartner Group anticipates that by the 2004 presidential election, all of the states in the United States will have a pilot election by using EVSs (Copeland and Verton, 2000). In the future, empirical research should investigate the specific factors impacting EVS adoption and the exact influence of EVS on different variables in elections, such as education level, race, election process, political tendency, technology usage, etc., in order to make a smooth and successful move to electronic voting.

REFERENCES

Associated Press. (2000). *Census Offer More Proof on Net Growth*. Found at: http://www.cnn.com/2001/TECH/internet/09/06/census.computers.ap/index.html).Retrieved from the WWW in September 2000.

Benschoten, E. V. (2000). Technology, Democracy and the Creation of Community. *National Civic Review*, 89(3), 185-192.

Chaum, D. (1981). Untraceable electronic mail, return addresses, and digital pseudonyms. *Communications of the ACM*, 24(2), 84-88.

Clinton, B. (2000, May 24). *Internet Caucus Briefing Book, Pt. 3*: Should all information be treated equally? (p. 9). Found at: www.netcaucus.org/books/privacy/.

Copeland, L. and Verton, D. (2000). Arizona, California pilot voting over the Internet. *Computerworld*, 34(48), 8.

Council for Excellence in Government. (2000). *E-govern, The Next American Revolution*. Found at: www.excelgov.org. Retrieved on the WWW in May 2000.

Cranor, L. F. and Cytron, R. K. (1997, January 7-10). *Census: A Security-Conscious Electronic Polling System for the Internet*. Proceeding of the Hawaii International Conference on System Sciences. Wailea, Hawaii.

Done, R. S. (2002). *Internet Voting: Bringing Elections to the Desktop*. Research report at the PricewaterhouseCoopers Endowment for the Business of Government.

The Economist. (2002). Britain: Tony's watching you. *Local Government*, 363(8271), 29.

The Economist. London. Turner, R. (2001). *E-Government and Digital Divide*. U.S./Office of Management and Budget Watch. Found at: http://www.netcaucus.org/books/egov2001/. Retrieved from the WWW in August 2001.

Electronic Voting Hot List. (2001). Maintained by Lorrie Faith Cranor. Found at: http://www.research.att.com/~lorrie/voting/hotlist.html. Retrieved from the WWW in June 2002.

EzGov. (2000). *EzGov, E-government, Privacy, Security and Accessibility*. E-Government Technology Industrial Profile. Found at: www.ezgov.com. Retrieved from the WWW in August 2000.

Fujioka, A., Okamoto, T. and Ohta, K. (1993). *A practical secret voting scheme for large scale elections*. Advances in Cyptology - AUSCRYPT '92. Lecture Notes in Computer Science, 718, 244-251.

Gartner Group. (2000). *E-Government*. Seminar Series in the Capitol. Found at: www.gartner.com. Retrieved from the WWW in June 2001.

Hill, K. A. and John, E. H. (1998). *Cyberpolitics: Citizen Activism in the Age of the Internet*. Lanham, MD: Rowman & Littlefield.

Hiller, J. S. and Bélanger, F. (2002). *Privacy Strategy for Electronic Government*. Research report at the PricewaterCoopers Endowment for The Business of Government.

Hoffmann, D. L. and Tomas, P. N. (1999). *The Evolution of the Digital Divide: Examining the Relationship of Race to Internet Access and Usage Over Time*. Unpublished manuscript.

Hoffmann, D. L., Tomas, P. N. and Venkatesh, A. (1997). *Diversity on the Internet: The Relationship of Race to Access and Usage*. Unpublished manuscript.

Hunt, T. (2000, September 25). *President Urges Closing the Rich-Poor 'Digital Divide.'* Essential Information on an Essential Issue Letter, No.131.

Irvine, M. (2000, April 18). *Defining the Digital Divide: Is the 'Digital Divide' About Race, Income or Education?* Found at www.abcnews.com. Retrieved from the WWW in June 2000.

Larsen, K. R. T. (1999) Voting technology implementation, Association for Computer Machinery. *Communication of the ACM*, 42(12), 55-57.

Law, C. and Vanderheiden, G. (2000, November 16-17). *The Development of a Simple, Low Cost Set of Universal Access Features for Electronic Devices*. The Association of Computer Machinery Conference on Universal Usability. Washington, D.C.

Linden, M., Linna, P., Kivilompolo, M., and Kanner, J. (2002, June 19-22). *Lessons Learned in PKI Implementation in Higher Education*. The 8th International Conference of European University Information Systems.

National Telecommunications and Information Administration, United States. (1999). *Falling through the net: defining the digital divide: A report on the telecommunications and information technology gap in America*. (Rev.11/99) ed. Washington, D.C.: National Telecommunications and Information Administration U.S. Department of Commerce.

Nurmi, H., Salomaa, A. and Santean, L. (1991). Secret ballot elections in computer networks. *Computers & Security*, 36(10), 553-560.

Population Registration Center (2002). *Electronic ID Card*. Found at: 222.fineid.fi. Retrieved on the WWW in July 2002.

Posner, R. A. (2001). Bush v Gore: Prolegomenon to an Assessment. *The University of Chicago Law Review*, 68(3), 719-736.

Powell, Jr., and Bingham, G. (1986). American Voter Turnout in Comparative Perspective. *American Political Science Review,* 80(1), 17-43.

Riera, A., Rifa, J. and Borrell, J. (2000). Efficient construction of vote-tags to allow open objection to the tally in electronic elections. *Information Processing Letters*, 75, 211-215.

SinaNews. (2001, September 3). *Hackers challenge security mechanism, 100,000 credit card records are stolen*. Found at: http://dailynews.sina.com/newsCneter/focusReport/5371/2910762-1.html. Retrieved from WWW in September 2001.

Solop, F. I. (2000a, May 18-21). *Public Support for Internet Voting: Are We*

Falling Into a 'Racial Ravine'? Paper presented at the American Association of Public Opinion Research Conference. Portland, OR.

Solop, F. I. (2000b, August 31-September 3). *Digital Democracy Comes of Age in Arizona: Participation and Politics in the First Binding Internet Election.* Paper presented at the American Political Science Association National Conference. Washington, D.C.

Squire, P., Wolfinger, R.E. and Glass, D.P. (1987). Residential Mobility and Voter Turnout. *The American Political Science Review*, 81(1), 45-66.

Symonds, M. (2000, June 24). *Government and the Internet: Haves and have-nots.*

U.S. Newswire. (2000). *Clinton-Gore Record on Closing Digital Divide.* Found at: www.usnewswire.com. Retrieved from the WWW in May 2000.

Verba, S. and Nie, N. H. (1972). *Participation in America: Political democracy and social equality.* New York: Harper and Row.

Verba, S., Sclozman, K. L., Brady, H. and Nie, N. H. (1993). Citizen Activity: Who Participates? What Do They Say? *American Political Science Review,* 87(2), 303-318.

Washington Post. (2002, June 21). Fla. Election Aide Predicts Confusion in Primary Poll; State Replaces Punch Cards but Fails to Fund Voter Education, Miami, P. A23.

Watson, R. T. and Mundy, B. (2001). A Strategic Perspective Of Electronic Democracy. *Communications of the ACM*, 44(1), 27-30.

Westen, T. (2000). E-Democracy: Ready or Not, Here It Comes. *National Civic Review*, 89(3), 217-228.

Chapter XI

SME Barriers to Electronic Commerce Adoption: Nothing Changes–Everything is New

Carina Ihlström
Halmstad University, Sweden

Monika Magnusson
Karlstad University, Sweden

Ada Scupola
Roskilde University, Denmark

Virpi Kristiina Tuunainen
Helsinski School of Economics, Finland

ABSTRACT

In this chapter we look into earlier empirical research on the barriers to e-commerce (EC) adoption and diffusion for small and medium-sized enterprises (SMEs). We explore research conducted in the context of information and communications technologies (ICT) in general, as well as EDI and Internet-based e-commerce. What we are interested in is whether these barriers are something new created by the new wave of Internet based technologies. We divide the barriers, inhibitors, or factors slowing down the diffusion of new technologies found in previous literature into those internal to an organization and those imposed by external forces. The basic premise of this chapter is that technologies advance or change, but the barriers for SMEs to adopt them do not. The authors hope that understanding this will help researchers, small companies, and policy makers to move on and do something active to reduce such barriers.

INTRODUCTION

As a majority of the large businesses now have entered the "new information society," the small and medium-sized enterprises are expected to be next in turn. SMEs have undoubtedly an important role in most economies and are fundamental, especially in less developed countries and peripheral European regions. For example, in UK SMEs represent over 95% of all businesses registered for VAT, employ 65% of the work force, and produce 25% of gross domestic product (Ballantine, Levy, and Powell, 1998). SMEs play a key role in the economy by generating employment, engendering competition, and creating economic wealth (Hay and Kamshad, 1994). They are also fundamental in promoting new innovations (ibid.) and providing society with new products (Walczuch, van Braven, and Lundgren, 2000). At the same time SMEs are characterized by a high degree of failures (Ballantine et al., 1998). Within five years 80% of all new small businesses have failed (ibid.). Because of their importance, small businesses need to be embraced in the new information society as the Internet in the long run might affect their productivity, market access, and competitiveness (Walczuch et al., 2000). To be able to survive and prosper SMEs need to keep up with their larger counterpartners' way of doing business.

In recent years one of the most apparent trends in business is e-commerce. Even if the growth in e-commerce still has not been able to fulfil the optimistic prognosis, it is certainly here to stay. E-commerce in SMEs has become an important subject both in policy formulation and in research. For example, OECD (1998) believes that the adoption and diffusion of e-commerce among SMEs could contribute to increasing substantially their competitive advantage. Often e-commerce or electronic business is seen almost as the latest "miracle cure" for SMEs. Various national and regional (e.g., EU) projects on "SME awareness" to facilitate SME involvement in e-commerce are becoming more and more common on national and regional political agendas. Research studies on this subject are increasing as well (e.g., Chen and Williams, 1998).

It is feared, however, that because of a number of barriers and inhibitors, SMEs are left out of the developments in the information society. The high capital investment involved in IT adoption and the need of skilled manpower make the barriers larger for SMEs than for larger businesses (Thong, 2001). According to OECD (1998), the most significant barriers of e-commerce for SMEs in the OECD countries are lack of awareness, uncertainty about the benefits of e-commerce, concerns about lack of human resources and skills, set-up costs and pricing issues, and concerns about security.

The development of the Internet has opened up e-commerce between businesses (B2B) as well as between businesses and consumers (B2C). The big difference from earlier communication methods is the wide availability and low cost of the technology. Start-up costs and transaction costs are far lower than before, and an increasing part of companies and consumers are using the Internet to conduct their business. Still the small and medium-sized companies are hesitating.

In this chapter we look into earlier empirical research on the barriers to e-commerce for SMEs. What we are interested in is whether these barriers are something new created by the new wave of Internet-based technologies. Our grounding argument is that these barriers have remained the same since SMEs got involved in IS/IT and are not particularly specific to the new Internet-based technologies. We look at adoption and diffusion barriers of different information technologies in SMEs, with the focus on information and communications as well as e-commerce technologies, including different inter-organizational systems (IOS), EDI, and Internet-based solutions.

The chapter is structured as follows. In the following section we present definitions of e-commerce and SMEs and argue for the importance of looking at e-commerce adoption barriers among SMEs. The section "What's In It?" briefly touches upon the reasons why SMEs might benefit from e-commerce, and therefore the necessity to look at the reasons why e-commerce is still not spreading. The section "Barriers to E-Commerce" discusses barriers of Internet-based e-commerce adoption found in previous literature, as well as relating and comparing them, where it is possible, with SMEs' adoption barriers of EDI and IS/ICT in general. Finally, the last section summarizes the findings of the chapter and gives some suggestions for further research.

E-COMMERCE AND SME

Much confusion surrounds the definition of e-commerce. Some see e-commerce as Internet-based activities only, while others include any kind of business or exchange of information on any type of network. Our approach is closer to the latter one: we define e-commerce as a process, where electronic connections facilitate economic transactions between various parties in the value chain. This wide definition includes the usage of different types of information and communication technologies and systems, trade in both physical and digital products, and different types of services (Tuunainen, 1999). Even though this definition of e-commerce includes a range of technologies from proprietary IOS and EDI to Internet-based solutions and mobile or wireless technologies, for the purposes of this study we distinguish between the different technologies when such has been done in the reviewed literature.

There are different definitions of what SMEs are. The number of employees and turnover are two factors used to categorize businesses. According to the European Parliament, SMEs are businesses with up to 500 employees, net fixed assets of less than ECU 75 million, and with no more than one-third of their capital in the hands of a larger company. The European Parliament divides SMEs into different sub-groups based on the number of employees, for instance small undertakings with 10 to 50 employees and medium-sized undertakings with 50 to 250 employees (European Parliament, 2000).

A long-debated issue is whether SMEs substantially differ from larger ones or not. SMEs are not homogeneous and some even claim that it is impossible to draw any general conclusions about them. Still company size has been found to be a critical factor to adoption of e-commerce technologies (Premkumar, Ramamurthy, and Crum, 1997; Premkumar and Roberts, 1999). There also seems to be a significant difference in use of e-commerce between large and small companies. A Swedish study shows that 87.5% of companies with more than 500 employees had their own Web site in 1999. The corresponding figure for companies with 10-19 employees was 48.2% (Jönsson, 2001). The difference is even more substantial when looking at EDI adoption. While more than 62% of the largest companies have adopted EDI, only 7% of the micro companies (10-19 employees) have EDI (ibid.). This is problematic for the small companies that may be able to save money and increase revenue with the help of e-commerce technologies. The poor spreading to small companies, however, also cripples their larger business partners' possibility to gain optimal advantages from their e-commerce investments. Once a company has implemented any form of e-commerce, it is a large advantage to be able to connect all of its partners to the new system. In that way they avoid working with double routines and can reach maximal benefits.

Most companies today live under a strong economical, as well as technological, pressure. Welsh and White (1981) describe this special condition that distinguishes SMEs from their larger counterparts as "resource poverty." The increased globalization has intensified competition, the technical development is fast, and the information overload puts new demands on organizations (Turban, Lee, King, and Chung, 2000). For small businesses to strengthen their competitive ability and face the increased competition, both nationally and internationally, they need to adopt new technologies for production as well as management of the company (Julien, 1995). Some even claim that SMEs in the long run will be the real beneficiaries of IT (Chesher and Kaura, 1999).

A lot has been written about SMEs' poor ability to use IT as a strategic resource. For example, SMEs lack both business and IS/IT strategy, they have limited information skills, and when they modernize their equipment, the planning process is less structured and more incremental than in larger businesses (Ballentine et al., 1998; Julien, 1995). The strategic decision-making process is short-termed and reactive rather then proactive (Blili and Raymond, 1993). SMEs often use intuitive methods when monitoring new technologies and collect information in a more iterative and less organized manner (Julien, 1995). In small businesses the CEO is often the same person who owns the company. This makes his or her vision and commitment essential, especially to get the adequate resources and support to implement an innovation (Premkumar and Roberts, 1999).

The perhaps mostly discussed difference between SMEs and large businesses is the resource constraints that the former have to deal with. SMEs are usually poor in human, as well as financial, resources (Blili and Raymond, 1993). Their weak financial standing makes them more vulnerable to risk-taking, and an innovation (such as e-commerce) can represent a disproportionately large financial risk (Rothwell and Dodgson, 1991). Also, the level of IT-knowledge is generally low in SMEs. Small businesses often have difficulties recruiting and keeping well-trained IT personnel and their financial standing prevents them from employing their own IT expertise (Thong, 2001). Even though there is often a general lack of IS expertise in SMEs, small companies are unfortunately also less inclined to use external advice-giving services (Thong, Yap, and Raman, 1996).

There are also some advantages with being small. Small companies are claimed to be more flexible and they can more rapidly adapt to new demands and changes in the external environment (Rothwell and Dodgson, 1991). This is facilitated by an efficient internal communication that takes place in informal networks (Rothwell and Dodgson, 1991). The ability to reorganize fast is a valuable property, since a high level of uncertainty usually characterizes the environment of smaller businesses. Small businesses are also less bureaucratic and more willing to take risks to grasp new opportunities (Rothwell and Dodgson, 1991).

WHAT'S IN IT?

There are reasons to believe that many SMEs can gain from e-commerce. Advantages of early e-commerce technologies such as EDI typically include reductions in transaction costs and delays, higher quality service, and improved operations management (Raymond and Bergeron, 1996). Raymond and Bergeron (1996) also point out that SMEs could gain more benefits from EDI. This could be achieved by providing a higher level of organizational support for EDI, such as management support, employees training, and obtaining the collaboration and support of all the departments and business partners involved.

Newer communication technologies, such as the Internet, are claimed to have opened up new markets and made geographic locations irrelevant (Premkumar and Roberts, 1999). This brings interesting opportunities to small companies, as well as additional risks (ibid.). The spread of the Internet has changed the way consumers and companies collect information and conduct their businesses. The Internet has brought the possibility to reach new markets and new customers, but has at the same time made it more difficult to keep old customers. Buyers can, with the help of the Internet, relatively easy find competing suppliers and compare their offers. As an increasing number of enterprises and consumers are using the Internet to seek information before their final purchase, the risk is obvious for companies without a Web presence: if the company does not exist on the Internet, it does not exist.

E-commerce is driven by a number of factors on both buyer and supplier sides: access to an affluent customer base, lower information dissemination costs, lower transaction costs, broader market reach, increased service, additional channels for customer feedback, and consumer and market research (Auger and Gallaugher, 1997). Small businesses using Internet commerce have perceived a decrease in communication costs and the rise of new opportunities (Poon and Swatman, 1999). These opportunities can, for example, consist of the discovery of new business partners or business networks as well as useful feedback from customers (ibid.).

E-commerce applications, whether external or internal, are expected to improve coordination with trading partners or internal business units, and facilitate information exchange within organizations as well as market creation to reach new customers (Riggins and Rhee, 1998). One way to increase the potential benefits for the small players is the use of different kinds of cooperative arrangements between a number of SMEs. For instance, Kettinger and Hackbarth (1997) claim that to the extent that small firms can leverage their limited resources with other small firms via cooperative electronic network connections, they may achieve economies of scale and create new sales opportunities that were not available prior to e-commerce. Network members are believed to often have complementary resources that make the total benefits from being a network member larger than the sum of the individual parts (Poon, 2000).

The Web also offers an inexpensive way to market the company and to get new information (Turban et al., 2000). For companies with niche products or those wanting to conduct market research, the Web provides good possibilities (ibid.). Furthermore, the Web is said to be sparking an explosion of entrepreneurial activity by encouraging rapid experimentation with new business organizations and systems (Tenenbaum, 1998). Evidence has also been found that Internet commerce is increasing the competitive advantage of small businesses and the quality of information support (Poon, 2000). The benefits that Internet commerce brings to a corporation depend, however largely, on the percentage of customers and business partners that participate in Internet commerce (ibid.) This is due to the fact that the success of e-commerce and other inter-organizational systems depends on the number of external participants, while with internal IT systems, the success depends on the number of internal users.

According to this it seems that e-commerce can bring a number of benefits to SMEs. Small businesses are also under increasing pressure to use information systems to stay competitive or simply to survive (Thong, 2001). Even so the SMEs are hesitating. The crucial question is: *What's hindering the spread of e-commerce to SMEs?*

Barriers to E-Commerce

In the literature concerning barriers or inhibitors to implementing and adopting e-commerce technologies by SMEs, the issues discussed fall mainly into two categories: internal and external to the organization. Internal or organizational issues relate mainly to the lack of awareness and knowledge in SMEs and resource limitations. External issues, outside the sphere of influence of SMEs, include mainly technical considerations and the topic of external influence or support.

Internal Issues

There are a number of barriers related to information and communication technologies (ICT) that prevent SMEs from adopting and exploiting them for inter-organizational purposes (Chapman, James-Moore, Szczygiel, and Thompson, 2000). In this paragraph we discuss the internal issues that may hinder the adoption, summarized in Table 1 at the end of the paragraph. Many barriers relate to SMEs' lack of understanding of e-commerce potential opportunities and how to implement these techniques (ibid.). SMEs have been found to lack both an awareness of the potential benefits of the technology and the organizational readiness needed for the development of integrated EDI systems (Iacovou, Benbasat, and Dexter, 1995).

The diffusion of IT and EDI may in many cases be delayed because the managers fail to see the advantages of the technology (ibid.). Difficulties in perceiving any direct benefits may hinder both the adoption of Internet (Walczuch et al., 2000) as well as EDI adoption (Kuan and Chau, 2001). The lack of recognizable or measurable financial gains from Internet-based commerce is one such example (Vassilopoulou, Keeling, and Macaulay, 1999; Walczuch et al., 2000). The owner attitude towards growth and his or her perception of the business value of the Internet is another factor that is instrumental to the adoption decision (Levy and Powell, 2002). Similarly Poon and Swatman (1999) found that the lack of experiences of tangible benefits is a major e-commerce adoption barrier among SMEs.

Several studies describe lack of IT knowledge and technological expertise as a major hurdle to the adoption of different e-commerce technologies and procedures by SMEs (Iacovou et al., 1995; Damsgaard and Lyytinen, 1998; Bennet, Polkingham, Pearce, and Hudson, 1999; Kuan and Chau, 2001). In a study among Finnish SMEs supplying the automotive industry, Tuunainen (1998) found that particularly the smallest subcontractors rarely have the sufficient IT knowledge to fully utilize EDI. This is found to be still true in a more recent study conducted by Chau (2001). Again, in the Internet usage context, the lack of knowledge of technology has been cited as a major factor differentiating SMEs from larger firms (Haynes, Becherer, and Helms, 1998). In other studies this has been expressed as unfamiliarity with the Internet (Walczuch et al., 2000), lack of understanding of the e-commerce medium (Vassilopoulou et al., 1999), and limited knowledge of how the Web pages could contribute to the organizational strategy (McCue, 1999).

Small firms often lack suitable qualified technical specialists (Rothwell and Dodgson, 1991). They also tend to postpone the implementation of internal IS due to insufficient knowledge of how to implement it successfully (Thong, 2001). Most owners are aware of their lack of knowledge of IS and this results in doubts about given advice (Levy and Powell, 2000). The lack of knowledge also makes them reluctant to spend their limited resources on an area that they feel they do not control (ibid.).

Regardless of the technology in question, the technological development in SMEs is claimed to suffer from poor ability to manage technology as a strategic weapon, negative attitudes, and limited human resources as in-house expertise (Poon and Swatman, 1997; McCue, 1999; Buratti and Penco, 2001; Chau, 2001). Together, this indicates an insufficient organizational readiness. SMEs are also found to suffer from a lack of staff and time to investigate new technologies and systems (Bennett et al., 1999), as well as a reluctance to dedicate time and resources to resolve their lack of skills and understanding (Chapman et al., 2000).

Similarly, findings of a study conducted by Chen and Williams (1998) among UK small businesses also pointed out that SMEs tend to lack resources and experience, and seem to have difficulties in planning, designing or implementing EDI systems. Only few SMEs are recorded to have a full time IT professional, since IT-based systems are not regarded as an economically viable alternative (Stymne, 1996). This is in line with a study by Poon and Swatman (1999) who found that among the major barriers for SMEs not using Internet for their financial transactions is the fact that traditional transaction ways are perceived as robust and sound.

Table 1: Adoption Barriers of E-Commerce in SMEs — Internal Issues

Internet-based Electronic Commerce (EC)	**Electronic Data Interchange (EDI)**	**Information Systems (IS)/ICT in general**
Lack of understanding of opportunities (Chapman et al., 2000). *Owners perception of the business value* (Levy & Powell, 2002). *Lack of measurable financial gains* (Vassilopoulou et al., 1999; Walczuch et al., 2000; Poon & Swatman, 1999).	*Lack of awareness of the potential benefits* (Iacovou et al., 1995). *Perception of (too few) direct benefits* (Kuan & Chau, 2001).	*Lack of understanding of potential advantages* (Iacouvou et al., 1995).
Lack of IT-knowledge and technological expertise (Walczuch et al., 2000; Vassilopoulou et al., 1999; McCue, 1999; Haynes et al., 1998). *Lack of understading of implementation techniques* (Chapman et al., 2000).	*Lack of IT-knowledge and technological expertise* (Tuunainen, 1998; Chen & Williams, 1998; Iacovou et al., 1995; Damsgaard & Lyytinen, 1998; Bennett et al., 1999; Kuan & Chau, 2001).	*Lack of IT-knowledge and technological expertise* (Rothwell & Dodgson, 1991; Levy & Powell, 2000). *Lack of knowledge of implementation issues* (Thong, 2001).
Perceived cost (Deschoolmeester & Hee, 2000; Walczuch et al., 2000).	*Perceived cost* (Kuan & Chau, 2001; Saunders & Clark, 1992; Iacovou et al. 1995).	*Lack of financial resources* (Tuunainen, 1998; Bennett et al., 1999; McCue, 1999; Chapman et al., 2000).
Insufficient organizational readiness (Poon & Swatman, 1997; McCue, 1999). *Lack of human resources and time to investigate new technologies and systems* (Bennett et al., 1999). *Reluctance to dedicate time and resources to resolving their lack of understanding and skills* (Chapman et al., 2000).	*Insufficient organizational readiness* (Iacovou et al., 1995; Chau, 2001).	*Insufficient organizational readiness* (Buratti & Penco, 2001). *Lack of human resources to investigate new technologies and systems* (Stymne, 1996).

A weak financial position of SMEs and their resistance to invest in sophisticated systems involving complex telecommunications have been found as major barriers in several studies (Tuunainen, 1998; Bennett et al., 1999; McCue, 1999; Chapman et al., 2000). Saunders and Clark (1992) found that perceived cost has been a significant barrier to EDI adoption among small vendor firms. This result is consistent with findings of Iacovou et al. (1995) on SME EDI adoption and with a recent study conducted by Kuan and Chau (2001) on small businesses EDI adoption. Also the adoption and use of Internet technologies is found to be hindered by the cost and speed of Internet access, as well as by the cost of the start-up investment (Deschoolmeester and van Hee, 2000; Walczuch et al., 2000). Table 1 shows a summery of the internal issues that can hinder the adoption of different e-commerce technologies.

External Issues

Empirical investigations (e.g., MacKay, 1993; Iacovou et al., 1995) have suggested that a major reason why small companies become EDI-capable is due to external pressure, especially from trading partners. Insignificant influence by the industry and poor promotion campaigns by vendors and consultants are still found to play a role in slow diffusion of EDI (Chau, 2001) as well as Internet technologies (Poon and Swatman, 1997). Large firms wanting their smaller trading partners to adopt EDI can use a coercive or a supportive strategy (Premkumar et al., 1997). If the smaller trading partner is reluctant to adopt EDI, a coercive strategy consisting of creation of competitive pressures and threat of loss of business is sometimes used. The supportive strategy involves marketing the technology in such a way to help the smaller firms understand its advantages and sharing expertise with them (ibid.). Financial and technical assistance can be used to reduce the problems related to the smaller firms' organizational readiness (Iacovou et al., 1995). The latter strategy, even if costly, might be better in the long run to get as many partners connected as possible (Premkumar and Ramamurthy, 1995), but as both customer support and competitive pressure have proved to impact the adoption decision most firms need to use both strategies (Premkumar et al., 1997).

Another important barrier is the lack of a critical mass of electronically connected business partners. Previous studies have showed that low volumes of EDI transactions (Tuunainen, 1998), low volume of messages received over the Internet (Poon and Swatman, 1997), as well as concerns that suppliers and customers are not on-line (Walczuch et al., 2000) are barriers that prevents SMEs from investing time and money in new technologies. To be motivated to make a costly investment such as EDI, it is necessary that a majority of partners in the distribution chain, such as customers, suppliers, carriers, and banks adopt the technology as well (Premkumar et al., 1997). Otherwise it may be impossible to obtain adequate benefits because the organization has to maintain a paper-based system in parallel with the EDI system (ibid.). Electronic marketplaces and databases of products or suppliers are other examples where there have been problems reaching the critical mass.

Furthermore, lack of security or perceived security hazards have been and still are a major concern among SMEs, whether in EDI, Internet, or other ICT adoption (Tuunainen, 1998; Poon and Swatman, 1999; Vassilopoulou et al., 1999; Deschoolmeester and van Hee, 2000; Walczuch et al., 2000). Legal issues (Deschoolmeester and van Hee, 2000), lack of standards (Tuunainen, 1998), still experimental payment systems, and limited services offered on the Internet (Poon and Swatman, 1999) are other important factors contributing to slow adoption of different e-commerce technologies.

Table 2: Adoption Barriers of E-Commerce in SMEs — External Issues

Internet-based Electronic Commerce (EC)	Electronic Data Interchange (EDI)
Insignificant influence by industry (Poon & Swatman, 1997).	*Insignificant influence by industry* (Chau, 2001). *Lack of external pressure from trading partners* (MacKay, 1993; Iacovou, 1995; Premkumar et al., 1997).
Poor promotion campaign by vendors (Poon & Swatman, 1997).	*Poor promotion campaign by vendors* (Chau, 2001).
Lack of critical mass (Poon & Swatman, 1997).	*Lack of critical mass* (Tuunainen, 1998; Premkumar et al., 1997).
Lack of security or perceived security hazards (Poon & Swatman, 1999; Vassilopoulou et al., 1999; Deschoolmeester & Hee, 2000; Walczuch et al.; 2000). *Lack of secure payment systems* (Poon & Swatman, 1999).	*Lack of security or perceived security hazards* (Tuunainen, 1998).
Legal issues (Deschoolmeester & Hee, 2000).	*Lack of standards* (Tuunainen, 1998).
Limited services offered on the Internet (Poon & Swatman, 1999).	

External consultants and IT vendors could play an important role in assisting small businesses to successfully adopt IS (Thong et al., 1996). However, the lack of impartial advice (Vassilopoulou et al., 1999) and the difficulty of access to expert help (Bennett et al., 1999) are still inhibiting the adoption of new technologies among SMEs. A further problem is that the attitudes towards consultants are ambiguous in SMEs (Stymne, 1996). Table 2 shows a summary of the external issues that can hinder the adoption of different e-commerce technologies. The table compares only barriers to EDI adoption with barriers to Internet adoption since the adoption of proprietary IS are expected to be mainly an internal decision, and therefore less influenced by external forces.

SUMMARY AND CONCLUSIONS

In this chapter we have analyzed e-commerce adoption and diffusion barriers in SMEs discussed in previous literature, with the intention to find similarities and differences between the barriers associated with the adoption of different technologies: ICT/IS in general, EDI, and Internet-based e-commerce. After having discussed the importance of small companies in any country's economy, the chapter has presented different definitions of SMEs and advantages and disadvantages of being small. The chapter has then touched upon some benefits that e-commerce can bring to SMEs and posed the question of why SMEs still are reluctant to adopt e-commerce. This leads to the second part of the chapter that looks in depth at e-commerce adoption and diffusion barriers.

We do not claim to have conducted an exhaustive literature review on barriers to e-commerce for SMEs. We believe, however, that we have produced a representative sample of a wide range of often-cited pieces of research on the topic. We divided the barriers or inhibitors found in earlier empirical studies into internal and external issues. Barriers created or maintained by external factors, such as weak industry influence, poor promotion campaigns, lack of critical mass, lack of security or perceived security hazards, as well as lack of standards are essentially areas where ICT vendors, industrial partners or associations, as well as authorities and policy makers can have an impact. Nevertheless, much more factors were found to fall into the internal or organizational category, including issues such as lack of awareness or understanding, lack of knowledge and skill, and lack of financial resources to invest into the ICT technologies. External players can influence the level of awareness. Furthermore, it could be expected that the significance of many organizational problems will diminish as the more computer literate generations take over the SMEs; but then again, the pace of technological development is unlikely to slow down, creating all new possibly hurdles particularly for non-IT professionals. Furthermore, the same factors that are hindering the adoption seem to go on being problematic once the SMEs have implemented e-commerce. Factors such as lack of IT expertise, limited resources, and lack of support have been found to also inhibit SMEs' ability to derive benefits when using e-commerce (Chau and Turner, 2002).

What can be deduced from our analysis is that whether we are talking about ICT in general, EDI, or lately Internet-based e-commerce, the barriers to adoption and use of them for SMEs have mostly remained the same. This is to some extent confirmed by a recent empirical study (Mehrtens, Cragg, and Mills, 2001). Both similarities and differences between EDI adoption and Internet adoption seem to exist (ibid.). In Internet adoption as in EDI adoption perceived benefits, organizational readiness, and external pressure were found to have impact on the adoption decision. However, the internal factors of these categories varies to some extent between EDI adoption and Internet adoption (ibid.) At the adoption of the Internet it is the level of knowledge of the non-IT professional, often the owner/manager, that is important rather then the knowledge of IT professionals. While the perceived benefits of EDI for example might include reduced inventory levels, the benefits expected from Internet adoption consist of cheap and effective customer interaction and information gathering as well as image building (ibid.) In EDI the external pressure often comes from major customers. According to Mehrtens et al. (2001) external pressure has an impact on Internet adoption too. This time the pressure comes from a wide group of Internet users, not only customers, but also suppliers and potential employees (ibid.).

What are the implications of this study? Certainly *not* that industry players, authorities, and researchers should drop the topic of looking into barriers of e-commerce for SMEs. The implication is, rather, that we have to stop reinventing the wheel, so to speak, in form of creating new lists of old barriers. What we have to do is to move on, and develop new tools for SMEs to bring them into a mutual information society. Researchers for example could develop normative research to help SMEs overcome some of the internal barriers, such as lack of knowledge and ability to manage technology as a strategic weapon, while policy makers could develop more and better programs to make it easier for SMEs to embrace e-commerce.

REFERENCES

Auger, P. and Gallaugher, J.M. (1997). Factors Affecting The Adoption of An Internet-Based Sales Presence For Small Business. *The Information Society*, 13 (1), 55-74.

Ballantine, J., Levy, M. and Powell, P. (1998). Evaluating Information Systems in Small and Medium-sized Enterprises: Issues and Evidence. *European Journal of Information Systems*, 7, 241-251.

Bennet, J., Polkinghorne, M., Pearce, J. and Hudson, M. (1999, April). Technology transfer for SMEs. *Engineering Management Journal*, 75-80.

Blili, S. and Raymond, L. (1993). Information technology: Threats and Opportunities for Small and Medium-Sized Enterprises. *International Journal of Information Management*, 13, 439-448.

Buratti, N. and Penco, L. (2001). Assisted technology transfer to SMEs: Lessons from an exemplary case. *Technovation*, 21, 35-43.

Chapman, P., James-Moore, M., Szczygiel, M. and Thompson, D. (2000). Building Internet Capabilities in SMEs. *Logistics Information Management*, 13 (6), 353-360.

Chau, P.Y.K. (2001). *Inhibitors to EDI Adoption in Small Businesses: An Empirical Investigation*. Journal of Electronic Commerce Research, 2 (3). Available at: http://www.csulb.edu/web/journals/jecr/issues/20012/paper4.pdf.

Chau, S. B. and Turner, P. (2002). A framework for analyzing factors influencing small to medium sized enterprises (SMEs) ability to derive benefit from the conduct of Web: *Proceedings of the 10th European Conference on Information Systems,* 625-639.

Chen, J. and Williams, B. (1998). The impact of EDI on SMEs: Summary of Eight British Case Studies. *Journal of Small Business Management*, 36 (4), 264-278.

Chesher, M. and Kaura, R. (1999). *Electronic commerce and business communications*. London: Springer-Verlag.

Damsgaard, J. and Lyytinen, K. (1998). Contours of diffusion of electronic data interchange in Finland: Overcoming technological barriers and collaborating to make it happen. *Journal of Strategic Information Systems*, 7, 275-297.

Deschoolmeester, D. and van Hee, J. (2000). SMEs and the Internet: On the Strategic Drivers Influencing the Use of the Internet in SMEs. In *Proceedings of the 13th International Bled Electronic Commerce Conference*, 754-769.

European Parliament. (2000). *European Parliament Fact Sheets. Small and medium-sized enterprises (SMEs)*. Available at: http://www.europarl.eu.int/factsheets/4_14_0_en.htm?redirected=1 (12/07/2002).

Hay, M. and Kamshad, K. (1994). Small Firm Growth: Intentions, Implementation and Impediments. *Business Strategy Review*, 5 (3), 49-68.

Haynes, P., Becherer R. and Helms, M. (1998). Small and Medium sized businesses and Internet use: Unrealized potentials? *Internet Research: Electronic Networking Applications and Policy*, 8 (3), 229-235.

Iacovou, C.L., Benbasat, I. and Dexter, A.S. (1995). Electronic Data Interchange and Small Organizations: Adoption and Impact of Technology. *MIS Quarterly*, 19 (4), 465-485.

Julien, P-A. (1995). New Technologies and Technological Information in Small Businesses. *Journal of Business Venturing*, 10, 459-475.

Jönsson, C. (ed). (2001). Det nya Sverige - fakta om informations- och kommunikationsteknik 2001. Värnamo: Statens institut för kommunikationsanalys.

Kettinger, W. J. and Hackbarth, G. (1997). Selling in the era of the "Net": Integration of electronic commerce in small firms. In *Proceedings of the Eighteenth International Conference on Information Systems*, 249-262.

Kuan, K.K.Y. and Chau, P.Y.K. (2001). A perception-based model for EDI adoption in small businesses using a technology-organization-environment framework. *Information & Management*, 38, 507-521.

Levy, M. and Powell, P. (2000). Information systems strategy for small and medium sized enterprises: an organisational perspective. *Journal of Strategic Information Systems*, 9, 63-84.

Levy, M. and Powell, P. (2002). SME Internet Adoption: Towards a Transporter Model. In *Proceedings of the 15th Bled Electronic Commerce Conference,* Slovenia, 507-521.

MacKay, D. (1993). The impact of EDI on the components sector of the Australian automotive industry. *Journal of Strategic Information Systems*, 2 (3), 243-263.

McCue. S. (1999). *Small Firms and the Internet: Force or farce?* International Trade Forum, Geneva, 27-29.

Mehrtens, J., Cragg, P.B. and Mills, A.M. (2001). A Model of Internet Adoption by SMEs. *Information & Management*, 39, 165-176.

OECD (1998, October 7-9). *SMEs and electronic commerce*. Ministerial Conference on Electronic Commerce. Ottawa, Canada.

Poon, S. (2000). Business Environmental Impact on Internet Commerce Benefit - A Small Business Perspective. *European Journal of Information Systems*, 9(2), 72-81.

Poon, S. and Swatman, P. (1997). Small Business Use of the Internet: Findings from the Australian Case Studies. *International Marketing Review*, 14 (5), 385-402.

Poon, S. and Swatman, P. (1999). An exploratory Study of Small Business Internet Commerce Issues. *Information and Management*, 35, 9-18.

Premkumar, G. and Ramamurthy, K. (1995). The role of interorganizational and organizational factors on the decision mode for adoption of interorganizational systems. *Decision Sciences,* 26 (3), 303-336.

Premkumar, G. and Roberts, M. (1999). Adoption of new information technologies in rural small businesses. *Omega International Journal of Management Science*, 27, 467-484.

Premkumar, G., Ramamurthy, K. and Crum, M. (1997). Determinants of EDI adoption in the transportation industry. *European Journal of Information Systems*, 6, 107-121.

Raymond, L. and Bergeron, F. (1996). EDI success in small and medium-sized enterprises: A field study. *Journal of Organizational Computing and Electronic Commerce*, 6 (2), 161-172.

Riggins, F.J. and Rhee, H.S. (1998). Toward a Unified View of Electronic Commerce. *Communications of the ACM,* 41 (10), 88-95.

Rothwell, R. and Dodgson, M. (1991). External linkages and innovation in small and medium-sized enterprises. *R&D Management,* 21 (2), 125-137.

Saunders, C.S. & Clark, S. (1992). EDI adoption and implementation: a focus on inter-organizational linkages. *Information Resources Management Journal*, 5 (1), 9-19.

Stymne, B. (1996). *Improving competitiveness of SMEs through business engineering and targeted research technologies: A methodological approach to the setting up of pilot cases in three European countries.* Progress report in the Compete project, Commission of the European Community, Espirit.

Tenenbaum, J.M. (1998). WISs and Electronic Commerce. *Communications of the ACM,* 41 (7), 89-90.

Thong, J.Y.L. (2001). Resource constraints and information system implementation in Singaporean small businesses. The International Journal of Management Science, 29, 143-156.

Thong, J.Y.L., Yap, C-S. and Raman, K.S. (1996). Top management support, external expertise and information systems implementation in small businesses. *Information Systems Research*, 7 (2), 248-267.

Turban, E., Lee, J., King, D. and Chung, H.M. (2000). *Electronic commerce a managerial perspective.* Upper Saddle River, NJ: Prentice-Hall, Inc..

Tuunainen, V.K. (1998). Opportunities of Effective Integration of EDI for Small Businesses in the Automotive Industry. *Information & Management*, 36 (6), 361-375.

Tuunainen, V.K. (1999). *Different Models of Electronic Commerce – Integration of Value Chains and Business Processes*. Dissertation thesis, Helsinki School of Economics and Business Administration, A-153.

Vassilopoulou, K., Keeling, K. and Macaulay, L. (1999). E-commerce – Barriers and Facilitators for SMEs: A study in the Northwest region of England. In *Proceedings of the 2nd International Conference IeC'99*, 269-274. Manchester.

Walczuch, R., Van Braven, G. and Lundgren, H. (2000). Internet Adoption Barriers for Small Firms in the Netherlands. *European Management Journal*, 18 (5), 561-572.

Welsh, J.A. and White, J.F. (1981). A Small Business is not a Little Big Business. *Harvard Business Review*, 59 (4), 46-58.

Chapter XII

E-Business Development Issues in UK SMEs

Fiona Meikle
Leeds Metropolitan University, UK

Dianne Willis
Leeds Metropolitan University, UK

ABSTRACT

Using a case-study approach, this chapter aims to assess the development issues for e-business within small to medium enterprises (SMEs) in differing regions across the UK. The research documents the issues faced by three SMEs as they have embarked upon an e-business delivery. All of the case studies are SMEs that come from different industry sectors, but all have established an e-commerce service in the last 18 months. Our definition of e-commerce aligns with those principles set out by the Organisation for Economic Cooperation and Development (OECD) working party on Indicators for the Information Society WPIIS. The outcome is an evaluation and discussion of the underlying factors influencing each company's progress within a regional UK framework. Issues raised in the study include lack of training and awareness in SMEs, the need for government-funded initiatives, reliance on personal networks, and a lack of clarity about funding sources and schemes.

INTRODUCTION

This chapter traces some of the current e-business development issues in selected regions of the UK and looks at the extent to which take-up of e-business has been facilitated by government initiatives.

The aim of the research is to present a pilot study for situational analysis of e-business/e-commerce development within three different Midland and Northern UK regions, considering key issues and support mechanisms and the impact on growth.

To place the work in an appropriate context, here are some background figures. There were an estimated 3.7 million SMEs in the UK at the start of 2000 (UK online for Business). The vast majority of these (99%) had less than 50 employees and they provided 45% of the UK non-government employment and 38% of turnover. This gives an indication of the relative importance of SMEs to the success of present UK government e-commerce initiatives.

The International Benchmarking Study 2000 undertaken by the Department of Trade and Industry suggested that only 1.7 million smaller firms were connected to the Internet, and still less, 450,000 of them, were trading online. A later survey by the UK Office of National Statistics (later referred to as ONS) revealed significant variations in e-commerce implementation across the UK, with London and the southeast region "considerably" outpacing Internet sales in other regions (Saliba, 2001). The UK bought $28.6 billion in goods and services, London-based companies accounting for $7 billion, while regions such as the northeast and east Midlands spending less than $1.5 billion. It is the aforementioned "significant variations" that were of interest to the researchers in this case.

Having noted this regional variation, the research undertaken has focused on the lower spending regions to try to ascertain what are the limiting factors for companies in these regions. Further research will need to be undertaken to discover whether these regional variations are still present, and also whether or not a series of factors can be isolated that apply to different companies.

The period 1997-1999 saw exceptional e-commerce growth within the UK through many new "get rich quick" ventures supported by significant venture capital input. At the same time, established businesses looked to Internet technologies to support or revolutionize their existing business processes. After a series of dot.com collapses, 2000-2001 venture capital has largely dried up, but the market has continued to grow steadily with many mergers and acquisitions between new and old economy firms each supporting the other by exploiting their experiences and core competencies. In September 1999, the Performance and Innovation Unit (PIU) published a report, "e-commerce@its best," which found that the UK was the leader in e-commerce developments within Europe, but still behind the USA, Canada, Australia, and Scandinavia on key measures of business e-commerce use.

Figure 1: Consumer Online Spending at UK Sites 1997-2002

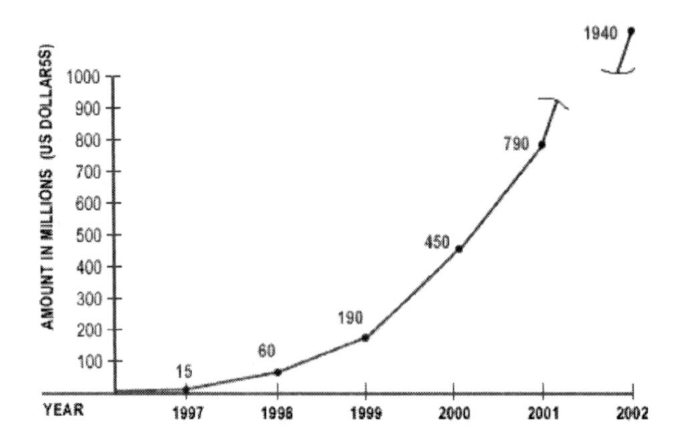

(www.mediamatrix.com)

METHODOLOGY

A range of possible methods was considered as potential vehicles for conducting the research. The approach to be taken was that of an in-depth exploration of the factors that affect each of the companies studied. It was decided that interviews would be the most appropriate main data collection method, with supplemental data being provided by documentation related to each of the businesses. In effect, each interview would be taped and these transcripts used as the basis for a case study of practice in each organisation studied. The advantages of using an interview approach are many, but the chief consideration from our point of view was that of the time-cost analysis (Gillham, 2000). Setting up and travelling to the interviews proved very expensive in terms of resource time and meant that one interview was eventually carried out over the telephone to alleviate these problems. One possible further refinement to the research would be the use of "experts" in the field of e-commerce as the companies studied. In fact, two of the companies studied had applied for UK Department of Trade and Industry awards for excellence in e-business, and one of the companies studied had won an award for its Web site design and e-business operation. It was decided that the focus of regions where e-commerce spending was low would not in fact lend itself well to the use of an expert panel when the sample of companies was widened.

The SMEs were selected from three of the key regions identified by the ONS survey as having significantly less e-commerce activity. Three companies were chosen across three different industries to provide the necessary data for this largely explorative pilot study, with a view to identifying potential trends to test in a larger UK-wide study. The interview consisted of 25 questions divided into three key sections: e-commerce strategy, project resources, and technology. The interview combined open and closed questions, though there was an emphasis on the need to draw out underlying reasons and rationale for actions, so open questions were more suitable. The divisions followed a similar structure to some other research undertaken by one of the authors, which had proven to be very effective. Due to the number and depth of the questions is was deemed necessary to tape the responses in order to allow for questioning and clarification as well as some interesting diversions from the original questions. Each person interviewed was invited to view the transcript and to change anything they wished to after reading what they had said in print. It must be stated that things said in the one-to-one interview situation were later acknowledged to be unsuitable for wider publication and amended or omitted. It was interesting to note that in the one-to-one situation, the interview was relaxed and friendly and the interaction between the interviewer and the interviewee allowed a real dialogue to build up. This dialogue contributed to the richness of the findings and allowed some very open comments, which the authors feel they would have been unlikely to get from a questionnaire approach.

All of the case studies are SMEs that have established an e-commerce service in the last 18 months. The rationale behind this choice of time period was that we wished to look at companies that had had the opportunity to get an established e-commerce delivery and also to avoid the prevalence of those companies who were unable to complete a full year's operation.

Our definition of e-commerce aligns with those set out by the Organisation for Economic Co-operation (OECD) working party on Indicators for the Information Society (WPIIS).

Company A is a wine and spirit merchant based in the Midlands, employing 10 people. Company B is a pump manufacturer based in the West Midlands and employs 14 people. Both of these companies use clicks and mortar business models. Company C is a furniture retailer based in Yorkshire, employing 10 people and has a pure play business model. All three of these companies are operating successfully, though with different approaches and attitudes.

RESEARCH FINDINGS

The findings are divided into a series of headings based around the interview schedule.

E-Commerce Activity

The UK has experienced a proliferation of business use of the Internet in terms of the volume and variety of business processes supported via e-mail, Web, and other means of information distribution and dissemination (Duan, Mullins, and Hamblin, 2000). All three of the case studies have access to the Web, a hosted Web site, and external mail to communicate with customers, which means that a comparison of their operations is likely to provide interesting insights. All three Web sites are categorized as catalogue sites; however, although this would normally equate with a situation where the level of customer engagement is relatively low, two of the companies relied heavily on the use of the telephone to build customer relationships after the initial Web contact had been made. In terms of historical technological issues, only Company A actively sought the integration of legacy systems. Company C was operating as a "pure play," but still categorised itself as an SME as opposed to a dot.com. The reasoning behind this categorisation may lie in the negative press coverage dot.coms have received in the last year since the bursting of the dot.com bubble.

The findings to date suggest a lack of business to business (B2B) e-commerce supported by integrated networks through the supply chain. In terms of Company C, who deals with very large manufacturers down to the individual artisan who makes a piece of furniture from scratch in a little workshop, despite a stated wish for more supply chain integration, this is not likely to be possible in the near future. Other issues, such as that raised by Company A, where the customers did not want to see supply chain integration mean this is a goal for the future rather than an immediately achievable situation. Comments from those interviewed included the following: "Our suppliers are not geared up to extranet"; "We are not large enough to support that kind of system and we don't have large orders."

Amongst those reasons identified by the research were cost of development, infrequency of orders, and fear of being tied into to a stronger companies system. It is important to remember when dealing with SMEs, especially those with a small workforce, that it may not be possible to devote many resources to e-commerce development if the immediate effects cannot be seen. Issues such as the availability of grants and other monies to undertake development were also explored and it became apparent that this is problematic. Company A also did a considerable amount of trade with other companies that did not wish to be tied to a minimum order level or a minimum delivery period. There is obviously a niche in the market for the flexibility provided by the company and that may well be lost if supply chain integration continues.

E-Commerce Strategy and Managers Perceptions

E-business is now a permanent fixture within the new economy and it is no longer optional for UK businesses to have an e-strategy, but methodical development of sustainable strategies seems to be non-existent in many areas, and in particular within SMEs.

The research findings to date suggest that manager's perceptions of e-commerce differ significantly. The managers of the two click and mortar companies recognized a need for an alignment between business and e-commerce strategy, but both insisted that e-commerce strategy did not take precedence because e-commerce revenues remain relatively minor. The pure play manager answered that e-commerce and business strategy "are the same for us."

E-commerce drivers differed greatly. Company C, as the only pure play, has built its business model on e-commerce, and fundamentally their driver is survival. It is interesting to note that to pursue that aim of survival, they need to provide a quality service, build a good relationship with their customers, provide a quality product, and hope that the larger players in the field allow them to maintain their niche. Company A's key drivers were a combination of first mover advantage and competitor pressure. However, the need to have a successful operation is not so great for this company – it is doing fine with the brick and mortar operation and sees any business coming from the e-commerce operation as purely "extra" or "over and above." This is partly because they are driven very much by the seasonal nature of their sales ("Christmas is crazy for us") and the homogeneous nature of their product —known and branded wines are available from a variety of sources. Company B's key drivers were competitor pressures. Although Company B gets regular queries and occasional orders from international customers, it has never pursued an aggressive e-commerce strategy. International orders via the Web, although occasionally significant in size, are considered an additional bonus and these clients are not considered core customers, the majority of which are local. This is interesting because whereas their competitors repackage solutions, they offer completely tailor-made solutions and as such the company believes itself to have a niche market — a usually very successful model for a successful e-business.

Interestingly, although all of those interviewed believe that their e-commerce projects have met their business objectives, only Company C (who tracks customers' activities while on their Web site) conducts any formal evaluation or independent appraisal of the effectiveness of their e-commerce activities. All those interviewed maintained sales records, but one could not identify which sales were orchestrated via their Web site and e-mail as opposed to telephone orders. There is no evaluation of the customer Web interface.

It is also useful to note that the e-commerce activity is generally driven by the younger generation in the two click and mortar operations. There are perhaps some issues here, which need to be teased out about perceptions of e-commerce activity and the age profile of those running SMEs – this may actually be a factor in the regional variations!

Project Resources

All three businesses developed their e-commerce projects using strictly limited resources, with no dedicated e-commerce budget. The core applications behind the Web sites were developed by a single person, usually those interviewed: the CEO or MD. In the case of Company A the underlying database was developed by the CEO. The Web site and application integration was outsourced using 40% Business Link funding. The underlying architecture for Company B's Web site is their product catalogue. This catalogue was developed by the MD over a period of two to three months and turned into a Web site in a very short period of time by a personal friend. The MD was aware of potential funding claims, but did not seek any funding due to previous experiences. Even the development of Company C was initially small-scale, with the CEO the principal designer, supported by a friend within the IT business. The only form of investment came from private investors identified through local networks.

The following quotes from those interviewed help to illustrate these points:

- "we knew funding was available, but not how to get it"
- "government schemes are inaccessible generally"
- "there is very little information and the Business Link Web site is not helpful"
- "government schemes in our experience tend to be all talk and no money"
- "we have used Business Link and DTI, but I would not use these sources again. I would prefer a cheap loan from a bank"

Training and Support Needs

Interview evidence suggests that the businesses discussed are open to any support offered from the private sector, but have a great suspicion of local and government training schemes. It would be interesting to track how this came about. The main area of training is in the development of e-commerce applications and integration of back office systems. At least two of the three interviewed had their Web sites hosted by an external party, with very little integration of their own systems with another company's Web server.

One issue that was brought up was the fact that SMEs need more flexibility in the availability of training courses. As training time is limited (often as staff cannot be released for any significant period of time), there is a need for training programmes to be ready as and when the company wants to take advantage of them. Presently, this does not appear to be the case.

CONCLUSIONS

While the authors are aware that given the small sample size interviewed here, any extrapolation of the results needs to be done with care, it remains the case that some themes have come up in each interview situation and that the three organisations have produced some strikingly similar results. This encourages us to feel that these issues are pertinent and can be explored in greater depth in an extension of the work to date.

There is some evidence to suggest that training and awareness-raising remains an issue for SMEs; of those interviewed there was a lack of awareness of the options for businesses. Many organisations appear to be prejudiced from prior knowledge or experience of having to buy into expensive EDI network integration through traditional hub and spoke models. One firm in particular showed a lack of awareness of Web alternatives to the expensive and standard controlled EDI network configurations of the previous decades. The research suggests that further information about alternative technical solutions and evaluation of implementing these solutions is necessary, and that the role should be facilitated by impartial sources—possibly through more focused government initiatives.

Two out of the three case studies referred to their work as constantly "fire fighting" and therefore individuals within the business had no time to look at possible initiatives. In particular, one individual interviewed stated that the firm's profit margin had decreased substantially, an occurrence throughout their industry resulting in a fear of investing any funds or human resource into a "blue sky" project

There is some evidence within these preliminary findings that the actual e-commerce development within SMEs may rely very heavily on the personal networks of the managers. There was evidence from two of the firms of heavy reliance on friends who work within the IT industry or have an interest in developing home networks. Interestingly, this included the pure play business. This is something that needs to be explored in greater depth in future research and suggests that there is much untapped IT knowledge within the UK economy.

The results to date suggest knowledge of government and other independent initiatives for supporting e-commerce development within SMEs, but a significant number of poor experiences using these initiatives. At least one company had accessed the government's e-business support site, but found the site to be unhelpful, all documentation superficial, and full of unrealistic promises with no on-line support network available. Companies such as Business Link actively approached at least one business on a monthly basis, suggesting that SMEs are made fully aware of initiatives offered by local and national government. One company had such a bad experience with government initiative support that they asked the representative to leave the site. The main problem appeared to be that the representative had not had time to fully research the business environment and, as a result, had failed to establish trust with the managers of the business. The findings suggest the need for further research identifying why these initiatives are not working for SMEs. This will include a wider survey of SME experiences and interviews with the businesses such as Business Link.

Future Direction

Evaluation of the work to date indicates that this initial pilot study has barely scratched the surface of the myriad of reasons why e-commerce take-up may differ regionally within the UK.

It is intended to take the research further now by expanding the number of SMEs interviewed, while trying to balance the different categories already identified. We propose as the next step to extend the number of companies interviewed within the three regions already targeted and then to add companies from the higher take-up regions in the capital and the southeast.

The methodology chosen has worked well with a small number of pilot studies, but as each interview lasts in excess of an hour, consideration needs to be given as to whether this is feasible on a wider basis. One possible solution is to reduce the number of questions asked, particularly those covering financial issues, which companies were generally not happy to divulge. Some balance here must be preserved with the richness of the data and the previously mentioned rapport that was found in the interview situation.

A further issue that has been highlighted has been that we may be directed to the wrong person, which will have a significant impact on the results we get. A final point has been lack of understanding of the issues where the Web operation is outsourced. In at least one case, the interviewee has stated that they have no real depth of knowledge in this area and are unable to answer questions.

One further possible consideration is the prevalence of call centres in the north of England and the business that these have brought to regions where e-commerce has previously been less active. Integration of Computer-Telephony Integration (CTI) and outsourced call management systems will impact on both e- and m-commerce, and there are a number of potential studies that could be factored in.

In order to add a more academic dimension to the work, it is proposed to try two separate approaches to the expansion of the work. One approach will be a joint study with a colleague in Australia who is also working in this field. The interesting aspects here will be the different research approaches. In the UK we are working with a focused, in-depth analysis on a company by company basis; in Australia, the approach is the opposite, with a large sample size and less depth. The contrasting approaches may lead to some joint research when factors for each country have been identified.

A second and more easily achievable approach is that of using a methodology to assess the potential benefits of using an e-commerce strategy.

The preliminary findings have clearly shown that no methodologies were executed during the development of any of these e-business systems; indeed, the evidence from the interviewees suggests that none have seen their e-business as a system and have fallen into the bottom-up development trap. Strategic managers were aware of e-business activities, but have not identified stakeholders or mission statements/objectives to meet through any strategy development methodology. Extensive research has located only one example of an appropriate methodology for strategy development — that of Hackbarth and Kettinger (2000). They propose that use of their methodology will enable a company to break out of its existing constraint to alter existing business processes and open up new markets. Their methodology has been designed to support businesses in their move from what they term level 2 to level 3. Level 2 is defined as being where e-business supports, but is subservient to, current corporate strategy — mainly supporting existing business processes, and level 3 is defined as being where e-business transforms the organisation's strategy. While we are aware that it is a more process-based methodology, it is expected that using it will produce some interesting results.

Finally, as one of the important, identified issues for two out of the three companies is a lack of knowledge and understanding about UK government funding initiatives for e-commerce development in SMEs, the UK Department for Trade and Industry will be approached to discover the full range of information and grants available to SMEs and to ascertain how to make this information more accessible to those SMEs who are unaware of what help is available.

REFERENCES

Duan, Y., Mullins, R., Hamblin, D. (2000). Making Successful E-Commerce: An Analysis of SMEs Training and Supporting Needs. *Proceedings of the 1st World Congress on E-Commerce Management.* Hamilton, Canada

Gillham, B. (2000). *The Research Interview.* Continuum, London.

Hackbarth, G. and Kettinger, W.J. (2000, Summer). Building an E-Business Strategy. *Information Systems Management,* 78-93.

Myers, M.D. (1994). Quality in Qualitative Research in Information Systems. *Proceedings of the 5th Australasian Conference on Information Systems,* 763-766.

Office of National Statistics. Retrieved February 10, 2001 from the World Wide Web: http://www.statistics.gov.uk/.

Organisation for Economic Co-operation and Development (OECD). Retrieved February 10, 2001 from the World Wide Web: http://www.oecd.org.

Porter, E.M (2001, March). *Strategy and the Internet*. Harvard Business Review, Reprint R0103D.

Saliba, C. (2001). Study: UK Firms Tarry with E-Commerce Adoption. *E-Commerce Times*. Retrieved September 10, 2001 from the World Wide Web: http://www.ecommercetimes.com/perl/printer/13437/.

Timmers, P. (2000.) Electronic Commerce, Strategies and Models for Business to Business Trading. Wiley Series in Information Systems.

Travers, M. (2001). *Qualitative Research through Case Studies*. SAGE.

UK Online for Business. Retrieved September 10, 2001 from the World Wide Web: http://www.ukonlineforbusiness.gov.uk/. Last accessed 9/10/01

Yin, R.K. (1994). Case Study Research; Design & Methods (2nd ed.). Applied Social Research Methods, vol. 5. SAGE publications.

WEB SITE REFERENCES

www.mediamatrix.com. Retrieved January 23, 2001 from the World Wide Web.

Chapter XIII

The Game of Internet B2B

Thomas O'Daniel
Monash University Malaysia, Malaysia

Teoh Say Yen
Monash University Malaysia, Malaysia

ABSTRACT

Game theory accepts the expected utility hypothesis and reduces roles to the "informed" and the "uninformed" player in order to facilitate the process of constructing mathematical models. When quality is known to the seller, but not to the buyer, private markets can be modeled as a screening game, and public exchanges as a signaling game. In a private market, the buyer moves first by revealing acceptable quality. In a public exchange, the seller moves first by publicizing product information. Adoption of the technology will ultimately depend on perception of the game and payoffs relative to risks. Price competition is a significant negative externality, and opportunistic representations a real danger. When search costs are low, scope for differentiation limited, and information about quality is incomplete or imperfect, the conditions for a lemon's market are fulfilled. A focus on commodities, global reach, and building a positive brand image for Internet business-to-business (B2B) in general should prove effective.

INTRODUCTION

Recently, the public and private sector in ASEAN have taken the initiative in encouraging the development of Internet B2Bs. For example, the E-ASEAN framework has been set up to improve Internet penetration and develop a B2B e-commerce community for ASEAN's small and medium enterprises (SME) (Legard, 2000). FreeMarkets and the US-ASEAN business council have also formed strategic alliances to facilitate the growth of Internet B2B in ASEAN (FreeMarkets, 2001).

Numerous electronic markets are being formed worldwide; more than 750 were in existence at the beginning of the year 2000 (Seller Beware, 2000). However, AMR Research found that not even 1% of 600 B2B portals had reached the overall feasible trading volume in the business (The Container Case, 2000), and IDC reported that of the approximately 1000 B2B public exchanges launched between early 2000 and mid-2001, only about 100 are handling any genuine transactions ("Time to rebuild," 2001).

In this chapter, game theory and social theory inform the discussion of technology adoption decisions in general, and B2B electronic commerce in particular. Technology adoption is a risky proposition, even when it is limited to a firm's internal processes. It demands a collective decision to exchange one set of expertise for another, which changes the social context of work. E-commerce technologies reach beyond the bounds of the firm, extending the impact of process re-engineering. Adoption will ultimately depend on perception of the risks and payoffs, which is the realm of game theory. Modeling B2B e-commerce as games of asymmetric information offers insight into these perceptions, and the strategies of the players.

Turban, Lee, King, and Chung (2000) provide a succinct taxonomy of business models for B2B electronic commerce. "Intermediary-oriented marketplace" describes a World-Wide Web (WWW) site that acts as a marketing channel for products that are of interest to businesses rather than consumers, operated by a third party that does not produce or use the products in question. The "seller-oriented marketplace" is similar, except it is focused on the products of a single vendor. The "buyer-oriented marketplace" features facilities for bidding on RFQs, and are often run over closed networks or open by invitation only (pp. 204-206).

Here, the terms "electronic market" and "Internet B2B" will be used to refer to all three of these. "Public exchange" and "portal" include both intermediary-oriented and supplier-oriented marketplaces, while "private market" refers to the buyer-oriented marketplace model. The intention is to gloss over the wide range of possible business models in favor of uncovering common motivations for participation.

Implementation

When Wirtz and Wong (1999) surveyed selected industrial companies in Singapore, they found only one-third of the SMEs using or interested in using Internet B2B. The vast majority of their respondents cited "No Need" as a barrier to participation. Amongst firms that were interested in or already using Internet B2B, the top motivations cited were image and reputation, increase in sales, and the global reach of suppliers and customers. This group cited security, setup costs, and ongoing operational costs most frequently as barriers to adoption.

Firms implement strategic information technology (IT) applications to gain an edge over competitors or to prevent competitors from gaining an edge over the firm. King and Teo (1996) found that the implementers placed more emphasis on innovative needs and economies of scale than did the non-implementers, both as facilitators and inhibitors. The non-implementers emphasized top management guidance as an important facilitator, and the lack of adequate IT-related support as an important inhibitor. Both groups identified competitive position and environment as important facilitators.

Facilitators and Inhibitors

King and Teo's factors are more closely linked than they might appear. Innovative needs imply that firms can gain a favorable image or reputation by using technology to differentiate their products and services. Firms that do not seek to be unique or innovative may be more likely to adopt a "wait and see" attitude toward the strategic application of IT. Well-defined management objectives and top management support are prerequisites for the perceived importance IT to company strategy. It is entirely possible that the management support is simply taken for granted; when it comes to corporate culture, the absence of management support may be more notable than its presence. Moreover, investments that benefit only a limited part of the firm reduce the pool of resources available to all others, and political considerations may weigh heavily in the decision.

Competitive position refers to the need to improve or maintain market position, and the company's image or reputation. Favorable environmental change in the form of market growth and overall economic growth make it easier to increase investment in IT, since resources are more readily available. Finally, economies of scale make investment more feasible. The IT application described by the implementers was most often directed at internal operations and/or customers, and the group was biased toward companies with more than 10,000 employees. Large companies have more absolute capacity to invest, and the number of users is more likely to reach the critical mass required for maintenance of qualified full-time support staff. Large companies can also spread investments over a number of operational budgets.

Learning Curve

Mason, Bowling, and Niemi (1998) distill three other key points from the literature related to SME adoption of information technologies:

- Benefits from information technology are cumulative and synergistic, with a disproportional increase in benefits as the number of applications (and enterprise integration) increases. Firms that have implemented information technologies in both the administrative and engineering/production operations, for example, enjoy benefits that are greater than the sum of the benefits derived from each individual system.
- The cost of learning to use and integrate new technologies makes evolutionary change seem less risky. More advanced technologies may have greater productive potential, but the firm expects greater costs if it has less expertise in implementing such technologies. Firms with existing technological capabilities have higher "absorptive capacity" for new technology, and are able to integrate it quickly.
- The adoption of new technologies is related to the firm's linkages with other firms and industrial organizations. Informal but trusted conduits for sharing of technical know-how appear to lower the cost of learning for the firm. Public sector initiatives, such as technology transfer centers and assistance networks, act as a bridge between sources of knowledge about new technologies and the SMEs as potential users.

BACKGROUND

In the present context it would be useful to step back and look at the issues from somewhat different perspectives: social theory and game theory. A broader theoretical perspective allows generalization of these specific findings to the overall process of technology adoption and, indeed, to the development of these technologies themselves.

Fundamentals of Game Theory

Game theory assumes that when players face uncertain outcomes, they seek to maximize their expected payoffs. This "is known as the expected utility hypothesis, and has been controversial since it was first proposed by John von Neumann and Oscar Morgenstern in 1944" (Bierman and Fernandez, 1998, p. 220).

Essentially, any uncertain outcome is modeled as some type of "lottery." The nature of a lottery is determined by the probability of a payoff. A "fair lottery" offers a 50-50 chance of winning or losing, so the expected return over time is zero. In an "unfair" lottery, the chances of losing are greater than the chances of winning (expected returns are negative) and in a "superfair" lottery the chances of winning are greater than the chances of losing. A person who is willing to accept unfair lotteries can be called "risk loving," while a person unwilling to play even a fair lottery is "risk averse." A person's willingness to accept a given type of lottery may change based on the magnitude of the potential payoff or loss (Bierman and Fernandez, 1998, pp. 229-30).

In games of incomplete knowledge, a collection of probability assessments about the state of the world formed from observing the moves of opponents is called the player's "belief profile." Following the expected utility hypothesis, each player's strategy always selects moves that maximize the player's expected utility, given knowledge of the game up to that move, beliefs about the state of the world at that point, and beliefs about the other players' strategies (Bierman and Fernandez, 1998, p. 328). In this class of games there are two roles, which can be called "informed" and "uninformed." "Bayesian updating" of belief profiles during a game consists of simply replacing the prior probability of a state of the world with its posterior probability, after observing the moves of a better-informed player (Bierman and Fernandez, 1998, p. 323).

Beliefs and Roles

Game theory accepts the expected utility hypothesis and reduces roles to the "informed" and the "uninformed" player in order to facilitate the process of constructing mathematical models. Rossiter and Percy (1987) develop a more complete set of roles for purchase decisions. They stress that having an effect on group decision-making requires reaching the individuals who will have the most influential roles in the decision. Their taxonomy of roles (pp. 109-110) is made up of:

- Initiator: gets the overall purchase decision started
- Influencer: uses product information to either promote or retard the overall decision
- Decider: makes the overall "go/no-go" decision
- Purchaser: executes the decision (although there may be scope for change)
- User: ultimate consumer or user of the product

Simon (1959, pp. 51-2) describes a role more generally as:

> *... a social prescription of some, but not all, of the premises that enter into an individual's choice of behavior. Any particular*

concrete behavior is the result of a large number of premises, only some of which are described by the role. In addition to role premises there will be premises about the state of the environment based directly on perception, premises representing beliefs and knowledge, and idiosyncratic premises that characterize the personality . . . With our present definition of role, we can also speak meaningfully of the role of an entire business firm—of decision premises that underlie its basic policies . . . The common interest of economics and psychology includes not only the study of individual roles, but also the explanation of organizational roles of these sorts.

The key point here is that considering a company as a player in a game is not simple anthropomorphism. Communities of interest within the organization will determine the action, which is ultimately visible to other players. A company's belief profile is a collective interpretation of the payoffs, probabilities, and actions of the other players.

The Structurational Model of Technology

Orlikowski develops Giddens' theory of structuration into a social model of technology that can be used to add depth to further analysis. Structuration theory focuses on the interplay of "structure" and "action." Structure is a body of social learning embedded in each member of a society (and thus an organization or community as well). "Structure has no existence independent of the knowledge that [human] agents have about their day-to-day activity" (Giddens, 1984, p. 26). That knowledge is gained from monitoring actions and their consequences—both intended and unintended. "That is to say, actors not only monitor continuously the flow of their activities and expect others to do the same for their own; they also routinely monitor aspects, social and physical, of the contexts in which they move" (Giddens, 1984, p. 5). "According to the notion of duality of structure, the structural properties of social systems are both medium and outcome of the practices they recursively organise" (Giddens, 1984, p. 25).

The organizational context is defined by three fundamental elements of social interaction: meaning, power, and norms. Meaning is shared knowledge that informs and defines interaction, as distinct from the conventions and rules that govern "appropriate" behavior (norms). Power refers to the asymmetry of resources that participants bring to, and mobilize within, interaction. (Orlikowski, 2001, pp. 64-65) In other words, the rules and resources that constitute structure both enable and constrain action. At the same time, structure is reaffirmed as actors observe and understand what they are doing in the context of producing and reproducing day-to-day social encounters.

Technology is both the product of human action (design) and a medium of action (use). The structurational model of technology relates technology (material artifacts mediating task execution in the workplace), human agents (designers, users, decision makers) and institutional properties of organizations (both internal and environmental) (Orlikowski, 2001, p. 71). It assumes that these elements interact recursively, may be in opposition, and that they may undermine each other's effects (Orlikowski, 2001, p. 75).

Technology constrains and enables action, thus conditioning social practices. Designers embed rules reflecting knowledge about the task being automated and the organizationally sanctioned process for executing a sequence of tasks into a new resource for accomplishing the work. Once created and deployed, technology remains inanimate and, hence, ineffectual unless and until it becomes a medium of human action (Orlikowski, 2001, p. 73). When users conform to a technology's embedded rules they consciously or unconsciously reaffirm the institutional structures in which the technology is deployed. When users do not use the technology as it was intended they may undermine these structures and, hence, the strategic objectives of the sponsors and designers (Orlikowski, 2001, pp. 74-75).

Application

This perspective gives substance to the interplay of the facilitators and inhibitors described above. Organizational norms and shared meaning are the domain of management and strategic vision, which guides the participants in the collective decision-making process. Economies of scale and market expansion are resource issues. The firm's image and competitive position create and constrain strategic vision, as well as resources and alternative uses for them. All of these elements are known to a player in a game, but they are not known to all players, and will be subject to updates based on other player's actions.

While Orlikowski does not consider it explicitly, the structurational model of technology easily incorporates re-engineering designs that are meant to challenge organizational norms and shared meaning. It is important to recognize in this context that the rules to be embedded in a re-designed process are not simply received by the initiators and influencers. The actions they take in defining a set of costs and benefits associated with an option for action may themselves undermine the intent of other rules embedded in the larger process.

Thomas (1994) describes a case where a flexible machining system (FMS) was an investment alternative for a manufacturing company. Upper management had set high standards for return on investment (ROI), but uncertainty about the actual cost of the system and the development team's lack of experience made the exercise "...really silly. We had a number and we hit it" (Thomas, 1994, p. 207).

However, "... the operations manager gave credence to the R&D group's assessment of the importance of imagery in decision making. He preferred the FMS because 'harder working machines' and fewer people were something he thought his superiors could understand" (p. 203). Indeed, the R&D manager who had supervised the writing of the proposal had made an explicit effort to use the same words and phrases that the operations manager had used in describing an "antiquated factory" run by a competitor (Thomas, 1994, p. 202).

Thomas states, "The net result was that technological choices were made largely on the basis of personal and professional interests and what was perceived to be an archaic social context in the shop that could not be altered without the external pressure of technological change" (1994, p. 210). It is also interesting to note that in this case, the operations manager was promoted to a higher position in the company (Thomas, 1994, p. 211).

The Role of the Expert

Interpretation of action or choice of possible courses of action are frequently based on mediated knowledge rather than first-hand experience. Giddens (1991) points out that while in modern times there are plenty of claimants to authority, in reality there are no determinant authorities but "an indefinite pluralism of expertise" (p. 195).

> *Specialisation is actually the key to the character of modern abstract systems. The knowledge incorporated into modern forms of expertise is in principle available to everyone, had they but the available resources, time, and energy to acquire it. The fact that to be an expert in one or two small corners of modern knowledge systems is all that anyone can achieve means that abstract systems are opaque to the majority. Their opaque quality - the underlying element in the extension of trust in the context of disembedding mechanisms, comes from the very intensity of specialisation that abstract systems both demand and foster (Giddens, 1991, p. 30).*

The domain expert requires a vocabulary for describing the topic area, and a set of rules for combining terms and relations, which allow for extension of the vocabulary (an ontology) (Farhoodi and Fingar, 1997). In structuration terms, a community of experts forms around meaning and norms. When it comes to resources, Williamson's (1975, p. 111) characterization could apply equally to the purveyors of technology, and the technologies themselves:

> *Reputation, which is to say prior experience, is of special importance in establishing the terms of finance for transactions that involve large, discrete commitments of funds. ... Faced with incomplete information, suppliers of capital are vulnerable to opportunistic representations. Unable to distinguish between those unknown candidates who have the capacity and the will to*

execute the project successfully from the opportunistic types who assert that they are similarly qualified, when objectively (omnisciently) they are not, the terms of finance are adjusted adversely against the entire group.

In game theory terms, Williamson casts the resource provider as the uninformed player, and the community of experts as the informed player. In a signaling game, the better-informed player makes a move before the less-informed player; in screening games, the less-informed player moves first. "In short, the screen is essentially a set of hoops set by the uninformed player that the informed player can choose to jump through or not, depending on the rewards offered by the uninformed player" (Bierman and Fernandez, 1998, p. 336). Here, the suppliers of capital set up a screening game by demanding a higher payoff before they will accept the proposition.

Fact vs. Hope

Opportunistic representations are a real danger. They may be internal and deliberate, as illustrated by the FMS case mentioned above where management had set ROI as a screen for acceptable projects. On the other hand, they may be the result of imperfect knowledge on the part of external experts.

For example, when NASA (1998) looked at the acquisition process for Commercial Off-The-Shelf (COTS) software, they "... expected vendor interaction to be simple and to end with the purchase of a product. In reality, ... the [study] team found a strong dependence on bi-directional information flow" (pp. 5-2). The vendor was one more party with whom communication channels had to be established and maintained at different levels throughout the project. Project personnel had to rely on the vendor for a variety of technical issues, but vendor personnel were not always as helpful or available as promised (NASA, 1998, pp. 4-2). This led to reliance on a number of other parties, including other projects that use COTS, independent evaluation teams, and other customers of the vendor (NASA, 1998, pp. 5-2).

In sum, mediated information may add to rather than reduce the risk associated with the adoption decision. Development and deployment of technology requires a team of domain experts, each with its own set of shared meanings. "Narrative coherence with which the reader or viewer can identify becomes the way to commodify prepackaged theorems of how to 'get on' in life..." (Giddens, 1991, pp. 198-9). We could find an explanation here for the high degree of concern about Internet security, relative to startup and maintenance costs. To information security specialists, these are inseparable: security policies and mechanisms must be established before the system is brought on-line and audited over time to ensure proper implementation and timely evolution as new threats are identified (Northcutt and Novak, 2000, p. 390). However, the horror stories about computer "break-ins" are far easier to relate to than a rigorous routine designed to prevent them. When effectiveness of the measures themselves depends on the expertise of the software and system security vendors relative to the hostile experts attacking the systems, the situation seems even more opaque.

Summary

While dependence on technology does not really increase the risk of a failure that requires unique expertise to fix, adopting new technology requires a change of expertise that negates the value of a particular set of acquired experience. Small wonder then that Wirtz and Wong (1999) found an overwhelming majority of their respondents saw no need to adopt Internet B2B technologies. Multi-organizational systems are doubly abstract, in the sense that they use opaque technological systems to tie together the internal processes of a number of companies. Adoption will ultimately depend on the perception of the game, and the payoffs relative to the risks.

Within the organization, one community of experts that must form is the IT support team. Their expertise will replace the expertise of others that are left behind in the transition. Management guidance is also necessary to re-shape organizational norms. Visible investment of resources must be complemented by visible promotion of new ways to think about the firm and how work gets done. The drive for innovation may come from company norms, or communities of experts within the company.

Market expansion and global reach hint at economies of scale, although another angle on global reach is considered below. In the absence of clear competitive necessity and economies of scale, the management's perception of possibilities to enhance the firm's image will be a key motivation for investment. This will be moderated by the perception of successful implementation of IT applications, both within the firm and externally. Widely publicized concerns about Internet security will increase uncertainty and perceived risk.

B2B GAMES

As noted above, in a screening game the less-informed player moves first, effectively creating barriers to entry, while in a signaling game the better-informed player moves first. If quality is known to the seller, but not to the buyer, Internet B2B may take on the characteristics of either type of game.

Since these games involve participation in a network, payoffs will be affected by network externalities. An externality is a feature of a product that has no market price, and may be positive or negative (Whinston, Stahl, and Choi, 1997, p. 520). Network externalities correlate the size of the network with expected economic benefit to be gained from joining.

B2B Externalities

Positive network externalities may exist where a market maker creates an alternative channel for trading in a more distributed or fragmented environment. For example, The Economist (A Matter of Principals, 2001) describes Enron's efforts to act as a market maker for all sorts of energy, by treating it as a commodity and providing a platform for rapid execution of orders. Malone, Yates, and Benjamin (1987) might find this a clear example of the "electronic brokerage effect" as the number of users of the network grows, the benefits increase for both the market maker and each individual participant.

Competitive firms will generally not want consumers to engage in pure price shopping, and will instead try to differentiate their product and services so as to discourage price comparisons (Shapiro and Varian, 1998, p. 79). Limiting opportunities for differentiation creates negative externalities. When the participants are competing suppliers, the expected economic benefit to be gained from joining the network may be lower when the expected network size is larger (Riggins and Mukhopadhyay, 1999).

Both private markets and public exchanges may encourage price competition. A public exchange not only allows consumers easy access to prices, it also allows the participants themselves to monitor each other's price movements. If the buyer in a private exchange sets a standard of quality and makes it known to all sellers, pressure on prices is almost inevitable.

Effects on Prices

Varian (1999) points out that models in which some consumers search out the lowest price for a generic product while other consumers shop at random generate similar equilibria: sellers manage to charge a relatively high price on average by randomizing their prices to discriminate between searchers and non-searchers. In other words, companies compete for searchers by temporarily lowering prices; those who invest in the search may end up with a lower price, while the probability and magnitude of the discount will, to a degree, determine the propensity to search.

Moderating the tendency to search for lower prices in the short term is the fact that overly price-sensitive customers will give up the benefits conferred by loyalty.

Expectations of repeat business may discourage efforts to seek a narrow advantage in any particular transaction (Williamson, 1975, p. 107).

Global reach may mitigate local negative externalities, by providing a basis for price differentiation between local and foreign markets. The OECD (1998, pp. 86-87) cites research that shows many SMEs are using Internet B2B to open and/or maintain a presence in foreign markets. They raise the possibility that international markets can function as niche markets for start-ups that otherwise face greater competition at home. Once these have a certain brand reputation and expertise, they may then reinforce their position in domestic markets, especially if the domestic market is large.

Private Markets

Traditional EDI clearly fits the definition of a screening game. It is well documented that large companies can and will force smaller suppliers to adopt technology by making participation in the network a precondition for continued business. Indeed, the OECD (1998, p. 52) cites estimates that up to 70% of EDI links are established primarily because a major corporate or government customer specifies doing so as a term of contract.

While Malone, Yates, and Benjamin (1987) see the benefit of the "electronic integration effect" as lower transaction costs, this benefit often accrues to the larger partner at the expense of the smaller. Hammer (1990) for example, relates that when Ford moved to a paperless accounting system, some suppliers still printed invoices, but threw them away instead of sending them. If lower transaction costs are the goal, subsidies may be necessary for the network to achieve an acceptable volume of transactions. Riggins and Mukhopadhyay (1999) make a case for differential subsidies, to avoid the "moral hazard" of subsidizing participants who would join without help.

Private markets, where suppliers bid on packages of work, are growing in popularity and utility. General Electric began purchasing maintenance materials over the Internet, and realized cost savings in the range of 30-40% (Magaziner, 1998). By 2001, GE was doing more business through this private marketplace than all public exchanges combined (Older, Wiser, Webbier, 2001).

A Screening Game

It makes intuitive sense that pressure to join a private market would be seen as an element of the competitive environment. The element of coercion remains: if you want to do business with the company, you must use this channel. Migrating EDI systems to semi-private networks based on Internet technology will not change the way they are used; it simply lowers one of the hurdles that must be cleared to reach a powerful customer. If barriers to participation are low, there should be a wide variety of value-for-money propositions for the buyer to choose from.

Revealing private information is beneficial to consumers with low valuations, while those with higher valuations must be given sufficient incentives to reveal them (Whinston, et. al., 1997, p. 345). Sellers will always provide information about high-cost, high-value products, but will only provide information about lower value products when they can discriminate between buyers (Whinston, et al., 1997, p. 256). By moving first, publicizing product specifications that set a lower bound on quality, the buyer screens out sellers who are unable to meet the minimum quality. More importantly, the buyer screens out sellers who are unwilling to compete on price for products that meet the minimum quality standard.

Public Exchanges

Grewal, Comer, and Mehta (2001) study a public exchange for jewelry, where a monthly access fee allows members to buy and/or sell products, which are not, by their nature, commodities. The "open bazaar" environment makes it efficient to exchange information related to price, product specifications, and terms of trade. They conceptualize the nature of participation in terms of three distinct states: exploration, expert, and passive, and distinguish between them by the number of transactions executed in the market and the length of time a firm has been a participant. Firms in the exploration state are "testing the waters," trying to understand the new medium better. In the expert state, firms believe they have been successful in re-engineering their business processes to function effectively in the electronic market.

In the passive state, organizations maintain a presence, but carry out virtually no business in the electronic market. Their analysis suggests that the passive state is (1) propagated by firms entering on an experimental basis, including competitive hedging by firms that do not believe public exchanges are viable, but consider them a future opportunity or threat and therefore want to observe and learn; (2) perpetuated by low entry barriers, in that joining requires a commonplace computer and access to the Internet; and (3) reinforced because maintaining a presence is not expensive, requiring a firm simply to pay its monthly subscription fee (Grewal et al., 2001).

The argument for the public exchange to have a subscription-based revenue model rather than charging a per-transaction fee is strong. First, a company might establish a relationship with a supplier through a public exchange, and then invite that supplier to migrate to some other channel for their transactions. In this case, the continuing stream of transactions is invisible to the portal, and a business model based on per-transaction revenues would not reflect the value created for the trading partners. Second, what seems to be a market relationship may actually be based on trust and habitual use of the portal. The public exchange may simply be the most efficient channel for two trading partners with a long history of successful transactions. In this case a per-transaction revenue stream could effectively raise, rather than lower, transaction costs for the participants; again, a membership model is favored.

Market Presence

Chen (1998) makes a case for "Dual-Acceptance of Adoption" and "Crossed Reciprocal Interdependence" phenomena and the World Wide Web in general. He shows that the rate of adoption of Web clients will depend upon the number (or the utility) of Web servers, not the number of other Web users. Conversely, the rate of adoption of Web servers depends upon the number of users (or the usage), not the number of Web servers. Furthermore, the benefits from each additional adoption increase not only for all future adopters, but also for each previous adopter. However, the initial relationship still holds: the benefits from each additional Web server increase directly for all future and previous Web client (but not server) adopters. Similarly, benefits from client adoption increase directly for all future and previous Web server providers.

One conclusion that might be drawn is that as the number of public exchanges increases, it may be advantageous to be a passive participant in more than one. If barriers to entry for server providers are low, and clients are charged on a subscription basis rather than per-transaction, the cost of passive participation may well be calculated on the basis of "serendipitous" transactions that result from a widespread presence in many markets. Reinforcing this view is the fact that search costs increase for the potential customer as the number of portals increases. Maintaining a presence in many markets increases the chance that the firm will be visible to anyone searching a subset of them. A low transaction volume in any particular market could add up to substantial transaction volume for the firm, especially if the portal is actually facilitating transactions executed offline or through other channels.

A Signaling Game

Beyond simple cost calculations, the firm's image and reputation and innovative needs make electronic markets look more like a signaling game, especially for passive participants. Grewal et al. (2001) points out that if stakeholders view technologically sophisticated firms more favorably in comparison with technologically naive firms, then by virtue of a firm's entry into an electronic market, it is in a position to assert that it is ready for the challenges of the information age. By extension, organizations that embrace electronic markets to mimic a successful benchmark firm may believe that participation is a critical success factor, or that participation provides a better fit with the modern-day organizational profile.

The subscription model itself can be seen as a signal to market participants. The portal studied by Grewal et al. (2000), Polygon, does not enable participating firms to make payments electronically, but it does provide ratings for all participating firms based on their payment history. They report that Polygon has debated moving to a transaction-fee model, but concluded that its neutrality is important for the success of the market. The company believes that by taking a cut of transactions, it may become more interested in making the transaction and compromise its neutrality. In the words of Williamson (1975), "The reputation of a firm for fairness is also a business asset not to be dissipated" (p. 108).

CONCLUSION

When quality is known to the seller, but not to the buyer, private markets can be modeled as a screening game, and public exchanges as a signaling game. In a private market, the buyer moves first by revealing acceptable quality. In a public exchange, the seller moves first by publicizing product information.

Lemons Market

In both cases, the situation begins to look conducive to the development of a "lemons market." The lemons market comes about when quality is unknown to the buyer (but not to the seller) and the buyer is averse to the probability of paying a high price for poor quality. In these circumstances the buyer will offer a low price and obtain the product only if it is low quality. The next best outcome is to pay a high price for a good product; but a high price may attract opportunistic sellers with low-quality products (Bierman and Fernandez, 1998, p. 336, c.f. p. 399; Whinston et al., 1997, p. 37, c.f.p. 141).

Electronic markets may foster competition based on price alone, creating potentially significant negative externalities. Public exchanges limit the scope for price differentiation as more customers become seekers. Differentiation becomes equally difficult for participants (client adopters) and the portals themselves (server providers) as their number increases. The private market allows the buyer to screen out products that do not meet a certain standard. The buyer gains from lower transaction costs (as with traditional EDI), and the ability to choose from those that offer the best price; expectations of repeat business will limit opportunistic representations.

When search costs are low, scope for differentiation limited, and information about quality is incomplete or imperfect, the conditions for a lemon's market are fulfilled. But is it inevitable? Is it (in spite of the name) necessarily bad?

Commodities

Commodities are goods that are divisible and fungible. As long as a unit of the product can be divided into indistinguishable sub-units, it can be treated as a commodity. Since there is no scope for product differentiation, competition will be based on unit price for a particular quantity and value-adding services such as just-in-time delivery.

Given the discussion above, empirical evidence would be expected to show success with products treated as commodities in both private markets and public exchanges. Economies of scale should be evident, and innovative bundles of services should entice buyers to pay premium prices. Branding becomes a matter of the image and reputation of the firm for reliability in the fulfillment of transactions, rather than product characteristics. In this case, international differences in language and time should make Internet B2B an efficient marketing and fulfillment channel.

The Nature of Participation

The discussion of public exchanges implies that portals themselves may be treated as commodities by the participants. If this is so, having a critical mass of client firms in the expert state may encourage migration toward them, leaving the mass of server providers with clients in the exploration or passive states (as defined by Grewal et al., 2000). Empirical evidence might show that attaining that critical mass depends on the ability to allay fears about security, assist with process integration, and publicize success stories. On the other hand, it may show that successful portals are simply better at disseminating product information, order entry, and account management (O'Daniel, 2000).

Research along these lines should also focus on the true nature of passive participation. Passive participants deploy the technology, but do not make it a medium for action. There are a number of promising possibilities for research. The initiative might be driven by IT experts in the company without co-opting management and key members of the purchase decision team, for example. Firms may be using the medium simply for advertising, and executing transactions through other channels. A closely related question is reaching participants in the process of making the purchase decision. Do they actually search? Only when switching? Which role is most likely to be scanning the portals for potential business partners?

Facilitators

Branding concerns, shared meaning, and purchase behavior may largely be determined by conventions and rules. Beyond these factors, resource issues should also be investigated. One such issue might be the relationship between use of traditional EDI, participation in Internet B2B, and the growth of internal IT capability. Industry characteristics may have an effect on these relationships as well as the business model of the Internet B2B service provider. Expectations for ROI might also be quantified in terms of transaction costs, risk premiums for switching systems and/or business partners, and the real benefits of system integration.

This has important implications for public policy initiatives that seek to increase participation in Internet B2B through financial subsidies. Financial subsidies to encourage participation in public exchanges become a subsidy to server providers, effectively raising the price on offer. The chance of paying a high price for low quality increases as the number of portals proliferates, and expectations of subsidies may encourage passive participation by firms that have not made the internal commitment to the new business process. Subsidies may be better spent to allay fears about security, assist with process integration, and publicize success stories: in essence, building a brand for Internet B2B itself.

Technology adoption is a risky proposition, even when it is limited to a firm's internal processes. It demands a collective decision to exchange one set of expertise for another, and opportunistic representations are a real danger. Internet B2B is not entirely a special case, except that price competition creates a potential lemons market. On one hand, participation will require clear competitive necessity, economies of scale, and/or potential for market expansion. On the other, assurance will be necessary that the new expertise required by dependence on global networks is reliable enough to avoid greater vulnerability.

REFERENCES

A matter of principals. (2001, June 28). *The Economist* [Electronic version]. Retrieved July 10, 2001 from the World Wide Web: http://www.economist.com/displayStory.cfm?Story_ID=674210.

Bierman, H.S. and Fernandez, L. (1998). *Game Theory with Economic Applications* (2nd ed.). New York: Addison-Wesley.

Chen, H. (1998, June 3-5). Dual acceptance of web diffusion: A case of clients and servers. In Toms, Campbell and Dunn (Eds.), *Information science at the dawn of the next millennium*. 26th Annual Conference of the Canadian Association for Information Science. Ottawa.

The container case. (2000, October 19). *The Economist* [Electronic version]. Retrieved July 20, 2001 from the World Wide Web: http://www.economist.com/displayStory.cfm?Story_ID=388030.

Farhoodi, F. and Fingar, P. (1997, November). Developing enterprise systems with intelligent agent technology. *Distributed Object Computing Magazine*, Object Management Group. Retrieved July 9, 1999 from the World Wide Web: http://home1.gte.net/pfingar/docmag_part2.htm.

FreeMarkets and US-ASEAN Business Council form strategic alliance; alliance aimed at facilitating growth of e-commerce in ASEAN. (2001, March 20). *Business Wire*. Retrieved July 20, 2001 from the World Wide Web: http://attjcwl.newsedge.com/1stbin/read_story/FIRST/010701/38/7/617/11.

Giddens, A. (1984). *The Constitution of Society*. Cambridge: Polity Press.

Giddens, A. (1991). *Modernity and Self-Identity*. Cambridge: Polity Press.

Grewal, R., Comer, J. M. and Mehta, R. (2001). An investigation into the antecedents of organizational participation in business-to-business electronic markets. *Journal of Marketing*, 65 (3), 17-33.

Hammer, M. (1990, July-August). Reengineering work: Don't automate, obliterate. *Harvard Business Review*, 104-112.

King, W. and Teo, T. (1996). Key dimensions of facilitators and inhibitors for the strategic use of information technology. *Journal of Management Information Systems, 12* (4), 35-44.

Legard, D. (2000, November 27). E-ASEAN plan gets solid framework. *IDG*. Retrieved July 20, 2001 from the World Wide Web: http://www.idg.net/ic_296454_1794_9_100000.html.

Magaziner, I. (1998, May 27). Transcript of address at the opening of TM@B convention in Brussels. Retrieved September 24, 2001 from the World Wide Web: http://www.fabrimetal.be/secteurs/ict/news/12/magazinerspeech.htm.

Malone, T., Yates, J. and Benjamin, R. (1987). Electronic markets and electronic hierarchies: Effects of information technology on market structure and corporate strategies. *Communications of the ACM, 30* (6), 484-497.

Mason, R., Bowling, C. and Niemi, R. (1998). Small manufacturing enterprises and the National Information Infrastructure. In *The Unpredictable Certainty: Information Infrastructure Through 2000 (White Papers)*. Washington, D.C.: National Academy Press.

NASA. (1998). *SEL COTS Study, Phase 1: Initial Characterization Study Report*. (SEL-98-001). Software Engineering Laboratory, Goddard Space Flight Center, National Aeronautics and Space Administration.

Northcutt, N. and Novak, J. (2000). *Network Intrusion Detection: An Analyst's*

Handbook (2nd ed.). Indianapolis: New Riders Publishing.

O'Daniel, T. (2001). A value-added model for electronic commerce. *Electronic Markets,* 11(1), 37-43.

OECD. (1998). *The Ecnomic and Social Impacts of Electronic Commerce: Preliminary Findings and Research Agenda*. Paris: Organisation for Economic Cooperation and Development.

Older, Wiser, Webbier. (2001, June 28). *The Economist* [Electronic version]. Retrieved July 20, 2001 from the World Wide Web: http://www.economist.com/displayStory.cfm?Story_ID=679981.

Orlikowski, W.J. (2001). The duality of technology: Rethinking the concept of technology in organisations. In C. Bryant and D. Jary (Eds.), *The contemporary Giddens: Social theory in a globalising age* (pp. 62-96). UK: Palgrave.

Riggins, F. and Mukhopadhyay, T. (1999). Overcoming adoption and implementation risks of EDI (revised January 1999). Retrieved October, 1999 from the World Wide Web: http://130.207.57.82/papers/edi.html.

Rossiter, J. R. and Percy, L. (1987). *Advertising and Promotion Management* (International Edition). Singapore: McGraw-Hill.

Seller Beware. (2000, March 2). *The Economist* [Electronic version]. Retrieved July 20 2001 from the World Wide Web: http://www.economist.com/displayStory.cfm?Story_ID=288267.

Shapiro, C. and Varian, H. (1998). *Information Rules: A Strategic Guide to the Network Economy*. Boston: Harvard Business School Press.

Simon, H. A. (1959). Theories of decision making in organisations and society. In F. G. Castles, D. J. Murray, and D. C. Potter (Eds.), (1971) *Decisions, Organisations and Society* (pp. 37-55). UK: Open University Press.

Thomas, R. J. (1994). What machines can't do: Politics and technology in the industrial enterprise. In D. MacKenzie and J. Wajcman (Eds.), (1999) *The Social Shaping of Technology* (pp. 199-221). UK: Open University Press.

Time to Rebuild. (2001, May 17). *The Economist* [Electronic version]. Retrieved July 20, 2001 from the World Wide Web: http://www.economist.com/displayStory.cfm?Story_ID=627416.

Turban, E., Lee, J., King, D. and Chung, H. M. (2000). *Electronic Commerce: A Managerial Perspective*. New Jersey: Prentice-Hall.

Varian, H. (1999, May 25-26). Market structure in the network age. Paper prepared for the Understanding the Digital Economy conference, Washington, DC. Retrieved October 16, 1999 from the World Wide Web: http://www.sims.berkeley.edu/~hal/Papers/doc/.

Whinston, W., Stahl, D. and Choi, S. (1997). *The Economics of Electronic Commerce*. Indianapolis: Macmillan Technical Publishing.

Williamson, O. (1975). *Markets and Hierarchies: Analysis and Antitrust Implications*. New York: The Free Press.

Wirtz, J. and Wong, P. K. (1999). An empirical study of Internet-based business-to-business e-commerce in Singapore. In *E-Commerce and Official Statistics - Selected Papers from the ISI Cutting Edge Conference on the Measurement of E-Commerce* (pp. 133-156). Singapore: Department of Statistics, Ministry of Trade & Industry.

Section III

IT Addressing Globalization

Chapter XIV

Virtualisations and its Role in Business

Jerzy Kisielnicki
Warsaw University, Poland

ABSTRACT

This chapter presents some of the aspects of virtualisation and its role in modern society. In today's world, a controlled virtualisation process creates enormous opportunity for economic growth of those countries and organisations, which, so far, due to various restrictions, have had no chance to become competitive in the global market. Those people and organisations that know how to make use of the opportunities presented by virtualisation may become more effective in business. Moreover, virtualisation creates the best options for intellectual enterprise development. Virtualisation is a very complex process. The author would like to discusses both the positive impact virtualisation can have on society and also some dangers or problems.

INTRODUCTION

Virtualisation, which is a subject of this thesis, could not exist without information technology (IT). Most authors who write about the problem of virtualisation apply an object-centred approach. Within this approach, the analysis is based on organisations and their structure. Perhaps this approach should be supplemented by a process-centred approach, which allows presenting both a complex nature of the virtualisation process and the analysis of its impact on society. According to Percival-Straunik (2001), virtualisation triggers off the process of integration and creation of global organisations. It is the basis of new business quality measures such as e-business and e-commerce.

> *The hypothesis, which should be proved in this thesis, is as follows: In today's world, a controlled virtualisation process creates enormous opportunity for economic growth of those countries and organisations, which, so far, due to various restrictions, have had no chance to establish themselves on the global market and become competitive.*

In practice, the restrictions on development are of a varied nature. They might be economic, legal, psychological, and organisational. The hypothesis presented earlier may be developed further; in the modern world, only those people and organisations who know how to make use of the possibilities presented by virtualisation may become competitive on the global market. Moreover, virtualisation creates the best options for intellectual enterprise development. Barrenechea (2001) is perhaps completely right when he says, "e-business or out of business."

The reason for which the virtualisation process has to be controlled is the fact that it brings advantages as well as new unknown dangers. Some of these dangers have been described by Chenoweth (2001) in "Reality war on the information's highway." In most cases, virtualisation, according to Breier (2000), Gates (2000), and Maitland (2001), is a chance for a significant improvement of one's life situation or development of an organisation.

The term virtualisation describes the processes connected with IT application. It is facilitated in the following areas of activity:

- In traditional organisations that want to expand their range of activities and have access to IT and global computer network. Such organisations develop through creating new subservient organisational units, such as Internet kiosks or shops. Other steps leading to further development include expanding, through the IT, the already existing sphere of activity—for example marketing or human resources.

- Creating a virtual organisation, i.e., an organisation established in order to achieve a common goal or goals. In such an organisation, the participants enter various types of relationships. The participation in the organisation does not require any form of legal agreements. The duration of a relationship is determined by each of the participants of the virtual organisation. A decision to terminate or reconstruct may be taken by any participant who decides that the relationship is no longer beneficial for him or her. A virtual organisation operates in the so-called cyber-space. The duration of any relationship may be extremely short. A virtual organisation does not have one boss. It begins to exist precisely at the moment when the manager of any given organisation comes to a conclusion that he is unable to fulfil the task on his own and he needs to co-operate with other organisations.
- Supporting teaching in various areas, including distance learning and application of computer simulation models for teaching such subjects as decision-making processes or complex process analysis.

The influence of virtualisation on the society is both varied and significant. In this thesis, there are presented results of our own research on this problem and the analysis of the literature on application of virtualisation in practice. The thesis also focuses on the problem of virtualisation as a chance for small and medium-size enterprises (SME), and also on the role of virtualisation in stimulating professional activation.

Virtualisation in Traditional Organisations

Virtualisation allows for development of any organisation at a much lower cost than in the traditional way. The picture presents the diagram of an organisation whose core is formed by traditional, permanent structures. These structures are connected with the virtual members of the organisation. The virtual elements established within the virtualisation process are very flexible. Thus, the organisation may quickly adjust to the changing environment.

Development through virtualisation may be facilitated as follows:

- The organisation creates virtual kiosks or shops. For that, specialty software is required. Thus, the organisation that sells furniture, by using computer graphics, may present its products on a computer screen. It may also receive orders in places located outside their traditional locations. In exactly the same way, other organisations, e.g. travel agencies, real estate companies, book shops, the stock exchange, etc., may operate.
- An organisation places information about its activity on the appropriate Internet pages. Through the monitoring programmes it is available to its

Figure 1: Structure of a Modern Organisation

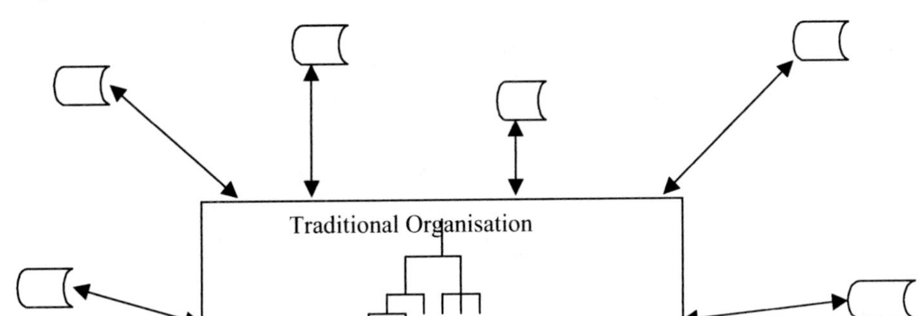

Virtual Branches or Kiosks

potential clients 24 hours a day. This way, the operations of the organisation are not limited to office hours only. Home banking services function in the same way. A client can perform banking operations from home. Compared to the situation described earlier (traditional) the expenses connected with the services of an organisation are shifted to the client. It is the client who has to pay for the terminal and access to the Internet or another network, for example Extranet. The organisation covers the cost of the development and exploitation of an appropriate system. It often provides the client with the software, which allows him to use the resources or services provided by the organisation.

- The organisation creates a possibility of working from home, the so-called Tele-work. In this way, the organisation may develop or restrict its activities depending on its needs. It is a very good way of increasing professional activity in those regions in which it is difficult to find employment in a traditional way. It should also be remembered that through Tele-work, a local organisation might become a global one.

Virtualisation allows traditional organisations to have a wider range of influence. A society is better-informed on the organisation's activities both by the organisation itself and by its clients. The restrictions on the development are varied. The most common include available financial resources to purchase the IT, language of presentation, and a necessity to have access to global, reliable computer networks. It should also be stressed that, unfortunately, virtualisation enables organisations that are not socially accepted (pornography, terrorism) to operate freely.

On the basis of the analysis of those organisations that utilise virtualisation in their activities, it can be assumed that their development requires five times lower investment outlays and costs connected with operational activities. Only in separated cases, the proportions were less favourable. Minimum savings obtained in result of virtualisation exceeded 60% of the financial resources, which would otherwise be spent on comparable development of the same organisation.

In the organisations where the development is achieved through Tele-work, the proportions are difficult to calculate. The analysis of a situation in the organisations in which Tele-work is connected with group work (workflow management) or in those that obtain employees from the countries where salaries are low confirms high effectiveness of virtualisation. Such a situation can be observed in software development. The companies from highly developed countries, such as the USA, Great Britain, or Germany, employ programmers from India, China, or Pakistan. This situation is beneficial for both the company and the countries the programmers come from. Whether it is beneficial for the tax system of the countries that buy such labour is another story.

It is a totally different situation when Tele-work is connected with professional activation of the disabled or the unemployed. Direct costs are higher as we deal with the poorer part of the society. Thus, additional costs have to be incurred for training, hardware, and software. Unfortunately, there is no data available to make a precise calculation. It is extremely difficult to establish how much money has been spent. In many countries, the cost of training and purchase of the equipment is covered by special social programmes. It is also difficult to estimate advantages. It may be said that social effect, which decreases the unemployment figures and, in the case of the disabled, enables them to live a normal life in the society, is the most important one. It is a very significant advantage possible only through virtualisation. Tele-work ensures reducing the necessity to directly invest in the development of an organisation, reducing overloading of communication systems, savings in the time spent on travelling to work, and savings in expenses connected with creating new parking spaces.

The issue of outlays and effects connected with virtualisation of work places will be analysed in further research. The analyses that aim at more precise estimation of profitability of the decisions to develop an organisation through virtualisation are the most significant.

Virtual Organisation as a Chance for Small and Medium Organisations

Virtualisation that leads to creating a virtual organisation forms a separate category. The term "virtual organisation" was used previously. In the literature on this subject, there are many terms used to define such organisations. Terms such as "network organisations" (Drucker, 1998), "organisations after re-engineering" (Hammmer and Champy, 1994), "crazy institutions" (Petersa, 1994), and "intelligent organisations" (Quinn, 1992) have also been used.

The analysis of the existing virtual organisations confirms the fact that they are not created by big companies. Their development is made through previously stated directions of activity such as kiosks and Internet shops and Tele-work. The reason for this situation might be fear of unethical conduct of other organisations that might destroy their reputation on the market (Kisielnicki, 1999).

One can state that SMEs, in order to establish themselves on the market and increase their competitiveness, create virtual organisations. To verify the above thesis, there were performed, in 2001 and 2002, investigations aiming at answering the following question (Kisielnicki, 2001):

- Do organisations' managers and entrepreneurs working for SMEs recognise a possibility of development by the way of virtual organisation?

A questionnaire distributed by myself during the course on application of the IT provided the following results: (the questionnaire was completed by 165 owners and managers of SMEs)

- Do you want to expand your activity? – *165 positive answers*
- Do you have a concept of actions necessary to take in order to do so? – *162 positive answers*
- What are the most important obstacles in the development of your organisation?
  - Lack of financial resources – *155 positive answers*
  - Fear of realising the concept in practice – *128 positive answers*
  - Lack of appropriate staff – *85 positive answers*

  Please note that two answers could be chosen.
- Do you think that virtualisation may be a good direction of development for your organisation? – *118 positive answers*

There were also many reservations as to the development through virtualisation. They were mainly connected with the fear of:

- Unethical behaviour of the co-operating organisations, for example not fulfilling their obligations, offering low-quality products, and also dishonest competition (the so-called economic sabotage)
- Operating in the conditions of total transparency, which may lead to the theft of an idea or new technology, especially by big organisations as they have the appropriate economic potential and staff and are able to perform the task independently

The questionnaire, as such, has a limited cognitive value. It was conducted once only, in one country, in a big industrial centre. The people who participate in professional skill development training are always those who search for new solutions. Their opinions may not always be the same as the opinions of the so-called average owners and managers. Also, the polled person was familiar with principles of virtual organisation and in their professional activity they had utilized IT.

The influence of virtualisation on the development of SMEs may be presented on the basis of two case-studies.

Case I: "Soft Enterprise" company creates application software. It employs 15 designers. In 2000, it won a bid for developing a concept of computerisation of a big public administration institution. The concept was accepted by the institution.

The work ordered was to design a system based on Date Warehouse, including the delivery of an appropriate hardware and installing a computer network. As the order exceeded the appointee's capabilities, they created a virtual organisation. The work on the design of the system was divided between mixed executive teams. The concept was realised by both home and foreign companies. In order to realise the task, a global organisation was created. The internal links were multi-levelled. It resulted from the fact that mixed project teams (virtual teams) were created to complete partial tasks. In corporate work, the Tele-work and group work software have been used. The process of creating virtual project teams is shown in Figure 2.

Figure 2: Creating the Virtual Project Team

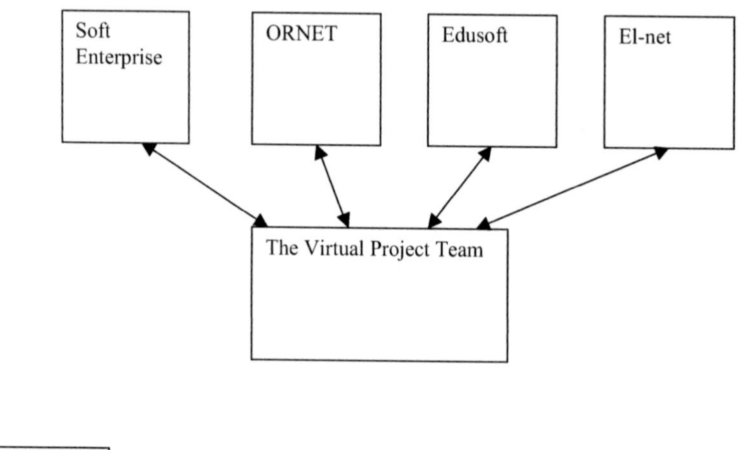

Case II: "Budex" company deals with housing constructions and repairs. It employs 60 people. In 1999 it constructed a building for a big development company. The company, being very satisfied with the services, ordered Budex to design and construct a housing development for 2,500 inhabitants. Budex was unable to fulfil the task on its own and thus created a virtual organisation. The organisation, after six months, becomes a holding company that deals with both design and construction.

The presented cases are typical of organisations that function using the virtualisation process. The organisations under analysis could establish themselves on the market only through virtualisation, as it enabled them to create one organisation. These organisations had not co-operated before. In the first case, the organisation was created only in order to perform a given task of computerising an institution. In the second case, virtualisation was the first step towards consolidation and creating a new, economically strong company. Virtualisation, in both cases, was about the process of acquiring producers, information on their reliability, and current cooperation for the sake of performing a task. And, although in both cases there were some traditional elements such as contracts and written agreements, the first step taken in order to fulfil the task was virtualisation. The contracts were concluded in result of agreements realised through the IT. The process of creating a new organisation—Budex holding—by virtual organisation is made by the three following phases:

- Phase I—the traditional organisations,
- Phase II—the virtual organisation,
- Phase III—the Budex holding.

Virtualisation is a chance for the transformation of SMEs into fully competitive organisations, even for the big and well-known companies. Virtual organisations perform the role of an incubator. And this is their positive influence on the society.

Virtualisation of Teaching

The research conducted by me and published previously suggests that a significant number of students, both in day studies and those working, feel the need to learn how to manage an organisation (Kisielnicki, 2001). The learning should be organised in circumstances as close to reality as possible. Virtualisation is the discipline of studies, which may cause the distance between the theory and practice to diminish. One may even risk a statement that it is the exact direction of the virtualisation, which, in the nearest future, shall have the most significant impact on the society. Virtualisation has influence on the increase of the effectiveness of the teaching process in the widest possible sense. It would be extremely difficult to find a discipline to which the virtualisation could not be applied. Perhaps not as the main subject, but most certainly as a subject supporting traditional teaching methods. Virtualisation may be applied in such areas as lowering the cost and decreasing time of training jet pilots, and also in improvement of military command, operating on the stock exchange, or cognitive analysis of genetic processes. In science, there are many examples of big discoveries that were first tried on computer-simulated models. It is virtualisation that allows for simulation of both the decision-making process and the analysis of complex technical or sociological processes. In virtualisation of teaching, two basic directions in which it develops can be identified.

The first one is the direction of common education in which everybody can, using the tools of IT, possess a given knowledge. A classic example is a virtual stock exchange. In many countries, a lot of people want to learn how to operate on the stock exchange before they actually start using it in an attempt to make money. Those people can get the necessary experience by using appropriate software. They can acquire necessary skills in the virtual world. This direction allows educating societies. There are also numerous games available through the Internet. These games not only provide pleasant time spent on playing, but also teach foreign languages or how to drive a car.

Another direction is dedicated teaching. There are the following activities to be identified:

- Self-control, i.e., your own evaluation of the possessed knowledge. For example, by using special software, the level of knowledge may be assessed, such as choice of the level of foreign language learning. Such method is applied by some language schools.
- Help in learning specific subjects. This includes, amongst others, enterprise laboratories, business games, and special simulators that teach how to use a specific technical equipment, e.g. flying simulators.
- Distance learning. A student who has a proper terminal and software may participate in classes from a distance. This direction of virtualisation is similar to the previously presented distance work.

Nowadays, all the decision-makers seem to appreciate the significant role of virtualisation in the process of education, although they do not always realise how complex it is.

Final Comments

Virtualisation is a very complex process. Nevertheless, it will certainly develop and be applied to an ever-expanding range of activities. It carries a lot of positive impact on the societies, but also some dangers. The author would not like the reader to get an impression that he treats virtualisation as a way to success. It should be remembered that, according to Thomson Financial Securities Data, for 20 Internet companies introduced at the stock exchange by Merrill Lynch Bank in 1997, the quotes of 15 of them dropped below the nominal value and two of them went bankrupt. The rates of eight companies, including the Buy.com virtual computer shop and 24/7 Media, an Internet advertising agency, dropped below 10% of the nominal value (Gates, 2000). The analysis of the reasons for this situation, as conducted by me, shows that very often the reason lies within the management errors. The most apparent example is Pets.com, an Internet animal food shop, which incurred a vast financial loss. The reason for this loss was the fact that the IT staff of the company could not solve the problem of defective codes. That was the reason for multi-million dollar losses.

Despite these negative experiences with virtualisation, the author remains an optimist and he would love to conduct research on this issue in various countries. The process of virtualisation has its features independent of the type of application. It also has its own character.

REFERENCES

Barrenchea, M. (2001). *E-business*. New York: McGraw Hill.

Breier, M. (2000). *Internet Man@ger*. London: Piatkus.

Chenoweth, N. (2001). *Virtual Murdoch-Reality War on the Information Highway*. London: Secker-Warburg.

Drucker, P. (1998). The New Organisation. *Harvard Business Review*, Nos. 1-2.

Elstrom, P. (2001, July). E-money. *Business Week*, 63.

Gates, B. (2000). *Business the Speed of Through*. Pingwin.

Hammer, M. and Champy, J. (1994). *Reengineering the Corporation.* Harper Business.

Kisielnicki, J. (1998). Virtual Organisation as a Product of Information Society. Informatics, 22, 3.

Kisielnicki, J. (1999). Management Ethics in Virtual Organisation. *10th International Conference of the Information Resources Management Association.* Hershey, PA.

Kisielnicki, J. (2001). Virtual Organisation as a chance for enterprise development. In M. Khosrowpour (ed.), *Managing Information Technology in a Global Economy*, (p. 349) Hershey, PA: IDEA Group Publishing.

Maitland, J. (2001) *How to Make Your Million from the Internet.* London: Hodder&Stoughton.

Percival-Straunik, L. (2001). *E-commerce, The Economist Book.* London.
Peters, T. (1994). *Crazy Times Call for Crazy Organisations, The Ton Peters Seminar*. Vintage Books.
Quinn, J.B. (1992). *The Intelligent Enterprise.* New York: The Free Press.

Chapter XV

Virtual Organization: Duality of Human Identities in Consciousness and Entity

Jinyoul Lee
State University of New York at Binghamton, USA

Bandula Jayatilaka
State University of New York at Binghamton, USA

ABSTRACT

This chapter discloses the social aspects of a virtual organization and identifies the role of human actors in a virtual organization (consciousness). This consciousness exists in the perceptual world that we create beyond the limits of time and space. However, its counterparts exist in various forms (entities) in the real world. To bridge the gaps between the consciousnesses and the entities, there exist dual identities of human interveners in both virtual and real worlds. This research provides the meaning of virtual organization, and proceeds to explain the relationship between the consciousnesses (virtual organizations) and entities (real organizations) with human intervention (human players) using structuration theory. This study uses a theory-building process to understand human activities in virtual organizations. The theory proposed in this study reflects the epistemological positions of virtual organization research.

INTRODUCTION

As with net-enabled organizations, the concept of virtual organizations has gained prominence among researchers and practitioners. As shown by the recent work of Schultze and Orlikowski (2001), virtuality can be understood through the perception of time and space. This research extends the scope of the virtual organization in terms of "virtual space," a metaphor used in *time* and *space* (beyond the constraints of the actual location we belong to) dimensions (Allcorn, 1997). As opposed to the virtual organization, time and space dimensions are constrained in traditional or "real" organizations. Time constraints occur in real organizations due to the operational time dimension of such organizations, while space dimension occurs due to constraints of location.

It is true that a virtual organization inherits the attributes of virtual dimensions —a newly defined concept of time and space. In other words, a virtual organization does not exist in our time and space, but rather exists only in virtual space (perceptual world), which is only a metaphor of our consciousness and not reality. A virtual organization, in this sense, is the metaphor of our designed and structured consciousnesses that exists in virtual space to perform the intended actions of interest. However, the most important thing in a virtual organization is to identify the role of human actors who get involved in both the physical and the perceptual world. We attempt to explain the relationships between the human actors, the real and virtual organizations, and our perceptions of these concepts.

MOTIVATIONS

Given that e-business is imperative in the modern business world, the definition or the dimension of virtual organization is necessary to set up competitive strategies in e-business. However, this is a very challenging task for many companies due to the ever-emerging, nebulous interpretations currently in existence. Many new business models have been created, experimented upon, and abandoned in the e-business area. E-business is still a fledgling field in terms of organizational strategies, structure, and behavior, which is indicative of the fact that virtual organization is not yet firmly defined within the dimensions of time and space (Ahuja and Carley, 1999).

Metaphors play a very powerful role in structuring virtual organizations because terms like "virtual space" and "virtual organization" originate from symbolic languages (Faucheux, 1997). These metaphors provide the meaning of existence, thus we can treat the organization like a real organization in virtual space. Continuous analogical processes between virtual and real organizations explain the existence of virtual organizations because there exist similarities and discrepancies in them (Ahuja and Carley, 1999). A virtual organization, operating within virtual space imagery, exists in our consciousness, while an actual organization physically exists in various forms (more tangible or definable manner) such as culture, politics, resources, etc. (Morgan, 1986). Although a virtual organization exists in our consciousness, it is associated with its physical counterpart in the "real" world. Allcorn (1997) described this counterpart as a parallel virtual organization and bureaucratic hierarchical organization counterpart. However, there is a possibility that in the near future a "real" organization will exist only when its virtual counterpart exists in virtual space. Mowshowitz (1994) described this as "a dominant paradigm" of virtual organization due to its unique advantages in the efficiency, cost, and effectiveness of goal-oriented activity. Surprisingly, human actors manage to control these two opposing ideas of real and virtual worlds — thus, it becomes obvious that humans possess duality of existence in both the real and the virtual world.

This research discloses the social aspects of a virtual organization and identifies the role of human actors in a virtual organization (or "consciousness") (Faucheux, 1997). This consciousness exists in the perceptual world that we create beyond the limits of time and space (Allcorn, 1997). However, its counterparts exist in various forms (entities) in the real world. To bridge the gaps between the consciousnesses and the entities, there exists dual identities in both virtual and real worlds. This research provides the meaning of virtual organization, and proceeds to explain the relationship between the consciousnesses (virtual organizations) and entities (real organizations) with human intervention (human players).

THEORETICAL FINDINGS

Schultze and Orlikowski (2001) examine rhetorical oppositions between real organizations and virtual organizations, and in doing so apply metaphors to the discourse. The visions or views of two opposing elements are not divergent or dichotomous; rather, they offer substitutes for the opposition through a process referred to as dualism. As Orlikowski (1991) proposed in her earlier paper, "The Duality of Technology," this dualism is not mutually exclusive. The dualism originated from the admirable work by Giddens (1984) — *The Constitution of Society*. Giddens's (1984) structuration theory integrated two main streams of sociology — objectivism, and subjectivism. It appears that the structuration theory adopts the notion of phenomenology, as it seeks to make explicit the implicit structure and meaning in human experiences (Sanders, 1982). Phenomenology searches for the essence of what an experience *essentially is* and is the intentional analysis between objective appearance and subjective apprehension. Structuration theory (the process of structuration of an organization), seeks a complementary essence in the structure of organization science and in the process of struggles between objectivism and subjectivism. Interestingly, the conflict of objectivism and subjectivism was reflected in metaphors, as Lakoff and Johnson (1980, p. 189) stated:

> *Objectivism and subjectivism need each other in order to exist. Each defines itself in opposition to the other and sees the other as the enemy. Objectivism takes as its allies: scientific truth, rationality, precision, fairness, and impartiality. Subjectivism takes as its allies: the emotions, intuitive insight, imagination, humaneness, art, and a "higher" truth… They coexist, but in separate domains. Each of us has a realm in his life where it is appropriate to be objective and a realm where it is appropriate to be subjective.*

Human players have very important roles in both phenomenology and metaphors due to their valuable experience. The key differentiator between objectivism and subjectivism is always human experience. Another important fact (usually overlooked by researchers) is that the use of metaphors appears in both the physical world and in the perceptual world (Harrington, 1991) because the terminology "organization" itself results from *dead* metaphors. Tsoukas (1991) describes the process in which metaphors "have become so familiar and so habitual

Figure 1: Dual Identities of Human Players in Both Real and Virtual Organizations

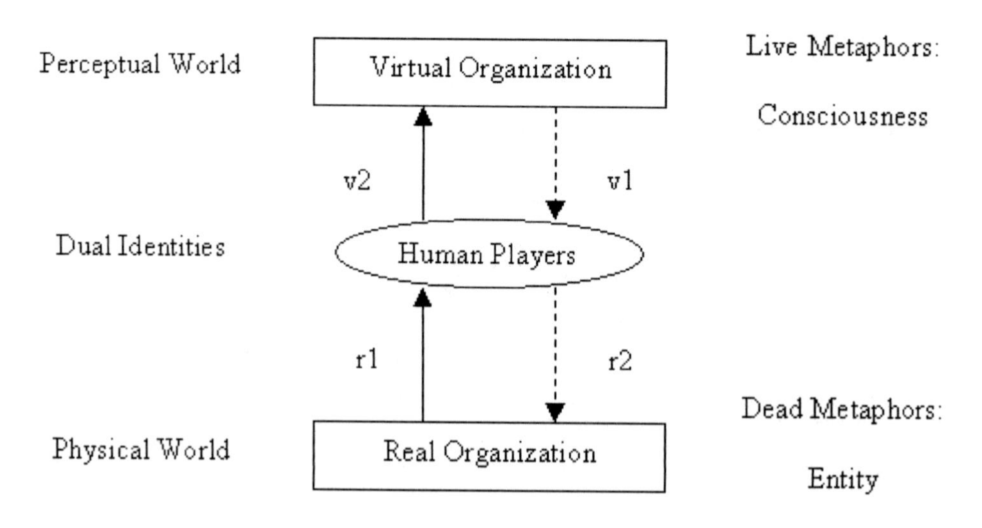

that we have ceased to be aware of their metaphorical nature and use them as literal terms" (p. 568) It implies that the metaphors of virtual organizations are *live* metaphors (Tsoukas, 1991) "knowing that these words are substitutes for literal utterances" (p. 568) that use dead metaphors (organization per se). Therefore, live metaphors are used to describe virtual organizations in another dimension where we can do things that are not possible in the real world, because the virtual world operates without the constraints of time and space unlike the real world.

The process of structuration involves the reciprocal interaction of human players and institutional properties of organizations (Giddens, 1984). As Orlikowski (1991) pointed out, "the theory of structuration recognizes that human actions are enabled and constrained by structures, yet these structures are the result of previous actions" (p. 404). Because we live in both real and virtual worlds, we have both objective and subjective understandings of each world—dual identities. Figure 1 shows the relationship between real organizations and virtual organizations in the presence of human interveners. Both real and virtual organizations consist of rule resource sets that are implicated in their institutional articulation, thus these rule resource sets act as structures of the organizations (both virtual and real), where a structure is the medium and the outcome of organizational conduct. The structural properties do not exist outside of the actions of the organizational actors. Therefore, structural properties, related to space and time, are implicated in the production and reproduction of the organizations. In other words, both real and virtual organizations undergo structuration across the different sets of dimensions of time and space based on the perspectives of each human player.

The previous model, which is adopted from the duality of technology of Orlikowski (1991), depicts four processes that operate continuously and simultaneously in the interaction between human players and both real and virtual organizations. These processes include: (i) institutional properties, represented by arrow r1 (objective appearance of the real organization) and arrow v1 (objective appearance of the virtual organization), which are the *medium* of human players; (ii) structures, represented by arrow r2 (subjective construction of the real organization) and arrow v2 (subjective construction of the real organization), which are the *product* of human players; (iii) the interaction of human players in both worlds, and the resultant influences on the social contexts of the real organization within which it is built and used (the direction of arrow r1 and v2); and (iv) how the virtual organization is built and used within particular social contexts in a real organization (the direction of arrow v1 and r2).

In Figure 1, there are two structurations from human players: one for the real organization (r1, r2) and the other for the virtual organization (v1, v2). The realms of virtual organization and real organization are objective while the consciousness of the human player is subjective. We have both objective and subjective understandings of each world (dual identities) because we live in both real and virtual worlds.

The maturity phase of the real organization (with its established tradition) and the fledgling state of the virtual organization (with its newly emerging phenomena) indicate that the objective appearance of the real organization (arrow r1) and subjective construction of the real organization (arrow v2) dominate the structuration process in modern organizations. Many observations show that the knowledge and experiences accumulated in real organizations enforce the formulation of the virtual organization in the abstraction process of efficient and effective goal-oriented activity (Mowshowitz, 1994). It is partly true that the creation of the virtual organization is only for the representation of the real organization in virtual space. A considerable amount of explanation arises from rethinking the basic assumptions of time and space. The real organization, whether tangible or intangible, is bound in time and space, while the virtual organization, an imaginative concept established in computer hardware and software, is free from the constraints of time and space.

IMPLICATIONS

Barley and Tolbert (1997) defined an institution as "shared rules and typifications that identify categories of social actors and their appropriate activities or relationships" (p. 97). As they explained in their recursive model (institutions and actions), institutionalization involves the behavior of revision or replication of organizational abstracts (work procedures), and entails objectification and externalization of behaviors. In this sense, the successful functioning of a virtual organization is reaching institutionalization in virtual space. Through this process, the virtual organization becomes stable and helps serve as the constitution where human players can follow their activities. Upon further inference, institutions from business processes of real organizations constrain human actors (constitutive nature, r1) who in turn construct institutions of virtual organization (constituted role, v2), and/or vice versa (from v1 to r2).

The above arguments provide complementary insights to the social process explained by the structuration theory (Giddens, 1984). In this theory, actions and institutions continuously interact, thereby determining the structure. The structuration theory lacks the explanation of how these interactions (revising and reproducing an institution or structure) are processed, although this is arguable as Giddens explains the role of reflection, interaction etc. However, Barley and Tolbert (1997) clearly stated that their work, "the aim of institutional theory" is "to develop the implications of structuration theory for the interplay between actions and institutions and to address the practical problem of how to study institutional maintenance and change in organizations" (p. 112).

The authors believe that the results of this study are compatible with the belief of Barley and Tolbert (1997) that "the institutional perspective must come to grips with institutionalization as a process if it is to fulfill its promise in organization studies" (p. 112). The focus of this study is the explanation of what is going on at a virtual organization. The result revealed by this research is a rich description of theoretical induction. A limitation of this process is that it only reflects one part of the recursive model of institutional theory (Barley and Tolbert, 1997).

CONCLUSIONS

Orlikowski (1996) studied organizational transformation. The approach of this study is similar to her work that organizational transformation is "the ongoing practices of organizational actors, and emerges out of their (tacit and not so tacit) accommodations to and experiments with the everyday contingencies, breakdowns, exceptions, opportunities, and unintended consequences that they encounter" (Orlikowski, 1996, p. 65). The above statement is identical to the findings of this study in that users of the system continuously interact with the system through producing, reproducing, and transforming work practices (Giddens, 1984).

This study reorganizes the ontology and epistemology in virtual organization. Similar to Mowshowitz's (1997) depiction of a virtual organization as a computer with a communication tool or computer network that increases the efficiency and effectiveness of organization performance (Mowshowitz, 1994) and a social system, the findings of this study complement the virtual organization as a social system giving the new meanings of time and space. This study rethinks the philosophy of virtual organization, providing insight into the concept of duality of human identity. It is not only a lens for understanding virtual organizations, but also a socio-technical understanding of virtual organizations through structuration.

The basic purpose of this study is to initiate a theory-building process in the Internet area. An analytical view of modern science alone does not provide a complete explanation of what we investigate. As IT has developed so rapidly along with science, researches have become one-sided, lacking epistemology (Reichenbach, 1958). Authors intend to make progress in the epistemology of virtual organization with the help of continuous, logical induction of previous theories and current phenomena. The theories proposed in this study reflect the epistemological positions of virtual organization research. Thus, the authors hope it would be the basis of other empirical studies in the future.

REFERENCES

Ahuja, M. and Carley, K. (1999). Network Structure in Virtual Organization. *Organization Science, 10* (6), 741-757.

Allcorn, S. (1997). Parallel virtual organizations: managing and working in the virtual workplace. *Administration & Society, 29* (4), 412-439.

Barley, Stephen R. and Tolbert, Pamela S. (1997). Institutionalization and Structuration: Studying the links between Action and Institution. *Organization Studies, 18* (1), 93-117.

Beer, Stafford. (1984). The viable system model: its prevalance, development, methodology and pathology. *Journal of the Operational Research Society, 35* (1), 7-25.

Faucheux, C. (1997). How virtual organizing is transforming Management Science. *Communications of the ACM, 40* (9), 50-55.

Giddens, A. (1984). *The Constitution of Society.* Berkeley, CA: University of California Press.

Harrington, J. (1991). *Organizational Structure and Information Technology.* Hertfordshire, UK: Prentice Hall International.

Lakoff, G. and Johnson, M. (1980). *Metaphors We Live By.* Chicago, IL: University of Chicago Press.

Morgan, G. (1986). *Images of Organization.* Beverly Hills, CA: Sage Publications.

Mowshowitz, A. (1994). Virtual Organization: A Vision of Management in the Information Age. *The Information Society,* 10, 267-288.

Mowshowitz, A. (1997). Virtual Organization. *Communications of the ACM, 40* (9), 30-37.

Orlikowski, W. (1996). Improvising organizational transformation over time: A situated change perspective. *Information Systems Research, 7*(1), 63-92.

Orlikowski, W. J. (1991). The Duality of Technology: Rethinking the Concept of Technology in Organizations. *Organization Science, 3* (3), 398-427.

Reichenbach, H. (1958). *The Philosophy of Space & Time.* New York: Dover Publications, Inc.

Sanders, P. (1982) Phenomenology: A New Way of Viewing Organizational Research. *Academy of Management Review, 7* (3), 353-360.

Schultze, U. and Orlikowski, W. J. (2001). Metaphors of virtuality: Shaping an emergent reality. *Information and Organization, 11* (1), 45-77.

Tsoukas, H. (1991). The missing link: A transformational view of metaphors in organizational science. *Academy of Management Review, 16* (3), 566-585.

Chapter XVI

Interorganizational Relationships, Strategic Alliances, and Networks: The Role of Communication Systems and Information Technologies

Keiichi Yamada
Nakamura Gakuen University, Japan

ABSTRACT

This chapter deals with roles and ways of interorganizational communication systems. Prior to the subject, author refers to three topics related to the subject: what are interorganizational relationships, strategic alliances, and interorganizational networks.

In order to understand interorganizational networks, the author utilizes Barnard's theory of cooperative system and formal organization, in which communication plays a significant role to formulate and to maintain interorganizational networks as organization of organizations. Furthermore, there are some problems for effective interorganizational communication systems – both human and machine: standardization of communication systems, impact of IT development, and interorganizational strategy using IT.

INTRODUCTION

Interorganizational relationship (IOR) is an interdisciplinary research theme that has been approached from various fields such as economics, game theory, strategic management theory, and organization theory, etc. (Child and Faulkner, 1998).[1]

In particular, IOR has both competition and cooperation – and they are dynamically changeable in accordance with the situation; therefore, it is the theme of competitive strategy in competition and the theme of interorganizational networks (ION) in cooperation on the contrary. Thus IOR is the domain spread over both theories of corporate strategies and organization theory.

On the other hand, on ION, there is another approach from information network system researchers. This is the perspective of how the information network system has to be utilized in order to enhance the effectiveness and efficiency of ION.

In this chapter, I will refer to the concepts and perspectives of IOR, strategic alliance as cooperative relationships, strategic alliance models based on core-competence, and ION as cooperative IOR. Then I will present models of ION as communication systems, and refer to issues about utilizations of IT in ION.

The objectives of this chapter are to discuss IOR and ION, both in the managerial standpoint and that of the information network system.

BACKGROUND

The studies about IOR and ION are not new. On IOR, sociologists carried out a series of studies in the late 1950s to early 60s (Dill, 1958; Levine and White, 1961; Litwak and Hylton, 1962). And on ION, studies were also carried out in the mid-60s (Evan, 1966; Caplow, 1964).

However, the reason why IOR and ION have been becoming significant is primarily that the development of information technologies (IT) change the way IOR and ION are.[2] Secondly, changes in organizational environments are so rapid and enormous. In other words, we are in an age of turbulence now.[3] In such an environment, a flexible organization, such as network organization, is more suitable to meet its environment than legacy bureaucratic organization. The concept of network organization covers both intra- and inter-organization (Rockart and Short, 1991).

On the other hand, progress of globalization and development of IT competition keener. In order to survive against such an environment, an organization needs to ally with other organization(s), formulate an ION, and try to overcome the difficulties that a single organization cannot do.

I will classify IOR first, and then study strategic alliance as a cooperative relationship. Then, I will refer to ION, as strategic alliance is actualized in the form of ION.

Barnard (1968) took up "communication" as one of the three basic elements necessary for formulating organizations. Simon (1976) grasped "organizations" as information processing systems especially for decision-making. Nonaka insisted that organizations are not mere information processing systems, but are also systems that create information (Nonaka, 1985) and even knowledge (Nonaka, 1991; Nonaka and Takeuchi, 1995).

In this regard, I think it is significant that we grasp ION as communication systems, information processing systems, information creating systems and knowledge creating systems. Among these systems, I will concentrate on the subject of "organization as communication system" and expand it to ION by using Barnard's theory here.

INTERORGANIZATIONAL RELATIONSHIPS

What is IOR?

IOR is simply relationships between/among focal organizations – if we borrow Evan's expression[4] (Evan, 1966) — and other single or more organizations. Generally, besides focal organization and others, there are other IOR between/among other organizations as well.

Patterns of such relationships are one-to-one, or one-to-many relationships with focal organizations, and many-to-many relationships among all of the organizations concerned.

Van de Ven and Ferry (1980, p. 298) classified these IOR into three models: dyadic or pairwise model, interorganizational set model, and ION model (Figure 1).

Classification of IOR

What kinds of IOR are there? I will argue about the static models and dynamic models by using the simple dyadic model.

Static Models

I will study static models of IOR between two organizations, A and B, here.

Static models indicate static relationship between objective organizations. In an analysis of static relationships one must consider firstly, relationships between objective organizations — whether other organizations are friend, enemy, or

Figure 1: Forms of Interorganizational Relationship

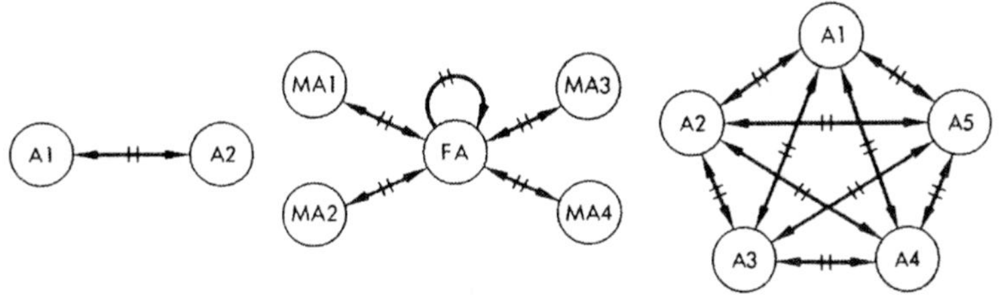

Dyadic or Pairwise Interorganizational Relationship — Interorganizational Set — Interorganizational Network

Source: Van de Ven, A.H. and Ferry, D. (1980). Measuring and Assessing Organizations. New York: John Wiley, p. 298

neutral; and secondly, the degree of dependence – whether interdependent, or one-sided; and thirdly, symmetry — whether bilateral or unilateral; and fourthly characters — whether homogeneous or heterogeneous.

Relationships between organizations

General classification of relationships between A and B is made on the basis of whether there are any relationships in organizations, and then, in case there are any relationships, whether such relationships are rival, neutral, or friendly. Those relationships can be broken down into three relationships: A and B (bilateral), A to B (unilateral), and B to A (unilateral). In the case of unilateral relationships, for example, if A considers B as its enemy, there are two cases – one is that B is neutral and the other is that B considers A as a friend. On the contrary, in case that A considers B a friend, there are two cases – one is that B considers A as an enemy and the other is that B is just neutral. And it is important that actions or even strategies of each party can be different according to how they consider their counterpart.

In case there are no relationships, two cases are considerable – one is that both parties have no relation with each other, and the other is that only one party thinks its counterpart has no relation (Figure 2).

Among these cases, the case that both A and B consider each other an enemy is called competitive relationships, and the case where both A and B are considered as friends is cooperative relationships. All other cases are basically not competitive or cooperative relationships. In these cases, one party unilaterally acts as a rival or friend to the others, or is completely neutral. But such actions can change their relationships and induce new competition and/or cooperation.

This chapter handles competitive relationships and cooperative relationship among them.

Figure 2: Patterns of Dyadic Relationship

	No Relationship	Enemy	Neutral	Friend
A and B		Rival or Competitive Relationship	Independent	Cooperative or Allied Relationship
A to B	B to A - Enemy - Neutral - Friend	B to A - Neutrality - Friend	B to A - Enemy - Friend	B to A - Enemy - Neutral
B to A	A to B - Enemy - Neutral - Friend	A to B - Neutral - Friend	A to B - Enemy - Friend	A to B - Enemy - Neutral

Dependence

Why does interorganizational competition and cooperation among organizations occur? Each organization has its own purpose (Barnard, 1968). And in order to attain its purpose or goals, one organization competes or cooperates with other organizations.

According to the open system theory, an organization has an interdependent relationship with its environments (Kast and Rosenzweig, 1972). An organization exchanges resources such as knowledge, information, energy, personnel, money, and material, etc., with its environments. And due to such exchange, an organization and the other organizations are interdependent over necessary resources for attaining their own purpose or goals. Such a relationship between organization and environment is interdependent in a macroscopic view, or thinking that the organization exists in its ecosystems, but there are two cases that the relationships with each organization — a part of environment — are bilaterally (or reciprocally) dependent and unilaterally dependent. Thus each IOR is different. Considering the dyadic relationships of A and B, there are the following three cases:

- A and B (reciprocal relationship or interdependence)
- A to B (one-sided relationship or parasitism)
- B to A (one-sided relationship or parasitism)

The degree of dependence is determined by importance (or necessity) and scarcity (or availability) of resources (Pfeffer and Salancik, 1978).

Symmetry

In relation to the "dependency" as described above, the "symmetry" of the relationship is whether two organizations are in an equal relationship or either organization is in a dominant position to the other one.

In other words, the symmetry of the relationship is the relationship of power between two organizations. Considering the dyadic relationship between A and B, there are the following three cases of symmetry:

- $A = B$ (equal)
- $A > B$ (unequal)
- $A < B$ (unequal)

The case A = B is a symmetrical relationship, and the others are not symmetrical ones. Depending on the cases, the autonomy of each organization is greatly different, and the degree of difficulty of attaining its purpose or goals is determined. In this case, one organization is in a dominant position to another organization; one organization can compete more advantageously to the others than in the case of an equal relationship in competitive relationship, and it can make more advantageous decisions than the others in a cooperative relationship.

The degree of symmetry is determined by the relativity of an organization's resource-dependency to its environment.

Character – Homogeneous versus Heterogeneous

In the analysis of IOR, it is necessary to make clear whether the relationship is homogeneous or heterogeneous. Then the way of competition or cooperation becomes distinct.

In a homogeneous relationship, there are rivalries among existing firms in the industry, new entrants, emergence of substitutes, etc., in competition; and various kinds of cooperative (or joint) activities of business associations, and joint research and development (R & D), etc., in cooperation.

On the other hand, in a heterogeneous relationship, there are bargaining powers of suppliers (or sellers) and customers (or buyers) in competition; and outsourcing and division of labors based on strategic alliances, etc. in cooperation.[5]

Dynamic Models

Dynamic models of IOR are models of IOR in which relationships change dynamically.

There are two meanings in such changes. One is that the relationships themselves change situationally, and another is the outcome that IOR bears.

Change of Relations

Static models can only illustrate the structure of relationships between A and B, but in the real society the relationship between A and B may change as time goes by and the situation changes.

Brandenburger and Nalefbuff (1996) studied interactions of competition and cooperation between/among organizations, which are based on the game theory, and they stated "business is cooperation when it comes to creating a pie and competition when it comes to dividing it up" (p. 4).[6]

Gomez-Casseres (1996) pointed out that "business rivalries now often takes place between sets of allied firms" (p. 2) and took up the concept of "collective competition."

Thus, in dynamic models, IOR are considered to be diversely changeable in accordance with the situation. An organization has its own purpose or goals and, in order to attain such purpose or goals, it carries out its activities. And it sometime competes and sometime cooperates with other organizations as the need arises.

Outcomes of Dynamic Interorganizational Transactions

Another sphere that dynamic models possess is an outcome brought by the competition and cooperation in IOR.

Moor (1993) presented a very interesting concept of "co-evolution in a business ecosystem." He suggested, "a company be viewed not as a member of a single industry but as part of a business ecosystem that crosses a variety of industries" (p. 76). And in this business ecosystem, "companies co-evolve their capabilities around a new innovation" (p. 76). Namely, "they work cooperatively and competitively to support new products, satisfy customer need, and eventually incorporate the next round of innovation" (p. 76).

He created a concept of "life-cycle model of a business ecosystem" based on a concept of "co-evolution in a business eco-system" and developed four evolutionary stages of a business ecosystem – birth, expansion, leadership, and self-renewal.

I do not agree with his idea of the range or the unit of a business ecosystem and of the four-stage theory, but I think we have to appreciate his basic thought that each organization "co-evolves" through interorganizational competition and cooperation.

By the way, if outcome of the cooperative activities between A and B is shown as (A + B), and outcome of the independent activities of A and B is shown as A + B, then there are the following three cases:

- $A + B > (A + B)$
- $A + B = (A + B)$
- $A + B < (A + B)$

The first case is that the outcome of independent activities is better than that of cooperative activities of two parties, and it is better that two parties do not cooperate and act independently as a result. The second case is that the outcome of independent activities and that of cooperation are equal, and it is all the same thing whether two parties do cooperate or not. It all depends on their options. The third case is that the outcome of cooperation is better than that of independent activities, and interorganizational cooperative activities become effective.

The third case can be further divided into two cases. One is that cooperation brings an outcome, which both parties cannot attain independently by making up for necessary resources with each other. And the other is that cooperation creates new resources – including knowledge and technologies, etc., products, and markets, etc., through "interorganizational learning" with many trials and errors in the cooperative activities.

With respect to "innovation," it is much significant that cooperation in IOR should be carried out to create new resources. Especially, on the subject of "knowledge management," interorganizational cooperation should be made towards creating new knowledge.

On the other hand, what about competition between/among organizations? In an interorganizational competition, it is necessary for an organization to win against its competitors for its survival or growth. In order to do it, an organization has to know who its competitors are and how to cope with them.

The competition against its opponents stimulates the activities of the focal organization. And then by concentrating its resources for the victories, and by continuing their activities through trial and error (with interorganizational learning), an organization can innovate various kinds of revolution of technologies, develop new products, saturate existing products, and develop or create new markets. As a result, "natural selection"—where only the winners can survive in the competition —works and then revolution as the "species" occurs.

Thus both interorganizational competition and cooperation have dynamic aspects of creating resources (such as new technologies or new products), of saturating existing products, and of creating and developing new markets.

STRATEGIC ALLIANCE AS COOPERATIVE RELATIONSHIPS

What is a Strategic Alliance?

An alliance is one of cooperative relationships between/among organizations. Child and Faukner (1998) defined alliance as partnerships between firms and a normal agent for cooperative strategy. An alliance is formulated strategically or tactically, for mutual benefit by two or more parties having compatible or complementary business interests and goals (Segil, 1996).

It is different from mere arm's length market transactions. Rather it is the particular kinds of interorganizational bonds that emphasize the relationship aspect of the exchange as much as the goods or services being exchanged (Kanter and Meyer, 1991).

In addition to exchanging these goods or services, partners can obtain unanticipated benefits from cooperation, such as mutual learning (Child and Faukner, 1998), which can bear some sort of innovation – new products/services, processes, markets, and resources, including knowledge.

According to Yoshino and Rangan (1995), a strategic alliance is defined as:

> *A strategic alliance links specific facets of the businesses of two or more firms. At its core, this link is a trading partnership that enhances the effectiveness of the competitive strategies of the participating firms by providing for the mutually beneficial trade of technologies, skills, or products based upon them (p. 4).*

And they added the following three determinants of strategic alliances.

- Uniting the members independently in the form of alliance to pursue their shared goals.
- Partners share the benefit of alliance and control over the performance of assigned tasks.
- Partners contribute to one or more key strategic domains on a continuing basis.

Konsynski and McFarlan (1990) took up a concept of "information partnerships" through information or information systems, and listed the following five points as success factors of such partnerships.

- Shared Vision at the Top
- Reciprocal Skills in Information Technology
- Concrete Plans for an Early Success
- Persistence in the Development of Usable Information
- Coordination on Business Policy

Guiding Principles of Strategic Alliances

Value Chain

Generally, the concept of "value chain" is used as a guiding principle of strategic alliances. Porter (1985) paid attention to "value," which the firm generates, and made linkage between intra-firm activities and those that generate such value as value chain.

In the alliance between/among firms, he developed such value activities from intra-firm level to inter-firm level, and made the concept of "value system." It specifies the existence and the location of the source of value — or competitive advantage — in the inter-firm business processes. And with this method, we can point out the significant points in the inter-firm alliances and lead the strategies for competitive advantage.

Although the concept of value chain that Porter advocated was oriented to vertical integration of the value activities, there emerged new concepts such as "value chain integration" (Pine II, 1993) and "value constellation" (Normann and Ramirez, 1993, 1994) in the early 1990s.

Value chain integration is the concept that Pine II advocated. He stated that, in turbulent times like today, there needs to be more flexibility than that of the legacy value chain, and in order to realize such flexibility, we need value chain integration instead of a legacy value chain – a vertical integration system.

Value Chain Integration

Value chain integration is based on the "open communication lines that allow everyone in the entire chain to focus on the next customer, and most of all on the end customer, combined with activities that proceed concurrently rather than sequentially" (Pine II 1993, p. 229). He added that value chain integration focuses on process capabilities, while vertical integration focuses on product competencies.

For example, in the Dell Computer's direct model, all the parties (such as suppliers of the parts, Dell Computer, and Federal Express) who manage logistics, including inventory management and delivery of products, share the ordering information and work as if the process is carried out almost concurrently rather than sequentially.

Value Constellation

Value constellation is the concept that was advocated by Normann and Ramirez (1993, 1994). They indicated that the paradigm shift from adding value step by step to co-producing value is needed.

They stated that, in the turbulent environment, corporate strategies cannot cope with the new environment only by the value chain, which arrange value activities in line with the pre-determined order based on value chain. Instead of adding values, it is necessary to reinvent value. In order to realize value creation, various parties concerned, such as suppliers, partner firms, allied firms, and even customers, etc., must get together and co-produce value.

The key strategic task of successful companies is to reconfigure roles and relationships among constellation of the parties concerned "to mobilize the creation of value in new forms and by new players" (Normann and Ramirez, 1993, p. 66).

They took up the case of IKEA, which is the largest furniture retailer in the world, and illustrated the concept of value constellation.

Thus, at present, guiding principles of strategic alliance are changed from the vertical integration of value chain — in other words from sequentially adding value — to synchronous value offerings or co-production of value.

As Norman and Ramirez (1994) stated, "words like synchronous, parallel, concurrent, distributed, co-processed, or co-produced denote the new possibilities which break the time, space, interface and role constraints inherent in traditional strategic models" (pp. xvi-xvii).

Significance of Strategic Alliances

According to Lewis (1990), strategic alliance provides access to far more resources than any single firm owns or could buy. The firm can strengthen the following abilities:

- Create new products
- Reduce costs
- Bring in new technologies
- Penetrate other market
- Preempt competitors
- Reach the scale needed to survive in world markets
- Generate more cash to invest in core skills

Doz and Hamel (1998) pointed out the following three points as primary purposes of strategic alliances. I think these are not purposes but rather characters that effective alliance should possess.

- *Co-option.* Co-option is a kind of cooperative strategy with the potential competitors or complementors who offer complementary products/services. There are two purposes of co-option (Doz and Hamel, 1998).
  - Potential rivals are effectively neutralized as threats by bringing them into the alliance
  - Firms with complementary goods to contribute are wooed, creating network economies in favor of the coalition
- *Co-specialization.* Co-specialization is "the synergistic value creation that result from the combining of previously separate resources, positions, skills, and knowledge sources" (Doz and Hamel, 1998, p. 5).

  An alliance can be successful through the contribution of partners by offering their own unique and differentiated resources – skills, brands, relationships, positions, and tangible assets – with each other. When these resources are co-specialized and bundled together, these resources become more valuable and may create new value.

I think there are two types of synergistic effects: complementary and reinforced. Complementary synergy is obtained through the combination of different types of resources. Reinforced synergy is that which is reinforced by bundling the same type of resources.

- *Learning and Internalization.* Skills that are tacit, collective, and embedded are not easy to transfer to another organization. And core competencies are not exchanged in an open market. The only thing that you can do to get these skills and competencies is to learn from the partners of an alliance. Skills obtained from partners should be internalized and exploited beyond the boundaries of alliance.

In addition to the above, innovations such as new products/services, new processes, new technologies, and new knowledge, etc., which were created by interorganizational learning through the interactions of organizations should be added to the significance of strategic alliance.

In the industries where there are such strategic alliances, there is a lot of "collective competition" (Gomez-Casseres, 1996), which is the competition between/among the groups of a strategic alliance. It is also important that such collective competition promotes innovation.

In addition to the above, one of the purposes of a strategic alliance is in the risk reductions. There are risks such as loss of assets, decrease of income, responsibility of reparation, loss of personnel, and business risk (speculative risk), etc. Risk management for such risks are indispensable, and consists of risk control — risk avoidance, loss prevention, loss reduction, segregation, combination, and risk hedge — and risk finance — risk retention and risk hedge.

Although the appropriate method of risk management is in accordance with the kind of risk, type of strategic alliances, and situation which organizations confronted; in any case, it is apparent that sharing risk between/among parties in strategic alliance can reduce risk compared to the case that each party acts alone.

Classification of Strategic Alliance

Kanter and Myers (1991) examined particular kinds of interorganizational bonds (alliances) that emphasize the relationship aspect of the exchange as much as the goods or services being exchanged. And they classified such interorganizational bonds into following three major types:

- Multiorganization Services Alliances or Consortia
- The Opportunistic Joint Venture
- The Complementary or Stakeholder Partnership

Konsynski and McFarlan (1990) listed following four types of information partnerships:

- Joint Marketing Partnerships
- Intra-Industry Partnerships
- Customer-Supplier Partnerships
- IT Vendor-Driven Partnerships

Yoshino and Rangan (1995) carried out more minute classification. At first, they roughly divided inter-firm links into contractual agreement and equity arrangement. Then they broke down the former into traditional contracts—arm's-length buy/sell contracts, franchising, licensing and cross-licensing—and non-traditional contracts. On the other hand, they broke the latter into no new entity, creation of entity, and dissolution of entity. They also defined the non-traditional contracts, the no new equity, and the non-subsidiary joint ventures as the "strategic alliances."

Thus the strategic alliances are not inter-firm transactions in the market and also not internalization of the other firms, such as M&A, etc. They can be considered as loose-coupling inter-firm relationships that exist in the middle of the market and the firm.

Strategic Alliance Based on Core-Competence

What is Strategic Alliance Based on Core-Competence?

I will introduce a strategic alliance model based on "core competence" as one of the new models.

Core-competencies are not mere individual skills or technologies, but the integrated multiple streams of skills and technologies. They enhance customer value, differentiate from competitors, and strengthen capabilities of the firm (Hamel and Prahalad, 1994).

For example, SONY has a capacity to miniaturize electric appliances such as compact cassette tape recorders (Walkman), and Yamato Transport has an expertise of delivering goods everywhere in Japan within next day.

Strategic alliances based on core-competence are aiming at combined effectiveness of core-competence by being allied with partners with its own core-competence.

Classification of Strategic Alliances Based on Core-Competence

There are two types of core-competence linkage. One is the "heterogeneous alliance model" and the other is the "homogeneous alliance model" (Figure 3).

- Heterogeneous Alliance Model

  This model is alliances of organizations that have different functions of core-competence in IOR.

  It is divided into the "outsourcing model," which focal organizations consign their non-core-part to external specialists who have core-competence in such non-core-part; and the "network-based division of labor model," which two or more organizations that have different core-competencies get together and allocate each function in accordance with core-competence.

  These are types of gaining competitive advantage by complementing necessary core-competence with each other and can be called a "complemented alliance."

  - *Outsourcing Model*

  Generally, outsourcing is that organizations consign a certain part of their activities or functions to external specialists.

  In this model, the non-core part or functions shall be outsourced to the external specialists by contracts. Through the outsourcing, the organization can concentrate its resources into its core competence and make its activities more effective and efficient.

  Also, through shifting its paradigm from the "possession" to the "utilization" (or from "stock" to "flow") of the resources, the organization can reduce the inefficiency and the risks of possessing the full set of the assets.

Figure 3: Classification of Strategic Alliance Based on Core-Competence

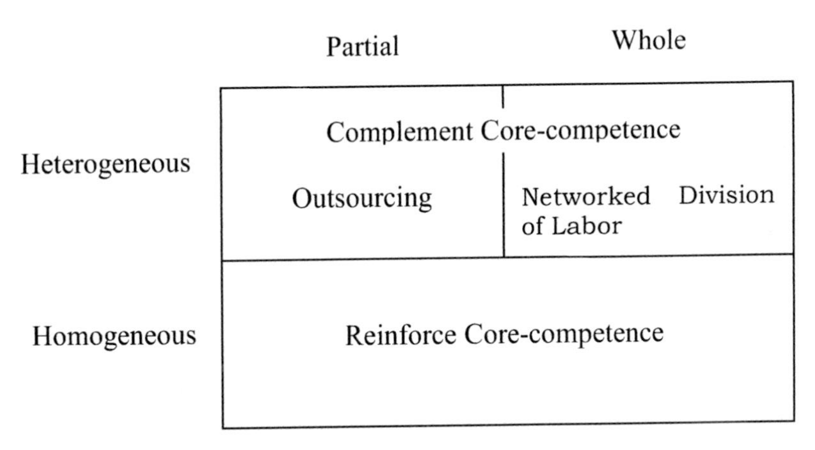

- Network-Based Division of Labor Model — Virtual Corporation Model
  In this model, two or more organizations share their core competence and share a series of the business processes, and act like a "virtual corporation" as a whole. Through the division of labor, the effectiveness and the efficiency of a "virtual corporation" can be improved.
  The members participate in the networks through reciprocal agreement, the contracts of memberships of the networks, or the contract with the leader of the networks. "Supply Chain Management" can be a sort of this model.
- Homogeneous Alliances Model
  Homogeneous alliance is that firms that have a similar core-competence organize for the purpose of reinforcing their core-competence, and thus it can be called a "reinforced alliance."
  In this model, for example, if one firm is not able to obtain a competitive advantage in the market by its own core-competence only, then it forms an alliance with other firms (those have similar core-competence) and strengthen their competitive advantage as a group of firms.
  On the other hand, there is an alliance for the purpose of expecting the effect of "co-option." This is a kind of strategy that one firm forms an alliance with current competitors or potential new entrants who have similar core-competence with a focal organization (Yamada and Arakawa, 1998) in order to reduce the competitiveness of its counterpart in the market — competitiveness of current competitors, bargaining power of suppliers, bargaining power of customers, threat of new entrance, and threat of substitute products or services (Porter, 1981).
  This model includes cartels, business cooperative associations in the same industry, joint ventures within the same industry, joint R & D, joint product development, joint manufacturing, joint marketing, and shared distribution services, etc.

INTERORGANIZATONAL NETWORKS

Networks and Interorganizational Networks

What are Networks?

Because the term "network" has broad meanings, it is very difficult to define precisely and perfectly. I use the term network in connection with the networks of organizations.

Rockart and Short (1991) stated that network concepts have been used primarily to study either inter- or intra-organizational activities. They listed seven key attributes of a network: shared goals, shared expertise, shared work, shared decision making, shared timing and issue prioritization, shared responsibility, accountability, and trust, and shared recognition and reward.

Therefore, these seven key attributes can be applicable to both the intra- and inter-organizational network.

Why Networks?

Lipnack and Stamps (1994) introduced five principles of organizing in the 21st century: the unifying purpose, the independent members, the voluntary links, the multiple leaders, and the integrated levels (Figure 4).

The traditional hierarchical organizations are not always effective at turbulent environments in the age of globalization and IT like today, and the "network organizations" with the above five principles can be one of the possible effective forms of organizations.

In the cooperative relationship, two or more organizations get together and formulate network(s); and there the above new principles can be effective. In this case, strategic alliances should be formulated between/among members.

What Shape Can ION Take?

Vertical Versus Horizontal

Imai (1984) classified the network into the vertical network (tightly connected, well-planned, and concentrated) and the horizontal network (loosely connected, self-organized, and decentralized).

Mechanistic Versus Organic

Network can be divided by character, such as mechanistic and organic. Burns and Stalker (1994) discovered there are two types of management systems: the mechanistic management system and the organic management system.

They stated that "a mechanistic management system is appropriate to stable conditions" (p. 119) and "the organic form is appropriate to changing conditions, which give rise constantly to fresh problems and unforeseen requirements for action which cannot be broken down or distributed automatically arising from the functional roles defined within a hierarchic structure" (p. 121). As for ION, mechanistic ION is suitable in a stable environment, and organic ION is suitable in a turbulent environment.

Homogeneous Versus Heterogeneous, or Complementary Versus Division of Labor

Network formulated by two or more organizations can be classified into the homogeneous network (members share the same function) and the heterogeneous network (members share a different function).

Figure 4: Five Key Organizing Principles for the 21st Century

Unifying Purpose	Purpose is the glue and the driver. *Common views, values, and goals hold a network together, A shared focus on desired results keeps a network in sync and on track.*
Independent Members	Independence is a prerequisite for interdependence. *Each member of the network, whether a person, company, or country, can stand on its own while benefiting from being part of the whole.*
Voluntary Links	Just add links. *The distinguishing feature of networks is their links, far more profuse and omnidirectional than in other types of organization. As communication pathways increase, people and groups interact more often. As more relationships develop, trust strengthens, which reduces the cost of doing business and generates greater opportunities.*
Multiple Leaders	Fewer bosses, more leaders. *Networks are leaderful, not leaderless. Each person or group in a network has something unique to contribute at some point in the process. With more than one leader, the network as a whole has great resilience.*
Integrated Levels	Networks are multilevel, not flat. *Lumpy with small groups and clustered with coalitions, networks involve both the hierarchy and the "lower-archy," which leads them to action rather than simply to making recommendation to others.*

Source: Lipnack, J. and Stamps, J. (1994). The Age of the Network: Organizing Principles for the 21st Century. New York: John Wiley. p. 18

The former is, for example, the joint R&D, or the cooperative distribution, etc. In this case, as each member carries out the same function in cooperation with others, the network(s) will be the "complementary network."

The latter is, for example, in the distribution channel. Each member — suppliers, manufactures, distributors, wholesalers, and retailers — carries out each function in the distribution process. This network will be called as the "division-of-labor network."

ION Model Based on Barnard's Theory

Barnard (1968) called "a complex of physical, biological, personal, and social components which are in a specific systematic relationship by reason of the cooperation of two or more persons for at least one definite end" (p. 65) a "cooperative system"; and a "system of consciously coordinated activities or forces of two or more persons" (p. 81) formal organization. And he listed communication, willingness to cooperate, and purpose, as the elements of formulating a formal organization.

Among them, communication is the first premise. It enables one to form and share the purpose, to induce the willingness to cooperate, and to enable the cooperative work.

The next subject he took up is on the elements for survival of organization: "organizational effectiveness" and "organizational efficiency."

Generally, effectiveness is considered as "the scale of matching the value or need of society and market" (Shimaguchi, 1986, p. 24), and efficiency is considered as "the scale of indicating the relationships between effort of input and effect of output" (Shimaguchi, 1986, p. 24).

Different from the general definition, on "effectiveness" and "efficiency" Barnard (1968) explained, "Accordingly we shall say that an action is effective if it accomplishes its specific objective aim. We shall also say it is efficient if it satisfies the motives of that aim, whether it is effective or not, and the process does not create offsetting dissatisfactions" (p. 20). According to his explanation, we can define effectiveness as "to what degree does organization achieve its purpose (or goal)" and efficiency as "to what degree does an individual satisfy his motivation of purpose." Organizational effectiveness is related to effectiveness and efficiency of the activities in organization. In this case, the terms effectiveness and efficiency shall be understood meaning as generally defined. Efficiency that Barnard defined is to what degree an individual satisfy his motivation of purpose; and we can call it "organizational satisfaction."

Morimoto (1985) illustrated the relationship between three elements of the formal organization, and the effectiveness of cooperation and the organizational efficiency (Figure 5).

He, at first, saw that the fundamental problem of organization is in the reciprocal-promotive progress of organizational effectives and organizational efficiency (or satisfaction). Organizational effectiveness is the degree of attainment of organizational purpose and its base is in organization structure. Organization structure is made of allocated tasks and a communication system that connects among tasks. A task is grasped in the unit of job or department and connected through formalized communication systems of authority and responsibility.

Once willingness of contribution of members as organizational personality is added to organization structure, and a certain communication is put into it, then organizational activity begins.

The outcome of organizational activity is organizational result. Organizational effectiveness is the degree of achievement of result compared to the initial purpose or goal. And the higher such effectiveness is, the better an organization can keep the balance with its environment.

An organizational result is also shared and distributed. As the result, it becomes an incentive of organizational members' willingness of contribution. The degree of satisfaction is organizational efficiency – the degree of satisfaction of individual purpose. And the higher such efficiency is, the better an organization can keep the balance with the individual.

Thus, an organization and its environment can keep good balance by organizational effectiveness, and the organization and the individual can keep good balance by organizational efficiency; then, an organization can survive.

In utilizing this model, the problem is whether a "member" of the interorganizational networks can be handled the same as a "person." or whether a "member" can be personalized or not.

Based on the general system theory, certain systems have sub-system components and are also a part of a supra-system. Thus, the general system has characteristics of hierarchy and whole-and-part (Kast and Rosenzweig, 1972). Using this theory, if we consider ION as organizations consisting of member organizations, then ION is a supra-system and member organization are subsystems; there is a recursive relationship in ION.

Thus, it can be explained by considering the relationships among ION, their members, and the persons in the members as the recursive relationship in the networks.

INTERORGANIZATIONAL NETWORKS AND IT

Interorganizational Communications and IT

Through Morimoto's illustration of Barnard's models, how IT is concerned with organization can be shown as Figure 5.

Communication plays the most important role in the entire ION. A communication system enables formulation and sharing of the purpose of network and willingness of cooperation between members of a network, and also has a function to harmonize by coordinating various activities among members of the network organization.

Furthermore, it furnishes information in order for each member organization to share organizational result and to acknowledge organizational effectiveness and efficiency.

As Simon (1976) pointed out, there are two types of communications in an organization: a formal system of communications and an informal network of communications, and to carry out interorganizational activities effectively, efficiently, and smoothly, an informal network of communications has to supplement the formal system of communications.

Figure 5: Elements and Problem Area of Ion and IT

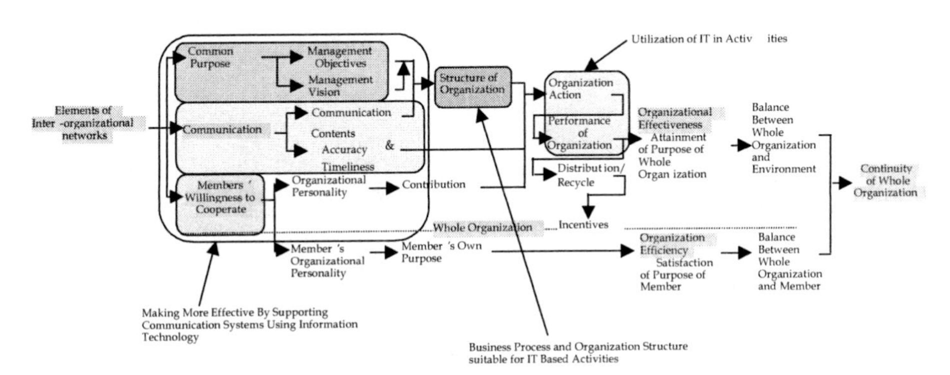

Source: Morimoto 1985. 7 with amendments of author

In ION, actual communications are made through boundary personnel in each member organization; in this case, both formal and informal communications are also indispensable.

Communication systems are made up of human communication systems and electronic communication systems, and work effectively when both human and electronic communication systems complementarily work together.

Simon (1976) listed oral communications, memoranda and letters, paper-flow, records and reports, and manuals as media for communication. But I will try to classify them in another viewpoint here. Communications consist of primary face-to-face communications and secondary other communications. I will classify them on the basis of time and place. If we make a matrix of time as the vertical axis and divide it into two—same time and different time—and place as the horizontal axis and divide it into two—same place and different place—then we will have four boxes: same time and same place, same time and different place, different time and same place, and different time and different place. And if we plot various procedures of communications in it, then we will have Figure 6.

Primary face-to-face communications (Nohria and Eccles, 1992) are indispensable for effective communications. The problem is how to transfer implicit nuances or even tacit information through secondary communications, though they may be transferable only through face-to-face communications.

Against this question, communications using hypertext, in which text, images, movie, and voice or sound, can be combined all-in-one are one answer. But in this case, the point is to what extent hypertext communications can realize the same function as face-to-face communications, and in order to enable them to do so, what kind of technologies are available and what technologies should be combined and utilized.

Of course, the best way of communication is:

- Each boundary personnel of member organizations gathers, shares place and time, and shares cognitive styles – or at least he has to understand what and how his counterpart thinks and acts, and further, make friendly relationships with him, if possible.
- In daily communications, he uses various media in human and electronic communications, including hypertext, in both formal and informal communications.
- To maintain good relationships, he periodically (or on occasion) has meetings with his counterpart, and confirms or reinforces what they are sharing.
- Towards intra-organizational personnel, boundary personnel also have to share place and time, make and keep good human relationships, and transfer information from boundary personnel of another organization to intra-organization personnel with necessary transformation in order to adjust cognitive difference between extra- and intra-personnel.

In addition, communication has both formatted and unformatted communication. In formatted communication, continuous and repeating daily transaction data is transferred. On the other hand, in unformatted communication, information that cannot be formatted is transferred in free format.

Anyhow, communication systems play a significant role in ION. However, when communication systems do not work well, the communication systems become constraints of ION.

Figure 6: Classification of Communication Measures (Examples)

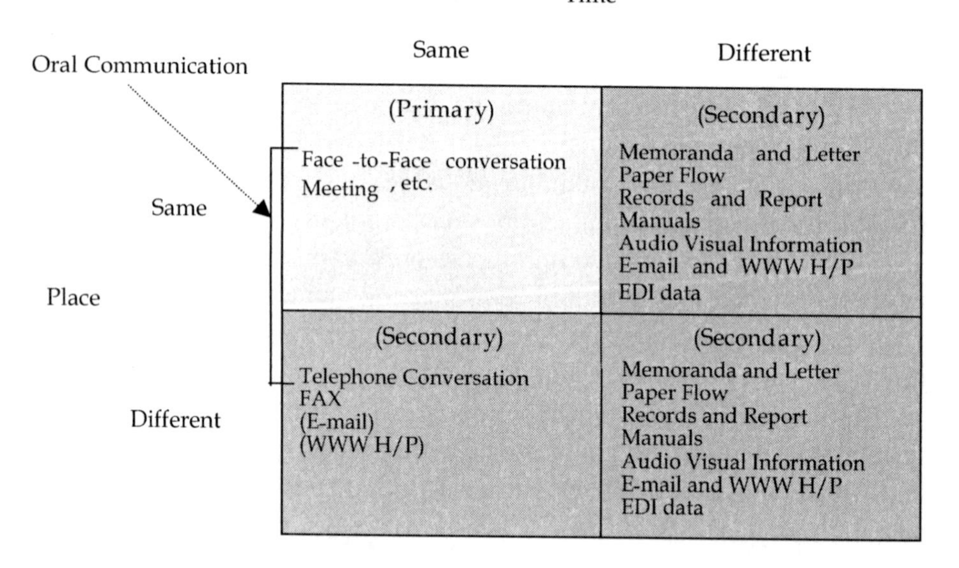

Especially, in ION, the organization culture of the member organization – which determines boundary personnel's way of thinking and doing — and intra-organizational network systems become constraints of ION. In order to solve these problems, face-to-face meetings between boundary personnel and standardization of communication protocols, both business and technical, etc., are necessary.

Johnston and Lawlence (1988) listed minicomputers and PCs with user-friendly languages, inexpensive general-purpose software packages, data standards and bar codes, information networking capabilities, computer-aided designs, and computer-aided manufacturing as new technological tools for creating a value-adding partnership.

INTERORGANIZATIONAL INFORMATION NETWORK SYSTEMS AND STANDARDIZATION

Today, the organizational environment is turbulent and its speed of change gets faster and the degree of change is greater. Under such a situation, IOR and ION cannot remain static. They are always changing dynamically. Therefore, interorganizational information network systems, which support ION, should meet such dynamic change.

Key to meeting this requirement is "standardization." Standardization of interorganizational information network system is that of platforms, application software, network protocols, and business protocols, etc. Standardization enables one to reduce switching costs of a network, and, although the effect of enclosure that the strategic information system aimed at is reduced, rearrangement of the network gets easier.

The problem is to what extent standardization should be carried out. Especially constraint of the best information system for specific business is specific business process and protocols. So, a fully standardized information system is not optimal for a specific business environment. In the light of effectiveness and efficiency, such a system tends to specialization.

In open-edi, which is not limited to specific customers, minimum standardization is carried out in order to enhance the generality of a system, and required parts for trade of specific customers are added on to a standardized system.

In considering an interorganizational information network system, in case IOR is in a turbulent environment and frequent rearrangement is needed, the level of standardization should be of infrastructure in order that the interorganizational information network system may have flexibilities. On the contrary, in case IOR is in a stable environment and frequent rearrangement is not needed, the level of standardization should be carried out to the level suitable for specific business.

By the way, considering security control of an information network system, in ION, situations such as "yesterday's friend is today's enemy, or vise versa" often happen; so timely and precise measures of access control should be taken. Quick alteration of passwords, access rights, and encryption rules, etc., should be modified in accordance with the rearrangement of dynamically changing ION.

FUTURE TRENDS

Development of Utilization of IT in Organization and Impact to ION

Utilization of IT in organization has been advancing and diffusing, with the progress of IT.

Tapscott and Caston (1993) explained about advancement of IT utilization in organization with a concept of "three critical shifts in the application of information technology" (pp. 14-18). The first shift is from personal to work-group computing; the second shift is from system islands to integrated systems; and the third shift is from internal to inter-enterprise computing. They listed eight technical shifts that enable the above three shifts: from traditional semiconductors to microprocessor-based systems, from host-based to network-based systems, from vendor proprietary software to open software standards, from single to multimedia (data, text, voice, and image), from account control to computer vendor-customer partnerships based on free will, software development from craft to factory, from alphanumeric to graphical, multiform user interface, and from stand-alone to integrated software applications.

Vekatraman (1991) pointed out that the role of IT in organization is shifting from a traditional supportive role to an emerging strategic role, and advocated "five levels of IT-induced reconfiguration" (pp. 127-128): localized exploitation, internal integration, business process redesign, business network redesign, and business scope redefinition.

According to him, these five levels of reconfiguration of business are that the higher the level is, the greater the degree of reconfiguration, and the broader the scope of potential benefit.

While localized exploitation and internal integration are piecemeal improvement, business process redesign, business network redesign, and business scope redefinition are reconfiguration of business at revolutionary level.

In ION, when we investigate how to utilize IT for effective and efficient business activities in order to compete and win in the competition among IONs, it is effective that we consider how we shall formulate competitive strategies in ION through utilization of IT, and reconfigures business in ION with IT.

Interorganizational Strategies Using IT

As aforementioned, Gomez-Casseres (1996) pointed out this "collective competition" between/among IONs. In order to meet such competition, IOR has to have its competitive strategies. There are three options that IOR can take using IT: effectiveness of existing business, efficiencies of existing business, and creating new business. A key concept of all these options is innovation. It has two dimensions: innovation of new products/services and that of new business processes.

Usually ERP and SCM are carried out for efficient operations or activities through "the best practice" of the industry. It is a kind of standardization based on the best practice, and only a necessary condition for survival. In order to win at the competition, a sufficient condition shall be satisfied; otherwise such competition will be an endless cost-reduction-race.

Therefore, prior to the introduction of ERP or SCM, existing business models should be reexamined and redesigned for sustainable competitive advantage. In other words, an innovation of business models or business processes is required as a sufficient condition.

As for "innovation," knowledge management systems shall play a very important role. In ION, it is the important theme how ION manages and enhances the collective knowledge of each member organization through utilizing IT support.

CONCLUSION

In interorganizational relationships (IOR), competition, neutrality, and cooperation are major types of relationships. These relationships are changeable in accordance with the situation. Organization grows up through competition and cooperation, or sometimes through natural selection. Competition and cooperation bring social interaction among elements in IOR, and interorganizational learning through social interactions bears innovation.

Strategic alliance is one cooperative relationship. It loosely connects relationships with organizations. It enables one to form agile and flexible IOR. Strategic alliance of organizations operates in the form of ION.

In this chapter, I considered ION as one of the systems, and tried to understand through Barnard's theory of cooperative system and formal organization.

Though there are various types of strategic alliances and ION, communications play a significant role for them to work effectively. Communication systems create purpose and willingness of members to cooperate, and coordinate interorganizational activities in ION as "organization of organizations." Communication systems consist of a human communication system and an electronic one. Both communication systems should work complementarily together.

Communications in ION are made through boundary personnel, whose cognitive style is usually different from his counterpart's because of the difference of organization culture he belongs to. For this reason, it is not sufficient to communicate only through secondary communication by electronic media, etc. The first thing that boundary personnel have to do is to promote mutual understandings with his counterpart by sharing place and time with him and through primary face-to-face communication, which can convey implicit nuance, tacit information, etc. On the other hand, in electronic communication, hypertext may be a powerful media. The problem is how shall we utilize this media effectively and efficiently.

As IT progresses, utilization of it is also developing. As utilization expands to ION, the way business should be or even the way ION itself should be has to be reexamined. Redesign of business and/or ION should be needed for their effectiveness and/or efficiency.

In order for ION to fit for a dynamically changeable environment, interorganizational information network systems, which support ION, should be also adaptable to such change. For the purpose of such a requirement, "standardization" is a key concept. A standardized open network environment, standardized business process and business protocol, and standardized information processing environment and applications, etc., are necessary.

But the problem is that a system tends to be specialized because network needs to meet specific conditions in order to enhance the effectiveness and efficiency of a network as the alliance of ION gets firm. To solve this problem, to what extent standardization should be made is the important theme. Levels of standardization should be decided in accordance with the necessity of rearrangement of ION.

In connection with this matter, information security measures should also be dynamic in order to meet the rearrangement of business process and ION timely and precisely.

In this chapter, I referred to interorganizational relationships, strategic alliance as cooperative relationships, interorganizational networks, and information technologies in interorganizational networks. Among them, on the last subject, I examined a communication system based on Barnard's theory.

However, in an interorganizational network, there is the dimension that interorganizational learning through social interactions among member organizations bears innovation — creating new resources, products and services, and markets for sustainable competitive advantage. And in this dimension, study about interorganizational knowledge management systems is indispensable.

ENDNOTES

1 Child and Faulkner (1998) listed four categories of perspectives for IOR: economics, game theory, strategic-management theory, and organization theory. In addition, they broke economics down into market-power theory, transaction theory, agency theory, and increasing-return theory; and also broke organization theory down into resource dependence and organization of alliance.

2 In MIT's research program on the management in the 1990s, Scott Morton (1991) listed the following six major findings of the research:
   - IT is enabling fundamental changes in the way work is done
   - IT is enabling the integration of business function at all levels within and between organizations
   - IT is causing shifts in the competitive climate in many industries
   - IT presents new strategic opportunities for organizations that reassess their missions and operations
   - Successful application of IT will require changes in management and organizational structure
   - A major challenge for management in the 1990s will be to lead their organizations through the transformation necessary to prosper in the globally competitive environment

3 Hall (1991) took up "general environment characteristics" as an important element of the framework for IOR analysis. Based on Aldrich's research (1979) on important dimensions of general environment, he listed turbulence, environmental complexity, homogeneous-heterogeneous, environmental capacity, stability-instability, and concentration- dispersion, as important dimensions of general environment

4 Evan (1966) introduced the concept of "organization sets" as the framework for IOR analysis by adopting Merton's role sets (1957) to IOR. He illustrated the relationships between organizations by using three basic elements: focal organization, input organization sets (supply resources to focal organization), and output organization sets (receive products from focal organization).

5 In this chapter, I use Porter's "forces driving industry competition" (1981) for an analytical framework of competition, and the concept of "strategic alliance" (Lewis 1990, 1995; Yoshino and Rangan, 1995; Gomez-Casseres, 1996;

Doz and Hamel 1998) for analytical framework of cooperation. By the way, Yamada and Arakawa (1988) introduced the strategic alliance as a strategy for neutralizing competitors by using Porter's above models.

[6] Brandenburger and Nalebuff (1997) created "Value-net" as a tool for analyzing relationships, and illustrated the relationships among the focal organization and its stakeholders. Generally these relationships consist of five parties: the focal firm, its suppliers, customers, competitors, and complementors. They regarded such competition and cooperation in the market as the "game," and listed players, added values, rules, tactics, and scope as five elements of the game (called "PARTS" by taking the capital letter of the name of each tools). And they analyzed the game of competition and cooperation in the market through various case studies.

REFERENCES

Aldrich, R. D. (1979). *Organizations and Environment.* Englewood Cliffs, NJ: Prentice Hall.

Barnard, C. I. (1968). *The Functions of the Executive Thirties Anniversary Edition.* Cambridge, MA: Harvard University Press

Brandenburger, A. M. and Nalebuff, B. J. (1996) *Co-opetition.* New York: Currency Doubleday.

Burns, T. and Stalker, G. M. (1994). *The Management of Innovation* – Revised Edition. New York: Oxford University Press.

Caplow, T. (1964). *Principles of Organization.* New York: Harcourt Brace Jovanovich.

Child, J. and Faulkner, D. (1998). *Strategies of Co-operation – Managing Alliances, Networks, and Joint Ventures.* New York: Oxford University Press.

Dill, W. R. (1958). Environment as an Influence on Managerial Autonomy. *Administrative Science Quarterly,* 2, 409-43.

Doz, Y. L. and Hamel, G. (1998). *Alliance Advantage – The Art of Creating Value through Partnering.* Boston, MA: Harvard Business School Press.

Evan, W. (1966). The Organization Set: Toward a Theory of Interorganizational Relations. In James Thompson (Ed.), *Approaches to Organizational Design* (pp. 173-18). Pittsburgh, PA: University of Pittsburgh Press.

Gomez-Casseres, B. (1996). *The Alliance Revolution – The New Shape of Business Rivalry.* Boston, MA: Harvard Business School Press.

Hall, R. H. (1991). *Organizations – Structures, Processes, & Outcomes* (5th ed.). Englewood Cliffs, NJ: Prentice Hall.

Hamel, G. and Prahalad, C. K. (1994). *Competing for The Future*. Boston, MA: Harvard Business School Press.

Imai, K. (1984). *Network Shakai* (Japanese). Tokyo, Japan: Iwanami Shoten.

Johnston and Lawlence. (1988, July-August). Beyond Vertical Integration: The Rise of the Value-Adding Partnership. *Harvard Business Review*.

Kanter, R. M. and Myers, P.S. (1991). Interorganizational Bonds and Intraorganizational Behavior: How Alliances and Partnerships change the Organizations Forming Them. In Amitai Etzioni and Paul R. Lawrence (Eds.), *Socio-Economics: Toward a New Synthesis* (pp. 329-344). Armonk, NY: M. E. Sharp.

Kast, F. E. and Rosenzweig, J. E. (1972, December). General System Theory: Applications for Organizations and Management. *Academy of Management Journal,* pp. 447-65.

Konsynski, B. R. and McFarlan, E. W. (1990, September-October). Information Partnerships – Shared Data, Shared Scale. *Harvard Business Review*, 114-120.

Levine, S. and White, P.E. (1961). Exchange as a Conceptual Framework for the Study of Interorganizational Relationships. *Administrative Science Quarterly, 5*, 583-601.

Lewis, J. D. (1990). *Partnerships For Profit – Structuring and Managing Strategic Alliances.* New York: The Free Press.

Lewis, J. D. (1995). *The Connected Corporation – How Leading Companies Win Through Customer-Supplier Alliances.* New York: The Free Press.

Lipnack, J. and Stamps, J. (1994). *The Age of The Network – Organizing Principles for the 21st Century.* New York: John Wiley & Sons.

Litwak, E. and Hylton, L.F. (1962). Interorganizational Analysis: A Hypothesis on Coordinating Agencies. *Administrative Science Quarterly, 6*, 395-426.

Merton, R. K. (1968). *Social Theory and Social Structure* (1968 Enlarged Edition). New York: The Free Press.

Moore, J. F. (1993, May/June). Predators and Prey: A New Ecology of Competition. *Harvard Business Review*, 75-86.

Morimoto, M. (1985). Keiei Sochiki Sosetsu. In Mitsuo Morimoto (Ed.), Keiei Soshiki (Japanese) (pp. 1-20). Tokyo, Japan: Chyuo Keizaisha.

Nohria, N. and Eccles, R. G. (1992). Face-to-Face: Making Network Organizations Work. In Nittin Nohria and Robert G. Eccles (Eds.), *Networks and Organization: Structure, Form, and Action* (p. 228-308). Boston, MA: Harvard Business School Press.

Nonaka, I. (1985). Kigyou Sinkaron – Joho Sozo No Management (Japanese). Tokyo, Japan: Nihon Keizai Shinbunsha.

Nonaka, I. (1991, November-December). The Knowledge Creating Company. *Harvard Business Review*, 65-77.

Nonaka, I. and Takeuchi, H. (1995). *The Knowledge Creating Company: How Japanese Companies Created the Dynamics of Innovation.* New York: Oxford University Press.

Normann, R. and Ramirez, R. (1993, July-August). From Value Chain to Value Constellation: Designing Interactive Strategy. *Harvard Business Review*, 65-77.

Normann, R. and Ramirez, R. (1994). *Designing Interactive Strategy: From Value Cain to Value Constellation*. New York: John Wiley & Sons.

Pfeffer, J. and Salancik, G. R. (1978). *The External Control of Organizations: A Resource Dependence Perspective.* New York: Harper & Row.

Pine II, B. J. (1993). *Mass Customization: The New Frontier in Business Competition.* Boston, MA: Harvard Business School Press.

Porter, M.E. (1981). *Competitive Strategy – Techniques for Analyzing Industries and Competitors.* New York: The Free Press.

Porter, M.E. (1985). *Competitive Advantage–Creating and Sustaining Superior Performance.* New York: The Free Press.

Rockart, J. F. and Short, J. E. (1991). The Networked Organization and the Management of Interdependence. In Michael S. Scott-Morton (Eds.), *The Corporation of the 1990s: Information Technology and Organizational Transformation* (pp. 189-219). New York: Oxford University Press.

Scott-Morton, M. S. (1991). Introduction. In Michael S. Scott-Morton (Ed.), *The Corporation of The 1990s – Information Technology and Organizational Transformation* (pp. 3-23). New York: Oxford University Press.

Segil, L. (1996). *Intelligent Business Alliances: How to Profit Using Today's Most Important Strategic Tool*. New York: Random House.

Shimaguchi, M. (1986). Togo Marketing: Hozetsu Jidai no Shijyo Shikoteki Keiei (Japanese). Tokyo, Japan: Nihon Keizai Shinbunsha.

Simon, H. A. (1976). *Administrative Behavior: A Study of Decision-Making Processes in Administrative Organization* (3rd Ed.) New York: The Free Press.

Tapscott, D. and Caston, A. (1993). *Paradigm Shift: The Now Promise of Information Technology.* New York: McGraw-Hill.

Van de Ven, A. H. and Ferry, D. L. (1980). *Measuring and Assessing Organizations.* New York: John Wiley & Sons.

Venkatraman, N. (1991). IT-Induced Business Reconfiguration. In Michael S. Scott-Morton (Ed.), *The Corporation of The 1990s – Information Tech-*

nology and Organizational Transformation (pp. 122-158). New York: Oxford University Press.

Yamada, K. (2002). Inter-Organizational Relationship and Networks. In Mehdi Khosrow-Pour (Ed.), *Issues and Trends of Information Technology, Management in Contemporary Organization, Vol 1.* Hershey, PA: Idea Group.

Yamada, K. and Arakawa, M.. (1998) "A framework for modeling business networks—focusing on market dominance. *9th International Conference of Comparative Management: New Waves in Contemporary Management.* Kaohsiung, Taiwan: National Sun Yat-Sen University, 133-145.

Yoshino, M. and Rangan, U. S. (1995). *Strategic Alliances: An Entrepreneurial Approach to Globalization.* Boston, MA: Harvard Business School Press.

Chapter XVII

The Internationalization Efforts of Small Internet Retailers

Anand Ramchand
National University of Singapore, Singapore

Shan-Ling Pan
National University of Singapore, Singapore

ABSTRACT

For the Internet retailers that have managed to dominate through the dot.com fallout, the next step for many is to leverage the technology to expand their operations to a regional or global customer base. However, the internationalization of e-tail differs significantly from traditional retail because of the compounding effect of the Internet, and empirical studies are deficient in the field. This chapter studies the internationalization efforts of three small Internet retail enterprises, highlighting the issues they faced in expanding their operations to service an international customer base. The study reveals their insights and experiences in terms of access to foreign markets, infrastructure considerations, and localization strategies. Through an understanding of these issues, it is hoped that further research will shed light into the intricate relationship between internationalization and Internet retail and the factors that influence it.

INTRODUCTION

Technology has always been a key enabler of change in retailing. The Internet, in particular, has played a vital role as an enabler in the adoption and execution of global business strategies. It is relatively unheard of these days to find an organization that has not established some form of online presence. After all, the Internet has affected many fundamentals of business: the structure of value chains, payment mechanisms, the speed and efficiency of the supply chain, fulfillment and delivery execution, inventory management, the retail store, customer service, and consumer expectations (Hopping, 2000). In particular, the worldwide proliferation and advances in Internet and e-commerce technologies have led to new paradigms in retailing. Power has shifted from the retailer to increasingly demanding consumers, who are further changing the face of retail by rapidly adopting the Internet into their mainstream.

This global growth of Internet usage and e-commerce technologies has led to greater opportunities for consumers and retailers worldwide. For consumers, the availability of detailed and relevant information, ease of use, convenience of access, added variety, and lower product, transaction, and search costs, warrant the use of the Internet as a medium for shopping. Likewise, for retailers the relative ease of setting up shop, lower overhead, property, and stock-keeping costs, the ability to disintermediate, and the global reach to consumers justify the decision to adopt the Internet as a channel or medium for retail (Kalakota and Whinston, 1996; Turban, Lee, King and Chung, 1999; Rosen and Howard, 2000).

For the many Internet retailers (e-tailers) that have managed to hold their own on the Internet, one of the next opportunities is to increase their reach. The use of the Internet eliminates geographical boundaries, and the lure of cheap and easy access to an expanding Internet customer base is too great an opportunity to ignore. Statistics (IDC, 2000; Ernst and Young, 2001) indicate international Internet users do not only purchase certain goods online, but also are willing and able to do so from foreign e-tailers as well. Organizations that do not market to international users are ignoring potential revenue streams. Furthermore, internationalization can be a strategic necessity, due to local and global competitive pressures, as well. Locally successful e-tailers must, therefore, begin to consider the importance of the global market in their operations, if they wish to continue to grow.

However, the internationalization of retail on the Internet can be tricky, and demands more than simply extending fulfillment structures. Corporate hesitation toward internationalization, because of implementation difficulties, has been one of the key barriers to more companies going global (IDC, 2000). Moving into foreign markets can be just as complicated for e-tailers as it is for traditional retailers. A sound internationalization strategy for Internet retailers should incorporate the relevant elements of the external and foreign environment, as well as consider a critical microscopic view of internal operations, to efficiently function on a global scale.

Literature pertaining to the adoption of global Internet strategies in retail is relatively deficient. While a vast amount of literature exists on Internet retail, and business literature on the internationalization of operations is abundant, Yip (2000) calls for a need to understand both Internet and globalization strategies ***together***, rather than separately, because "the impact of the Internet is more multiplicative than additive" (p. 1).

This chapter attempts to explore the issues pertinent to the internationalization of Internet-enabled retail by small Internet retail enterprises and investigate how these e-tailers are expanding their operations across national boundaries. Three case studies were conducted with competing Singaporean e-tailers to examine the various strategies in their expansion to international operations. This exploratory study draws attention to implications for future research by focusing on the commonalities across the cases and does not deal with any specific hypotheses.

BACKGROUND

Internet Retail and the Need to Internationalize

Emerging technologies have fundamentally changed many of the transaction-based and value-adding retail activities, and are moving them into cyberspace (Shaw, Blanning, Strader, and Whinston, 2000). Retailers are recognizing how Internet-empowered strategies can be used to deliver the set of attributes demanded by the changing customer, and are redesigning their business models to gain a competitive advantage. Katros (2000) describes the emerging trends and best practices of retailers in adopting Internet technologies, such as dynamic merchandising, targeted selling, ubiquitous retailing, and multi-channel retailing.

Internet retailing is driven by a number of benefits to both the retailer and the consumer, including the access to a more affluent customer base, lower information dissemination, and transaction costs, broader market reach, increased customer service, additional feedback channels, and access to consumer and market research (Auger and Gallaugher, 1997). The Internet has, therefore, become a strategic and critical medium and channel for retailers.

The widespread use of the Internet has affected the globalization drivers in many industries, thus having a direct affect on any organization's global strategies and operations (Yip, 2000). Various market, cost, governmental, and competitive factors drive the trend for organizations to internationalize. These include global customers and channels, economies of scale and scope, favorable logistics and trade policies, and competition from global organizations (Kuhn, 2000). The proliferation of the Internet internationally has accelerated the effect of these drivers. For instance, the Internet enables customers to be global, supports global marketing, exploits cost differences between countries, side steps trade barriers, and increases a commonality in consumer demands across countries (Yip, 2000).

Organizations need to adapt to these changes innovatively to survive. The Internet has made it easier for organizations to infiltrate global markets by enabling an instant global reach and global marketing. Furthermore, the Internet enables easier competitor monitoring, quick response, and effective inter-organizational linkages (Yip, 2000).

Multinational Strategies

Business studies dictate four strategic approaches to internationalization, varied on the symbiosis between the need to maintain responsiveness and gain a competitive advantage in a local setting, and the need to integrate across business processes and activities to obtain a competitive advantage globally (Griffin and Pustay, 1998; Kuhn, 2000). The *international* strategy utilizes a firm's core competency as a competitive weapon in foreign markets. The *multi-domestic* firm operates with independent subsidiaries, each focused on a particular domestic market, free to customize its product and strategies to the needs of the local customer. The *global* strategy views the world as a single marketplace, and strives to create standardized goods and services that will meet the needs of customers worldwide. A *transnational* strategy seeks to combine the benefits of global-scale efficiencies with the benefits of local responsiveness.

Internet retailing literature is riddled with studies on the trade-off between online-only retailing (*pure play*) and physical retailing (*brick-and-mortar*). Otto and Chung (2000) discuss the use of *cyber-enhanced retailing* to provide additional customer value and satisfaction by leveraging e-commerce technologies and the traditional shopping experience. However, many traditional brick-and-mortar retailers fear cannibalism of existing channels with the adoption of Internet strategies (Chen and Leteney, 2000). While early adopters hypothesize the exploitation of established brand names, physical infrastructure and distribution, and logistic networks to nourish e-tail success (Pottruck and Pearce, 2000), statistics and theory have yet to substantiate the claim. Birch, Gerbert and Schneider (2000) perceive synergies between established retailers and their Web sites to be fewer than anticipated, while the obstacles facing these organizations are substantially greater. Holistically, e-tailers who wish to succeed at global e-tail must find the correct balance between global integration of their operations and responsiveness to local consumer demands, while maintaining successful Web, or a combination of Web and physical, strategies.

However, studies relating to the issues faced by e-tailers adopting global strategies are lacking. Farhoomand, Tuunainen, and Yee (2000) identify many issues in global electronic commerce and propose a framework for classifying these issues into *technical, cultural/political, economic, legal and organizational* issues. However, as none of the case companies in the study were in the retail industry, it is motivating to take a closer look at Internet retailers.

Case Backgrounds

The three case companies provided a unique opportunity to conduct a study as each company stemmed from a spectrum of backgrounds, and each adopted distinct strategies in its e-tail and expansion approaches. Data was collected primarily from 13 semi-structured interviews with key personnel at the top and middle management levels in the companies in late 2000 and early 2001. Further data regarding the cases was accumulated from documentary evidence such as press releases and news and business reports. The interviews and documentation provided rich contextual data that is briefly summarized in following sections.

Company A is an Internet company that utilizes retail as a supporting function to its core consulting activities. Striving to be a knowledge resource for its customers, its online retail activities are the essence of the organization's services. The retailer operates on an online basis only, but a supporting physical office in Singapore acts as the organizational headquarters and service point for its local customers.

The company began its operations in 2000, and consists of 20 full-time employees, with 40 temporary *virtual* employees and partners situated worldwide. These virtual employees provide much-needed and necessary information and expertise of markets around the world. While the organization does not have its roots in its retail industry, it is privately funded by individuals and headed by a core management group with strong backgrounds in e-commerce.

The Web site aims to operate globally, not turning down deliveries to most parts of the world, e.g., its occasional orders from Vietnam and the U.S. However, because the organization has not marketed itself internationally, it has received few international orders. The company's strategy is to establish a critical mass in Singapore and use this as a test bed, while marketing itself aggressively in high-growth countries around Asia, including Malaysia and China, and eventually into the U.S. in the future.

Company B is owned by a large multinational conglomerate with a diverse business background in telecommunication and manufacturing. To reinvent itself for the digital economy, the conglomerate spawned a virtual retailer in Singapore, believing the country has a large growth potential in its retail industry.

Also launched in 2000, the online retail company aims to transform the attitude of online shoppers by providing a personalized and enriching shopping experience, and by enhancing its customer service to exceptional standards. Headquartered in Singapore, the pure play e-tailer operates with a nucleus management team of seven, and another 16 full-time employees.

The e-tailer operates in three countries — Australia, Singapore, and Malaysia — and prides itself on its price competitiveness, value proposition, and high standards of customer service and satisfaction. The company markets itself aggressively in all three countries, emphasizing on branding. Striving to remain virtual, the organization does not have any physical infrastructure in place, apart from its headquarters in Singapore, and a fulfillment centre each in Malaysia and Australia.

The organization is researching possible countries in the region to expand its operations, while trying to shorten delivery cycles, capture greater market share, and improve fulfillment.

Company C is owned by an organization with a relatively long history in retailing in the Asia-Pacific region. With many retail stores in countries around the region, the organization reinvented its strategies to deal with consumer demands. In 2000, it launched an online subsidiary of its retail outlets to fulfill the need for an e-tail channel.

The e-tailer subsidiary operates with a workforce of 60 employees in various functional departments, and maintains a strong but independent relationship with its parent company, operating with a synergistic *click-and-mortar* strategy. The e-tailer works closely with the network of physical stores around the region to promote its activities, to provide a personalized shopping experience and exceptional customer service, and to leverage off the existing distribution and fulfillment capabilities.

The e-tailer mainly serves customers from Singapore, Malaysia and Indonesia, but is technically and logistically capable of fulfilling global orders. It is attempting to establish itself in other countries around Asia — particularly China, the Philippines, India, and Thailand — through strategic partnerships and co-marketing.

DISCUSSION

The case companies revealed a multitude of viewpoints and considerations in their efforts to expand their operations regionally and globally. All three companies have adopted some form of internationalization strategy, varied along their strategies and needs for global integration and local responsiveness. The strategic issues identified from the experiences of these e-tailers have been classified into the following categories: **market access**, **infrastructure** and **localization**.

Market Access

The case companies identified access into a foreign market as a key issue, as well as gaining appropriate and relevant market information for their e-tailing needs. The companies approached this issue in a variety of ways, including forming strategic partnerships with in-country companies, which can ease the transition into a foreign market, as well as increase the efficiency of operations, while providing an e-tailer with a sustained source of information. A physical retail outlet location in the country would also serve that purpose, while providing an organizational presence, generating consumer awareness and confidence.

In adopting a global strategy, an executive from Company A found that "the biggest issue is market access and the unique value proposition." The company believes the first step is to find partners in foreign markets that can provide relevant market intelligence, allowing them to ultimately decide if the location is suitable for access, and then to slowly customize their Web site and operations to incorporate the new market. "We're going to establish partnerships with partners doing very focused work…our next target is to offer local currencies for these countries and use these partners to do our marketing."

Company B leverages off its parent company's international market experience and information to launch e-tail capabilities in Australia and Malaysia. The fulfillment centers in these countries play critical roles in acquiring sustained market information: "They should know the local conditions better than us, so we rely on them for a lot of market feedback and reports. We are dependent on them to a large extent — without their eyes and ears on the ground, we're operating fairly blind."

However, the company still finds difficulties in planning access to new markets, given its organizational objectives. "Each individual country's market is different. We'd like to use the same model — all this takes a lot of time."

To avoid start-up and promotion costs, Company C extended its influence in China through a series of strategic partnerships — first by investing in leading operators in the same industry, then by creating a strategic alliance to establish itself through joint marketing and co-branding. The partnership will, in effect, optimize the company's opportunities in China, reduce start-up and access risks, and enable the company to leverage off existing and established physical and online networks, domain knowledge, and market information.

The global e-tailer would find many advantages from forming strategic alliances with in-country partners to help minimize and handle the effects and complexities of communications with a new language and culture, local laws, financial issues; and to also provide an avenue for the e-tailer to monitor what happens after the transaction occurs in that country. Partners can provide quick and reliable market access information. E-tailers can adopt strategies with suitable local partners, such as co-branding, or can merge with or acquire the local partner as well. However, in choosing a partner, e-tailers need to ensure the partners have sufficient financial and personnel resources, demonstrated success, a willingness to form a partnership, familiarity with the e-tailer's practices, and knowledge about the obstacles to the e-tailer. The partner should also have good reach and reputation. Only then will the e-tailer be able to gain insight and access into the new market, and effectively localize itself at a more rudimentary level. Company A selects partners based on these: "The criteria is that they have something that is complementary with us, and they share the same vision with us, same passion, and certainly have very good knowledge about their markets."

Infrastructure

The issue of pure play and click-and-mortar retail modes frequently surfaced in each company's internationalization strategies. Would a physical outlet be critical in a foreign market regardless of its existence in the local market? The issue was reliant on two factors: the function played by the physical outlet, and the supply chain and logistics capabilities of the e-tailer. Companies A and B rely strongly on a virtual strategy, the advantages of unlimited "shelf space," and low infrastructural costs and risks. Company C, on the other hand, claims success with a multi-channel perspective.

Company A operates on a completely electronic JIT (just-in-time) strategy. The moment an order is placed on their Web site, it is placed electronically to the closest supplier worldwide and delivered via courier to the customer. The electronic integration with suppliers is deemed as a critical factor in increasing efficiency and lowering operating costs significantly. In effect, Company A does not maintain any warehouses, nor does it carry any inventory, keeping its operating expenses low. Furthermore, the electronic integration speeds up order processing, and ensures the flexibility needed to change processes easily. The organization believes this is sufficient at this point of time, using its partners to handle customer access. However, in moving full-scale into a foreign market, it believes the physical location is imperative. "We could use our partners' addresses to handle access for us. But when we're ready to move into other countries, we'd certainly need the physical office space. How else would we support our customers?"

Although Company B does not utilize a completely electronic logistics and supply chain, it is not convinced that a physical infrastructure is necessary. "Rental for a retail outlet is exorbitant, and there's never any guarantee that the location would be profitable...and then if inventory gets damaged, lost or outdated, you have to write it off. [The warehouse] has to be well-maintained and air-conditioned. And that's expensive — just the day-to-day operations cost is too expensive." However, the issue partly lies in the organization's priorities and implementation. Company B believes in minimizing physical asset costs and passing the savings on to the consumer. Its physical infrastructure in Australia and Malaysia act as points for reverse logistics, order consolidation and breaking bulk, with minimal staff at each location.

Company C, on the other hand, operates in synergy with its existing physical retail outlets around Asia to provide promotions on Web site activities, personalized customer support, and an access point for customer service. "Our offline and online integration offer our customers avenues to reach us. The physical and virtual businesses are inter-dependent for us. Without the physical facilities, we can't do the fulfillment, customer service and offer the warm human touch... We have counters at the physical stores to help our online customers who choose to pick up their [orders] or make exchanges." One executive attributes the lack of cannibalism to a close relationship between the physical and online stores: "Channel conflict is not an issue at all. We are after all the same shop and there's profit sharing between the two operations."

An internationalization strategy requires that e-tailers consider the implementation of physical infrastructure in the foreign markets. Offline assets affect customer service, branding, reverse logistics, and warehousing functions. With a physical store, shoppers can enjoy the ability to see, touch, and try merchandise and have instant gratification on purchases, and the ability to interact with in-store personnel (Rao, 1999; Calkins, Farello, and Shi, 2000). E-tailers adopting a click-and-mortar approach must find synergies between their Web sites and stores in each country, as well as customer service.

However, the economic issues of a physical infrastructure pose a large tradeoff, as does the issue of channel management and cannibalism (Katz and Rothfeder, 2000). Considering these issues, e-tailers must decide on an approach in each foreign market. Leveraging off a partner in a foreign market may provide the e-tailer with a "best-of-both-worlds" solution. However, finding a capable strategic partner may be difficult. In the case of Company A, it does not deal with many distributors for the sole reason that they lack sophisticated system integration capabilities. Similarly, for Company B, its supply chain is not electronically integrated because "some of [the suppliers] do not even use e-mail, how on earth would we integrate systems?"

Localization

Each e-tailer faced difficulties customizing their strategies, Web sites and systems to foreign market conditions. Economic, political, and cultural considerations, as well as localized content and technical implementations, have to co-exist harmoniously with the e-tailer's unique value proposition for success.

An executive from Company A expresses the importance of a unique value proposition: "What is unique about your product establishes you, and who you reach out to effectively." In providing value to a customer, the organization stresses on the importance of localization of Web site content, including currencies displayed on the Web storefront and the language used. "We can view over 30 currencies right away. The key thing is the localization of the content and language, and the knowledge about the customer locally—you can have a global market, but the local customization [is important]. The processes and methodologies can be global, but the last leg is that of personalizing it—the knowledge of your local customers is a problem."

The company also includes numerous "extras" in its value proposition, including the option of delivery to convenient locations, such as petrol stations located worldwide.

Company B, too, emphasizes the need for a differentiated identity: "You've got zero visibility—you're just a URL. You have to differentiate yourself." But the company also stresses on the need for political sensitivity and legal knowledge when entering foreign markets. For example, the company realized the necessity to register a separate organizational entity in Malaysia, while not in Australia. Similarly, some items sold to Australia are not charged taxes because they are considered imports, putting the e-tailer at an advantageous position.

Company C chooses to localize its content by decentralizing its Web site, based on the foreign market it serves. In this way, content can be localized, and the Web site easily maintained.

Entering a foreign market can provide the e-tailer with a number of advantages over traditional retailers because economic and legal restrictions and barriers are not effectively enforced over the Internet. However, e-tailers must be wary of political and cultural sensitivity, as well as manage risks in new and unfamiliar markets. All three companies agree that the key to a successful entry to a foreign market is to promote value and localize Web site content to the needs of the market, but each company differs on the extent of its localization measures.

FUTURE RESEARCH

Certain fundamentals of retailing are reinforced when e-tailers adopt a global strategy—they must focus on providing superior customer service and satisfaction and on obtaining more knowledge of the customer. The global e-tailer strives to entice global customers with quick fulfillment and a large product range at reasonable prices. To do so, the e-tailer's supply chain network must be prepared and capable before the internationalization process can be successful.

While the case companies are only a year old, and have not completely embraced global strategies, with only a small percentage of customers being from outside the SE Asian region, future research into similar and more established companies may unveil more issues to global e-tailing. Furthermore, it would be of great value to study the changes in strategies as these companies gain experience with global e-tail, depicting the evolutionary process of global e-tail strategy formulation and implementation.

However, of particular significance is the issue of adopting a physical infrastructure, and how to implement it. While much research has been done comparing the benefits and drawbacks of the click-and-mortar e-commerce strategy with that of a pure play model, the factors identified may not be suitable in the context of a global e-tail strategy. The innovative and effective use of physical infrastructure in a global setting, necessarily coupled with synergistic Web site strategies, may distinguish the successful e-tailer from the mediocre.

Furthermore, is the success of physical retail location largely dependent on the capabilities of the e-tailer's current supply chain and logistics network? Further research may identify the relevant factors in the relationship, possibly including the capabilities of suppliers and couriers, systems integration, and fulfillment cycle time.

The Internet has undoubtedly affected the process of retail internationalization as well. While retail internationalization could be charted along from a number of perspectives, empirical research has not addressed the changes caused by the use of the Internet as a driver and motivating factor in internationalization.

In managing the Web-store infrastructures, e-tailers should take into account the greater need for flexibility, as technologies to support the use of multiple languages and currencies are developed, Customer Relationship Management (CRM) applications are enhanced, and supply chains and logistics networks integrate. At the same time, e-tailers also need to differentiate themselves, while finding appropriate access to each individual foreign market, managing cannibalism among their channels, ensuring political, legal, and cultural conflicts do not ensue.

CONCLUSION

The global reach of the Internet, at its relatively low cost, has stirred many online retailers to extend their offerings across the globe. Traditional retailers, with their existing infrastructure and distribution and logistics channels, have also realized the potential advantages of Internet retail, and have hopped onto the bandwagon, selling their products globally as well. However, the actual adoption and implementation of a global e-tail strategy is not a simple matter.

Empirical studies on the issues facing Internet retailers in the process of internationalization are deficient. The changes brought about by the Internet in traditional retail have changed the dynamics of its internationalization tremendously.

In the process of achieving a global strategy, organizations must be aware of the pressure for local and global responsiveness, by balancing issues in the light of obtaining market access, maintaining a flexible infrastructure, and achieving adequate and suitable levels of localization in the foreign markets. The success of an e-tailer's endeavor will be dependent on its ability to creatively balance its contributing factors in its relationship between the Internet and international markets.

REFERENCES

Auger, P. and Gallaugher, J. M. (1997). Factors Affecting the Adoption of an Internet-Based Sales Presence for Small Businesses. *The Information Society,* 13, 55-74.

Birch, A., Gerbert, P. and Schneider, D. (2000). *The Age Of E-Tail: Conquering The New World Of Electronic Shopping*. Oxford, UK: Capstone.

Calkins, J. D., Farello, M. J., and Shi, C. S. (2000). From Retailing To E-Tailing. *McKinsey Quarterly,* 1, 140-147.

Chen, S. and Leteney, F. (2000). Get Real! Managing The Next Stage Of Internet Retail. *European Management Journal, 18*(5), 519-528.

Ernst and Young. (2001). *Global Online Retailing: An Ernst & Young Special Report*. Ernst & Young.

Farhoomand, A. F., Tuunainen, V. K. and Yee, L. W. (2000). Barriers To Global Electronic Commerce: A Cross-Country Study Of Hong Kong And Finland. *Journal Of Organizational Computing And Electronic Commerce, 10*(1), 23-48.

Griffin, R.W. and Pustay, M. W. (1998). *International Business: A Managerial Perspective* (2nd ed.). Reading, MA: Addison-Wesley Publishing Company.

Hopping, D. (2000). Technology In Retail. *Technology In Society*, 22(1), 63-74.

IDC Corporation. (2000). *Web-Site Globalization The Next Imperative For The Internet 2.0 Era.* IDC Corporation.

Kalakota, R. and Whinston, A.B. (1996). *Readings In Electronic Commerce.* Reading, MA: Addison-Wesley Publishing.

Katros, V. (2000). A Note On Internet Technologies And Retail Industry Trends. *Technology In Society, 22*(1), 75-81.

Katz, M. S. and Rothfeder, J. (2000). Crossing The Digital Divide. *Strategy and Business, 18*(1), 26-41.

Kuhn, J. (2000). The Role Of Continuous Improvement Within Globalization. *International Journal of Technology Management, 20*(3/4), 442-458.

Otto, James R. and Chung, Q. B. (2000). A Framework for Cyber Enhanced Retailing: Integrating E-Commerce Retailing With Brick-and-Mortar Retailing. EM - *Electronic Markets, 10*(3), 185-191.

Pottruck, D.S. and Pearce, T. (2000). *Clicks And Mortar: Passion-Driven Growth In an Internet Driven World.* San Francisco: Jossey-Bass.

Rao, B. (1999). The Internet and the revolution In distribution: A cross-industry examination. *Technology In Society, 21*(3), 287-306.

Rosen, K. T. and Howard, A. L. (2000). E-Retail: Gold Rush Or Fool's Gold? *California Management Review, 42*(3), 72-99.

Shaw, M., Blanning, R., Strader, T. and Whinston, A. (2000). *Handbook On Electronic Commerce.* Berlin: Springer-Verlag.

Turban, E., Lee, J. K., King, D. and Chung, M. H. (1999). *Electronic Commerce: A Managerial Perspective.* Prentice-Hall.

Yip, G. S. (2000). Global Strategy In The Internet Era. *Business Strategy Review, 11*(4), 1-14.

Chapter XVIII

Using the Web for Enhancing Decision-Making: UN Project Failures in Sub-Sahara Africa (SSA)

David King
University of South Australia, Australia

ABSTRACT

The purpose of this chapter is to highlight the use of the Internet to improve the reliability of information supplied to the United Nations (UN) from official sources in Sub-Sahara Africa (SSA). The focus of the chapter is that aid project failures in SSA need efficient project management, effective communication, and information openness to achieve socio-economic growth. The use of the Internet's potential(s) in a way that will benefit society at large and in particular vulnerable groups needs critical examination within a wider framework of the actual needs and existing facilities of these communities. An interpretive evidence data collection method is used through questioning and interviews with stakeholder groups, validated by observation where possible. The importance of aid project performance, assessment, and monitoring in

SSA is emphasised. The significance of public participation in decision-making processes is explored. This research also highlights the pragmatics of giving local people an international voice.

INTRODUCTION

The aim of this chapter is two-fold: (1) managing projects and (2) flow of public information. The framework and environment of managing projects have huge influence on the outcome of project work, and on how positively the management team experiences the entire process. The author stresses both the need and the opportunities of utilizing innovative environments and techniques to promote effectiveness in project management in SSA. This issue has become more topical by the increasing number of project works and management failures in these countries.

Another concern is that Sub-Sahara Africa needs good two-way flow of public information. This derives from a deeper concern about the lack of effective use of aid monies in SSA. This problem has also been identified in the UNDP Human Development Report (1998) and also announced in the World Bank Development Report (1987, 1999). This author argues that the Internet can be used to provide broader-based feedback essential for the effective use and allocation of aid monies on projects in SSA.

Kouzes and Posner (1987) claim that project management is essentially a problem-solving activity; yet, too often, the less experienced project manager is hindered rather than helped by the rules handed down. Though these authors have highlighted an important problem, this author also believes that an inexperienced project manager is not the only underlying issue. First, there is a need for both the donor organisations and the public to be involved in project works (see Figure 2); and secondly, ignored issues like corruption contribute to project failures. The chapter explores the circumstances and criteria for considering these factors to achieve project success. Major aspects considered include effective management risks, process, and techniques. This chapter also focuses on issues critical to achieving project objectives for socio-economic development, including project manageability; information reliability, and project decision-making. This section of the chapter amplifies these lessons with examples drawn from project management literatures and will appeal particularly to those project managers who have faced the gathering storm and wondered whether to bend or stand firm. Though the chapter is aimed at project management in general, the author is explicitly concerned with projects in the SSA.

Project managers in SSA have the need to improve the effectiveness of their requests and promises, and how team accountability, information openness, and performance are enhanced through the application of guidelines, suggestions, and recommendations. Projects in SSA must face the challenge of change. Aid projects represent the fulfillment of stakeholders' expectations (i.e., the orderly bringing to reality the concept of gratifying aid project objectives). Kouzes and Posner (1987) assert that investing in projects is consequently a strategy for reducing the uncertainty (or risk) in meeting the challenge of project change.

The author agrees with Dingle (1997), who uses the British Standard Guide to Project Management, to define a project as "a unique set of co-ordinated activities, with definite starting and finishing points, undertaken by an individual or organisation to meet specific objectives within defined schedule, cost and performance parameters." In this context, the specification of "performance" includes specification of *achieving* socio-economic development projects (e.g., health, education, and telecommunication infrastructure systems) in SSA. These "complex" projects, funded and non-funded, are still major problems in these countries as the achievement of completion is rare.

The job of managing a project has been described since early times in terms of organisational skills and capacity for wide-ranging forethought (Yuki, 1981). Project managers have to ensure that their projects are completed within budget and on time. They have to lay plans, anticipate problems, and see that objectives are met even when plans have to be changed. Project managers in SSA lack these disciplines; therefore, several project activities, such as communication and public information flow need to be improved to achieve these skills. If a project is regarded as an interconnected system of activities with predetermined objectives, schedule, and cost; project management is a discipline of conducting the necessary resources for execution of the project within the specifications of schedule, performance, and cost. Because of the lack of project management skills and discipline investments, many aid organisation projects have proven to be fruitless.

INTERNATIONAL CRISIS ON AID PROJECTS

Aid project crisis has crept up gradually over a number of years; therefore, its full extent is not appreciated. There is presently much more confusion about the basic purposes and aims of international aid than ever before in the past half century. This is reflected in UNDP (1996, 1999) that official aid on projects is now under attack from an extraordinary number of directions.

From political perspectives and some academic economists comes the argument that aid simply does not work, meaning that it does not increase economic growth. Rose-Ackerman and Stone (1996) and Riley (1998) indeed argue that aid must be positively harmful to poor countries because it conflicts with sound economics, causing distortions and misuse of resources and creating inefficiency through dependence on subsidy.

However, there is an increase of attack on official aid programmes for supporting corrupt governments on projects, proclaims Shihata (1996), and allowing aid itself to be used for corrupt purposes. SSA governments spend massive amount on armaments and their undemocratic governments are fulfilling neither the urgent nor long-term public needs. This appears sometimes as a general condemnation of "Third World" aid and sometimes as an argument for using aid to coerce recipient countries into more democratic behaviour. The tendency to think of "development" as consisting of promoting the political and social beliefs of donors (including, amongst other things, equality for women) has increased greatly in recent years. These beliefs must be encouraged to allow for project development resulting in socio-economic benefits in the SSA countries.

The implications of these far-reaching changes should be a central issue in the current debate about aid, but they are not. The international aid movement has only begun to address project failures and the issues that they raise for the priorities and methods of aid. Dingle (1997) and Knights and Willmott (1999) describe the ongoing and confused debate, most of which takes place in the First World rather than the Third—reflecting a general disillusionment about official aid. The confusion about objectives, and the consequent difficulty of assessing performance, must be one underlying reason for this disillusionment. Amongst the public in First World countries, attitudes range from outright hostility on to a passive indifference that simply accepts aid as part of the given order of things — an attitude that is more common in Europe. The International Monetary Fund (IMF) (1995) says neither attitude reflects any conviction that official aid projects achieve worthwhile results.

Ironically, however, in the First World, the aid business thrives and grows and Third World aid projects on socio-economic development have become a profession. The number of people engaged in socio-economic development in SSA, as mentioned in the UNDP (1996) Aid Accountability Initiative, is now very large and continues to grow. These are found in regional governments and a large number of international development agencies of all kinds, including many in the UN family; in institutes and research organisations devoted to analysing the problems of poor countries in extraordinary detail; and in colleges and universities where the popularity of "development studies" seems still to be on the increase. The volume of literature produced annually on the subject in its many aspects is far beyond the ability of one individual researcher.

The author is convinced that a new effort must be made to deal with this confusion and to bring more coherence and rationality to the whole subject. The author starts from a personal conviction that the effort to improve the quality of life for the majority of people in poor countries certainly deserves support in principle, but that it must be very clear about what the international community is trying to achieve and honest in assessing success and failure. This community must also beware of the insidious dangers that lie in the self satisfaction to be derived from doing good to the poor, and of the danger that the institutional interests of long-established development organisations and the career interests of those who work in them may override the essential aims of aid.

World Bank Report (1994) recommends that the International Aid Organisations (IAO) promote effective management procedures within projects by emphasizing the importance of monitoring as an integral part of day-to-day project operations. Communication is important in project works and the criteria that characterize project works indicate that communication among stakeholders (UN, IMF, local government, and the public) must be effective and efficient if project works in SSA are to be well directed and managed. How effective can this be?

In the SSA, Ghana for instance, the culture influences the way of thinking and doing things. Individual behaviour and organisational learning impacts on project culture, which in turn impacts on the outcome on the decision making process (Agyris, 1996; Argyris and Schon, 1996; Checkland, 1988). Most projects in SSA seek to improve the lives of their people and therefore the main users of the project outcome are those who must be responsible for development planning and design. Projects are run, created, designed, built, and operated by and for people. The Internet technology is the main open source of information and the appropriate tool that can effectively allow the public to voice and reach international settings. The author suggests that citizens of these nations must be involved in the monitoring process of any international aid projects, to help fight corruption and contribute to effective management.

PROJECT ASSESSMENT AND MONITORING

It is reported in GAO (1998) that a continuous assessment of project implementation in relation to agreed policies, and of the use of public controls, infrastructure, and open accountability services by project beneficiaries must be established in SSA. This is an integral part of good management by a project-implementing agency. The essence of this is to provide continuous feedback on implementation, and to identify actual or potential successes and problems as early as possible to facilitate timely adjustments to project operation. Dambia (1991), an

African expert in projects and economic development, has said that managing a development project is a complex task. The basic core of a good management work program should include the following (see Figure 1).

It is also mentioned in GAO (1998) that periodic assessment of the relevance, performance, efficiency, and impact (both expected and unexpected) of a project in relation to stated objectives is essential. Three types of periodic assessment are suggested.

1. An interim evaluation is undertaken by project management during implementation as a first review of progress and a prognosis of the likely effects of the project. This is intended to identify project design problems, and is essentially an internal activity undertaken for project management.

Figure 1: Monitoring and Assessment of Aid Projects in SSA

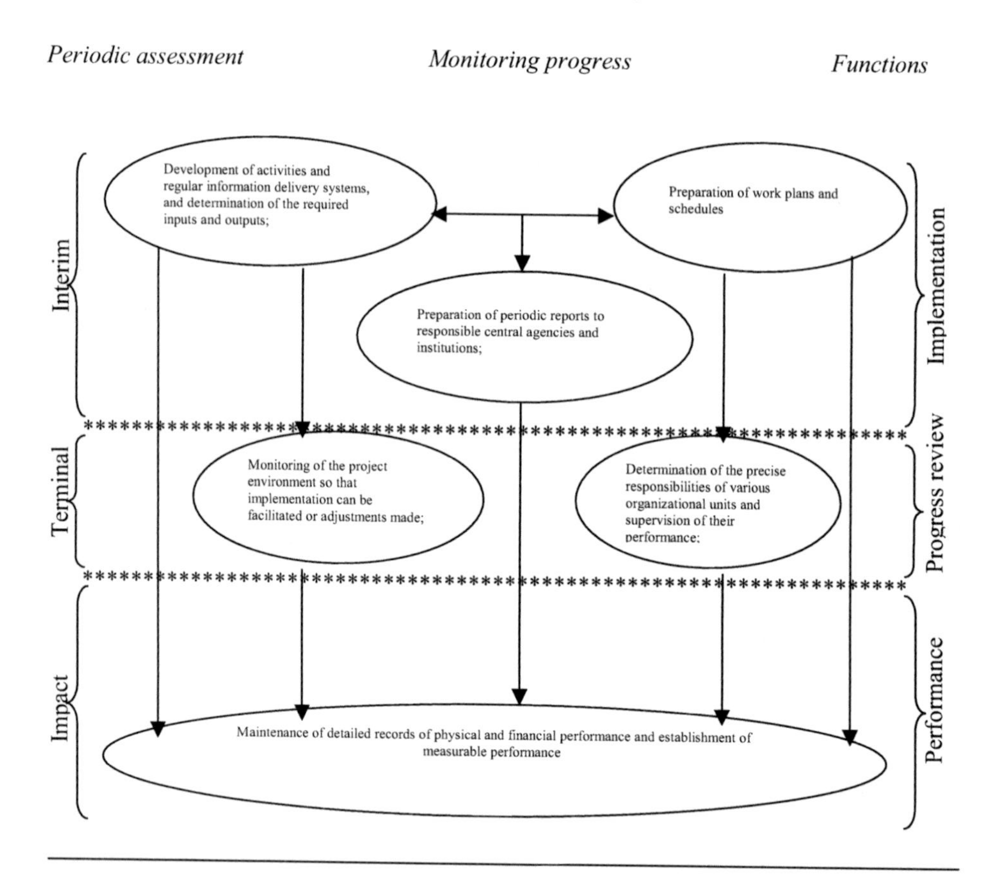

2. Terminal evaluation, a similar process undertaken at the end of a project, is required for the Project Completion Report (PCR) or Implementation Completion Reporting (ICP). It includes an assessment of the project's effects and their potential sustainability.
3. An impact evaluation is usually undertaken several years after final disbursement, and measures changes attributable to the project in terms of both direct and indirect causality.

National authorities or donor agencies normally undertake these measures. A more public, real-time reporting would seem preferable. Monitoring is a tool that project managers use to carry out functions. Schultz (1998) asserted that due to the immense amount of corruption that exists in these countries, unless good public flow of information and allowing the public to participate (monitoring and evaluating) in aid projects, project failures would continue to exist. The creation or strengthening of monitoring activities under a project is not a temporary requirement to meet the aid agencies' information needs, but an institution-building component, which should permanently improve overall management practice both within and outside aid agencies.

Moreover, GAO (1998) suggests that monitoring and evaluation are the responsibility of the borrowing organisations in project development. The common theme that stands out in interviews with stakeholder groups is that aid organisations seem to ignore the most obvious issue of corruption. Lenders simply want their money back; they have little interest in how it is actually spent, and thus, many projects do not get completed. Project implementation agencies need to be responsible for exercising the monitoring function consistent with agreed specifications. It is common in SSA that corruption takes the place of responsibility. SSA countries need a good, independent non-corruptible monitoring system, especially in complex projects with several agencies involved.

Whether an independent monitoring and evaluation unit is necessary to carry out the monitoring function will depend upon the complexity and scope of the monitoring function and the extent of evaluation requirements. For smaller projects, the responsibility for organizing, maintaining, and using a regular flow of publicly validated information throughout implementation must be included specifically in the terms of reference of any aid type.

The need for a reliable administrative unit for monitoring will be greatest in countries with a weak management history, or where project objectives are innovative and/or complex, or in projects with multiple components. When such an independent monitoring function is created, it should be integrated into the international aid management structure, since its purpose will be to serve the information needs of the implementing country. The World Bank Report (1994) stated that, in countries where corruption is very common like in SSA, leaders must be aware or informed that the public will also be involved in project assessment and supervision internally and externally using independent sources. The range of the information system and the scale of the monitoring process must be consistent with the administrative unit and financial resources available in the country and must be independent of governmental management procedures within the country.

COMMUNICATION AND COMMITMENT

From the perspective of project failures, it is obvious to say that most project managers do not communicate as effectively as they should in SSA. Project managers do not keep team members and upper management, or themselves, properly informed. Communication problems are experienced more often than project managers would like to admit. Previous studies in this field have highlighted some key problems. The author's personal experiences indicate that the following are major problems commonly found in SSA (Ghana being used as an example).

Barriers To Effective Communication

Often organisational barriers are much more important in communicating problems on projects. This is because of the very nature of a project. Projects in Ghana involve people from different ethnic (tribal) groups, who use different languages, have different objectives, have had different types of training, and yet must work together closely on a unique task. An example is given in Randolf and Posner (1998) who say "typical organisational barriers to communications include an organisational structure that separates the departments, information overload or sometimes underload (too little information), ambiguity leading to incomplete information or faulty transmission of information, and time pressures." In Ghana and some other SSA countries, the problem is generated primarily from tribalism, selfishness, greediness, bribery, and last but not least, control and power (UNDP, 1997).

Progress Report And Commitment

The author suggests that project leaders should adopt the "need to know" principle so that copies of written and unwritten communications are freely available to those who need the information. Electronic communication is nowadays in general use, and can very powerfully inform action. It is essential that efficient project management teams, including lower-level employees, make use of electronic communication to report to the "need to know" authorities on progress of a project and when things are going wrong. The best way to do this is make use of the Internet e-mailing system. It is cheap, easy to use, and free from monopoly.

In countries where project failures are common, progress reports are the main formal means by which project progress is communicated and recorded. As records, they are vital parts of the project's audit trail, so they must be prepared with all possible care. To eliminate unnecessary recording and information overflow, project progress reports should:

- State clearly the current status of the project
- Compare actual achievements with the planned target achievements
- Draw attention to critical issues
- Identify problems and propose solutions
- Promote effective management and control

In SSA project teams need extensive commitment in order to perform well in project managing. Below are some vital examples that the researcher believes SSA project managers need to follow.

- Generating a realistic plan, with realistic costs and reports
- Implementing straight-forward and easily-maintained report/approval procedures
- Producing and using "need-to-know" information strategy
- Straight-forward and effective change control, fault reporting, and cost control

A commitment plan and procedure must be put into effect decisively. The plan must make clear what is to be achieved, when it is to be achieved, and how it is to be achieved. A project manager needs to balance what needs to be done to maintain control over the long term. Having control of the project is a matter of maintaining control over a long term, which is also more a matter of managing risks and establishing effective monitoring procedures.

A project manager will have to balance challenging demands from different places, e.g., to satisfy the sponsor's management (who need to know what has happened) and to create space for the project's success. In SSA, where project failure is common, Chicken (1994) advises that there is a need to create effective risk management strategy to allow for project success.

PROJECT RISK MANAGEMENT METHODOLOGY

Effective risk management calls for an understanding of the totality of a project or part of a project under consideration, which may be helped by using checklists appropriately. As Dingle (1997) points out, many formal presentations of risk management methodology do not make it clear that the techniques must not be applied mechanistically. In addition, it is important that risk management calls for creativity, imagination, and lateral thinking. However, as communication is also a vital element in risk management methods, it is best to formalise communication and use it to best advantage.

The ultimate responsibility for risk management falls on the project manager. In SSA, subordinate responsibility should be allocated and delegated wherever and to whomever the project manager deems most appropriate for that project's circumstances. It follows that the project manager must understand and approve the methods used, and must delegate sufficient authority to the person acting as "risk analyst" to ensure that the analysis is independent and objective. Chicken (1994) emphasises that a project manager will use the findings of the risk analysis to develop risk management strategies; first, to reduce the likelihood of risks arising, and second, to minimise their impact should risks occur.

Harvey (1992) argues that efficient project risk management depends on recognition that proactive and judicious spending of some of the budget (e.g. time and/or cost) before any actual adverse event will provide better control than invoking a mitigation plan only when a potential risk has become an actual adverse event. The following basic steps in project risk management are recommended to project managers, including key project team members (Harvey, 1992; Chicken, 1994; Dingle, 1997).

- Identify the risks as early as possible
- Record what has been identified, for the purposes of information control
- Predict the likelihood of the risks, and how serious their impact may be
- Decide on suitable action
- Implement the decisions
- Monitor the implementation via a genuine and reliable method

Dingle (1997) suggests that in large projects someone responsible for coordinating and recording all risk management activities must be appointed and report immediately any possible risk that can endanger project development. In SSA, it is ideal to appoint someone who can be reliable and trusted. The public are the ones who, with anger and frustration due to socio-economic failures, may wish to contribute (through a reliable monitoring media, for example the Internet) to project progress and development. They can become part of a project team. The public in the SSA are likely to work together on suggesting how to overcome potential future project problems rather than counting on only government-appointed project leaders. It can be said that risk assessment does not guarantee correct decisions: however, it does enable people to make better decisions. Effective risk management should be seen as an important step for aid project "investment."

The very prevalence of risks (potential future problems), which could jeopardise a project's success, demands a systematic, methodical approach to risk awareness. It must also be noted that the identification of risks, the assessment of their likelihood and impact, linkages between risks, and prioritisation of a suitable response strategy is needed in the SSA.

For most projects, the perception of risk by the public influences the acceptability of national risk strategies. This influence is most rigorously imposed through higher authorities, but its perception may also be expressed through the Internet (media) reporting of project developments. It has become increasingly important for project decision makers to take account of public perceptions of project risk in the SSA.

INFORMATION OPENNESS

The control of information flow by official government sources in Africa is seen as a gatekeeper mechanism that has the potential to distort decision making within international aid organisations such as United Nations and the World Bank (Pettigrew, 1972; Bloomfield and Coombs, 1992). The Internet has the potential to be used by aid agencies in SSA as a tool for ensuring other sources than the official regional government sources of information are available to international aid organisations. Exactly how this might be undertaken needs to be researched in the context of the problem.

In response to obvious failures in the current SSA development investment where monies are not reaching the intended projects, the international community has begun to demand more accountability and openness of information flows (UNRISD, 1995). Seeking to promote improved information management and the increased efficiency and effectiveness of aid programs, Graeme and Weitzner (1996) recommended a government-wide requirement for agencies to set goals and report annually on projects' program performance. The author believes these reports could include local peoples' confidential feedback.

Jones (1995, 1998), Montealegre (1996), and Simon (1996) assert that the Internet serves as a medium for sharing knowledge, communicating knowledge, acquiring useful information, and knowledge transfer to allow communities to grow. This, however, downplays the power issues. In SSA those with the resources can ensure an unequal flow of information, especially given the large investment costs of the technology (Uimonen, 1997). This has particular application in SSA countries that are constantly seeking aid (World Bank, 1987).

It is believed that good flow of public information will assist the effective use of aid from overseas. The bias in feedback from governments to international aid organisations often makes it unreliable. This feedback needs to be evaluated, and it is believed that the best people to do this are the locals. Decision-making on project funding has often been hampered by the lack of accurate information on the results of international aid organisations (IAO) programs' efforts.

Allen (1984) suggests that the rapid advances in information and communication technology will create a democratic atmosphere in the areas needed. The Internet can allow "free" flow of information that will help progress of projects and socio-economic development. Madon (1999), in her paper on the "Internet and Social Development," asserted that the dominance of democratic institutions in a country is considered a key criterion for socio-economic development. Moreover, writers like Press (1996) and Mueller and Tan (1997) have also argued that Internet connectivity promotes democracy. Can the Internet be a democratic institution?

Kenney (1995) and Mansell and Wenn (1998) asserted that the importance of expanding the access of developing countries to the Internet has been recognised by governments and international agencies with increasing consensus that the Internet and related telecommunications technology should be regarded as strategic national infrastructure. However, Goodman et al. (1992) claim that the ways in which different developing countries are adopting these new technologies and supporting business strategies and entrepreneurial initiatives have received little critical attention.

With the advent of the Internet, Jones (1995) argues in his book *Computer-Mediated-Communication* that methods of accessing and disseminating information have been fundamentally changed, with profound implications for individuals, civil society, and governments. The Internet offers opportunities to exchange ideas and promote cultural and economic progress. The Internet is global in its reach to a degree that no other technology is: it transcends national borders and eliminates barriers to free flow of information for the common person at anywhere and anytime.

The Internet can be used to provide continuous feedback on project implementation, and to identify actual or potential successes and problems as early as possible to facilitate timely adjustments to project operation. The creation or strengthening of monitoring activities under a project is not a temporary requirement to meet aid organisations information needs, but an institution-building component, which should permanently improve overall management practice within borrower agencies

The Internet is infrastructure-independent, open, decentralized, abundant, interactive, user-controlled, and global in its reach, and can be used by the public. The World Bank (1999) experience on projects aimed at developing governance and policy-forming capacity in Africa, for example, finds that government failures in Sub-Sahara Africa are often attributable in whole or in part to governments' unwillingness to make themselves accountable to the citizens they are supposed to serve. The Internet has tremendous potential for fostering democratic participation, giving voice to the voiceless (Bimber, 1997). Figure 2 shows that the Internet could allow the public to communicate with aid organisations about the progress of a project. The author sees the Internet as multi-directional.

It is important that the reliability of the source and the accuracy of the information, as judged by data available at, or close to, their operational levels, are re-examined. Beacham (1997) argues that Internet technology can allow for participatory democracy in developing countries (Africa in particular) to enhance

Figure 2: The Internet is an Intelligence-Gathering Tool

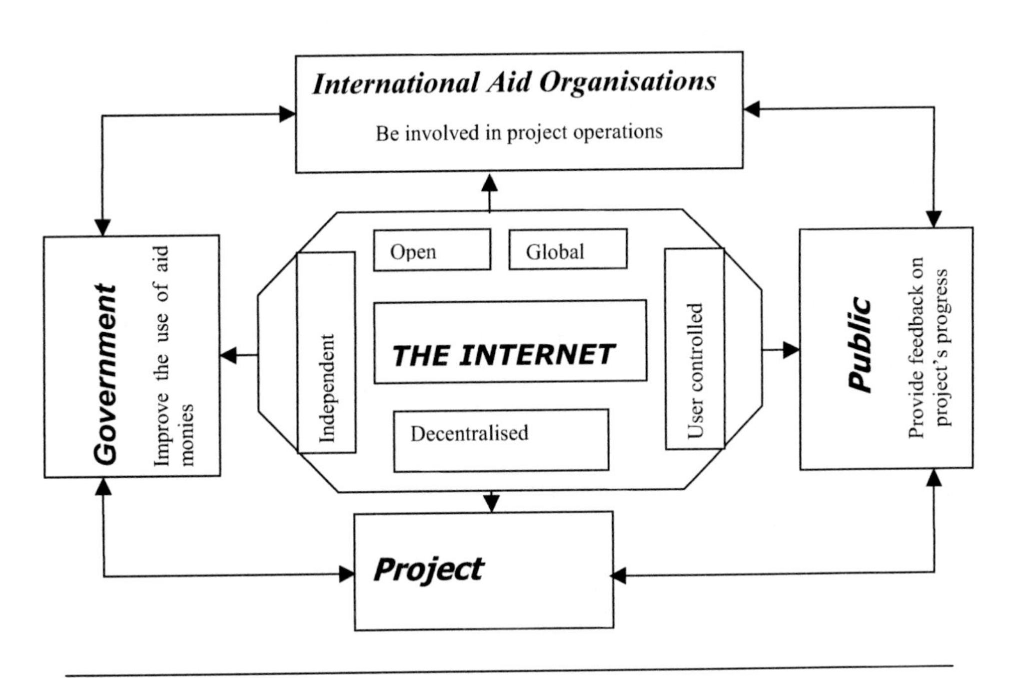

decision-making. Of particular interest is whether aid organisations are correctly informed about the application of their contributions.

United Nations Research Institute for Social Development (UNRISD) (1995) has already suggested that both the international aid organisations and the developing countries' governments need carefully evaluated information to help them make useful decisions about the programs they oversee. Also they need to implement information and communication technology (ICT) tools that tell them whether, and in what important ways, an aid project is working well or poorly, and why. Madon (1999) stated that, in the past, the tools for information evaluation have not proven to be reliable. This is supported by the uncountable number of project failures in most parts of the developing world. Rice and McDaniel (1987) also suggest that the Internet can allow developing countries' public to send and receive information on ongoing projects. This should help with their personal development through feeling of self worth and less feeling of helplessness.

Comments from UNDP (1999) indicated that "assistance" from the western world for developing countries' socio-economic growth has not been carefully utilised by their leaders. The chapter draws on the author's experiences and knowledge of international and regional organizations such as the United Nations (UN) and African Development Bank (ADB), respectively; national governments and non-government organisations (NGOs); as well as research from related regions of the world.

Professor K. Griffin, a former chairman of the UNRISD Board, discusses the intrinsic value of human development and cultural diversity, and also their instrumental value in promoting growth (Griffin, 1997). In discussing the ties that bind human development and economic growth, Griffin places emphasis on investing in human capacities, pointing out the positive economic repercussions of keeping such investments high and well-distributed across society as a whole. He argues that creativity—new knowledge, new technology and new institutional arrangements—is the fountainhead of economic growth, and these contribute to creativity in all fields of endeavour. United Nations and other aid organisations are in a strong position to achieve economic growth and higher rate of project success by encouraging public involvement and the use of the Internet.

The Internet is today's electronic medium that can profoundly influence economic and political development in developing countries. The extent of this influence, and its positive and sustainable effects, will depend on a myriad of factors—some predictable and others not. The potential contribution of electronic media to political outcomes in Sub-Sahara Africa, such as its impact on effective use of aid for socio-economic development, needs critical attention.

CONCLUSION

The administrative arrangements on a large project(s) are likely to be complex. The use of Internet, information openness, and effective communication can help ensure honest reporting. The aim of control procedures should be to enable the project management team to perform exactly what their commitments are for the completion of their work. It is important that the project plans are kept up-to-date, and that everyone concerned is kept informed about project changes.

From a project point of view, management have to ensure that adequate communication facilities are put in place and properly used. Communication problems cause project problems. Some of the more important communication problems relate to project organisation and discipline, the involvement of inexperienced managers, and also weaknesses in project management. Correcting the latter is the key to solving project failures.

The author suggests that the international aid organisations must assist in decisions on the way risks (large project failures) are reviewed, how new risk(s) will be identified, and on the level of necessary documents, and ensure that the results of all assessment are properly documented. The author suggests that when SSA proposes to undertake any investment for socio-economic development, it is wise to consider risk. The characteristics of a project make risk assessment not only necessary, but also a crucial feature of project planning.

REFERENCES

Allen, T.J. (1984). *Managing the Flow of Technology*. Cambridge, MA: MIT press.

Argyris, C. (1996). Actionable Knowledge: Design causality in the service of consequential theory. *The Journal of Applied Behavioural Science*, 32(4), 390-406.

Argyris, C. and Schon, D.A. (1996). *Organisational learning II – Theory, Method and Practice*. Addison-Wesley Publishing.

Beacham, F. (1997). *The Internet: Will it Become the Next Mass Media?* In Media and Democracy: A Collection of Readings and Resources. Washington D.C.: Institute for Alternative Journalism. At http://www.igc.apc.org/an/book/beacham7.html.

Bimber, B. (1997, August 28-31). *The Internet and Political Participation: The 1996 Election Season.* Paper prepared for delivery at the 1997 Annual Meeting of the American Political Science Association. Washington D.C.

Bloomfield, B.P., and Coombs, R. (1992). *Information Technology, Control and Power: The Centralization and Decentralization Debate*. Manchester School of Management, UMIST.

Checkland, P. (1988). Information Systems and Systems Thinking: A time to unite. *International Journal of Information Management*, 8, 239-248.

Chicken, J.C. (1994). *Managing risks and decisions in major projects*. London: Chapman & Hall.

Dambia, P-C. (1991). Governance and economic development. *AFRICA FORUM : A journal of leadership and development,* 1(1), 17-19.

Dingle, J. (1997). Project Management: Orientation for Decision Makers. London: Arnold.

GAO. (1998). *Performance Measurement And Evaluation Definitions and Relationships*. United States General Accounting Office GAO/GGD-98-26.

Goodman, S.E., Press, L., Ruth, S., and Rutskwski, A. (1992). The Global Diffusion of the Internet: Patterns and Problems. *Communications of the ACM*, 37(8), 27-31.

Graeme, B., and Weitzner, D.J. (1996). *Electronic Democracy: Using the Internet to Influence American Politics*. Wilton, CT: Online.

Griffin, K. (1997). *Culture, Human Development and Economic Growth.*

Harvey, C. (1992). *Analysis of project finance in developing countries*. Aldershot: Gower.

IMF (International Monetary Fund, Fiscal Affairs Department). (1995). *Unproductive Public Expenditures: A Pragmatic Approach to Policy Analysis*, Pamphlet Series 48. IMF: Washington, D.C.

Jones, S.G. (1995). *Cyber Society*. California: Sage.

Jones, S.G. (1998). *Cyber Society: Computer-Mediated Communication and Community* (revisited).

Kenney, G. (1995). The Missing Link – Information. *Information Technology for Development*, 6, 33-38.

Knights, D. and Willmott, H. (1999). *Management Lives: Power and Identity in Work Organisations.* London: SAGE Publications.

Kouzes, J.M., and Posner, B.Z. (1987). *The Leadership Challenge: How to Get Extraordinary Things Done in Organisations*. San Francisco, CA: Jossey-Bass.

Madon, S. (1999). *The Internet and Socio-economic Development: Exploring the Interaction*. London School of Economics.

Mansell, R., and Wenn, U. (1998). *Knowledge Societies: Information Technology for Sustainable Development*. Oxford, UK: Oxford University Press.

Montealegre, R. (1996). Implications of Electronic Commerce for Managers in Less-Developed Countries. *Information Technology Development*, 7, 145-152.

Mueller, M., and Tan, Z. (1997). *China in the Information Age, the Centre for Strategic and International Studies*. Washington DC: Praeger Publishers.

Pettigrew, A.M. (1972). *Information Control As a Power Resource*. An article discussed in the IS doctoral school. UNISA.

Press, L. (1996, February). The role of computer networks in development. *Communications of the ACM*, 39(2).

Randolph, W.A. and Posner, B.Z. (1998). *Effective Project Planning and Management: Getting The Job Done*. Englewood Cliffs, NJ: Prentice Hall.

Rice, R.E. and McDaniel, B. (1987). *Managing organizational innovation: The evolution from work processing to office information systems.* New York: Columbia University Press.

Riley, S. P. (1998). The Political Economy of Anti-Corruption Strategies in Africa. *European Journal of Development Research*, 10(1).

Rose-Ackerman, S. and Stone, A. (1996). *The Costs of Corruption for Private Business: Evidence from World Bank Surveys*. Washington, D.C.: The World Bank.

Schultz, T.P. (1998). Inequality in the Distribution of Personal Income in the World: How It Is Changing and Why. *Journal of Population Economics*, 11(3), 307-344.

Shihata, I.F.I. (1996, September 9). *Corruption: A General Review with an Emphasis on the Role of the World Bank*. Keynote address. Jesus College, Cambridge.

Simon, H. (1996). *A computer for everyman*. New York: The American Scholar.

Uimonen, P. (1997). Geneva: United Nations Research Institute for Social Development (UNRISD).

UNDP. (1996, July). *Aid Accountability Initiative*, Bi-Annual Report: 1 January-June 30, 1996. New York.

UNDP. (1997). *Management Development and Governance Division, Corruption and Good Governance*, Discussion paper #3, New York: UNDP, July 1997.

UNDP. (1998). *Human Development Report 1998*. New York: Oxford University Press.

UNDP. (1999). *Monitoring human development: Enlarging people's choices* (p. 262). Washington: UNDP.

UNRISD. (1995). *States of Disarray: The Social Effects of Globalization.* Report prepared for the World Summit for Social Development.

World Bank. (1987). *World Development Report.* Washington, DC: Oxford University Press.

World Bank. (1994). *Adjustment in Africa: Reforms, Results, and the Road Ahead. A World Bank Policy Research Report.* New York: Oxford University Press for the World Bank.

World Bank (1999). *World Development Report 1999/2000.* Washington: World Bank.

Yuki, G.A. (1981). Leadership in Organisations. Englewood Cliffs, NJ: Prentice-Hall.

About the Authors

Gerry Gingrich is a Professor of Systems Management in the Information Strategies Department of the Information Resources Management College at the National Defense University on Fort McNair, Washington, DC. Her research and teaching interests are organizational innovation and strategy, information technology and change, and executive leadership. Prior to teaching at the National Defense University, Dr. Gingrich was Co-Director of the Executive Masters in Information Systems in the School of Business and Public Management at The George Washington University. Earlier, she taught information systems strategy in the M.B.A. program at the University of Maryland. Dr. Gingrich obtained a Ph.D. in cognitive and organizational sciences from the University of Maryland in 1985 and a post-doctoral degree in information systems at the University of Minnesota in 1987. She has published her research in the *Proceedings of the International Conference on Information Systems, the Defense Intelligence Journal, the Journal of End User Computing, the National Defense University's Strategic Forum, Organizational Behavior and Human Processes*, and the *Proceedings of the Symposium on Human Factors in Information Systems*. Prior to entering the teaching profession, Dr. Gingrich was a Project Director for Louis Harris and Associates and for Westat, Inc., a corporate lending officer for NationsBank, and a certified public accountant for KPMG Peat Marwick. She obtained a B.S. in accounting and business from the University of North Carolina in 1972.

* * * * *

Stephen Burgess (M.Bus RMIT, Ph.D. Monash) is a Senior Lecturer in the School of Information Systems at Victoria University, Melbourne, Australia. He has a B.A. degree in accounting and a Graduate Diploma in commercial data processing, both from Victoria University, Australia; an M.Bus (information technology) from RMIT, Australia; and a Ph.D. at Monash University, Australia, in the area of small business to consumer interactions on the Internet. His research and teaching interests include the use of IT in small business, the strategic use of IT, B2C electronic commerce and management IT education. He has recently edited a book through Idea Group Publishing, *Managing Information Technology in Small Business: Challenges and Solutions,* and is track chair in the area of small business and information technology at the IRMA international conference (www.irma-international.org). Stephen is a co-founder of the new research group and IRMA Special Research Cluster on Small Business and Information Technology (www.businessandlaw.vu.edu.au/sbirit/).

Ming Chang is an Assistant Professor of MIS at the University of Houston-Downtown, USA. In addition to obtaining teaching experience in North Dakota and Washington states, he has extensive industry experience working with Boeing and e-commerce startups in the Seattle area. Dr. Chang also has a background in medicine and e-healthcare.

Stephen B. Chau graduated from the University of Tasmania in 1990 with a BEc. In 1991, he completed a Grad Dip Sci (IT), acquiring an Honours Degree in Computing in 1995. Currently he is in the final stages of completing a Ph.D. with the School of Information Systems at the University of Tasmania, Australia. Stephen maintains an interest in the SME use of electronic commerce and organisational change facilitated by Internet communication technologies. He has written a number of Australasian and international academic publications on the subject of electronic commerce and SMEs.

Jason C. H. Chen, Ph.D., is a Professor and the Coordinator of the MIS program in the School of Business Administration at Gonzaga University in Spokane, WA, USA. He designed and implemented an MIS system for a Chinese government agency to a World Bank project in 1994. He taught in the Beijing International MBA program at Beijing University in 1999. He is also the scholar-in-residence for an e-commerce and knowledge management firm in Taipei, Taiwan. His research interests include building and applying e-commerce models to business applications, the Pareto principle to business, and development of model and strategy of knowledge re-use to the enterprises.

P. Pete Chong is Martel Corp. Professor of CIS at the University of Houston-Downtown, USA. Prior to joining UHD, Dr. Chong taught at Gonzaga University,

University of Idaho, and Southeastern Louisiana University, where he also served as the Head of the Business Research Unit and the editor for *Southeastern Economic Outlook.*

Ta-Tao Chuang is an Assistant Professor of MIS at Gonzaga University, USA. Prior to coming to Gonzaga University, he taught at Wichita State University. Dr. Chuang has special research interests in business intelligence agents, e-commerce in international business environments, and the interdependence/integration of today's sometimes opposing organizations.

M. Gordon Hunter is an Associate Professor in Information Systems in the Faculty of Management at The University of Lethbridge, Canada. Gordon has previously held academic positions in Canada, Hong Kong, and Singapore, and visiting positions in Germany, USA and New Zealand. He has a Bachelor of Commerce degree from the University of Saskatchewan in Canada. He received his doctorate from Strathclyde Business School in Glasgow, Scotland. Gordon's professional designations include: Certified Management Accountant, Information Systems Professional, and Member–British Computer Society. He has extensive experience as a systems analyst and manager in industry and government organizations in Canada. Gordon is an Associate Editor of the *Journal of Global Information Management*. He is the Canadian World Representative for the Information Resource Management Association. He serves on the editorial board of the *Journal of Global Information Technology Management*, and the *Journal of Information Technology Cases and Application*. Gordon has conducted seminar presentations in Canada, USA, Asia, New Zealand, Australia, and Europe. His current research interests relate to the productivity of systems analysts with emphasis upon the personnel component, including cross-cultural aspects, and the effective use of information systems by small business.

Carina Ihlström received an M.Sc. degree in Informatics from Göteborg University, Sweden, in 1999. She is currently working toward a Ph.D. degree and is affiliated with the Viktoria Institute. She works as Director of Studies in Informatics at Halmstad University, Sweden, and lecturers in e-commerce and HCI. Her research interests lie within the areas of online newspapers and e-commerce, in particular the evolution of online newspapers since their launch in the mid-nineties.

Bandula Jayatilaka is an Assistant Professor of Management Information Systems at State University of New York at Binghamton, USA. He holds his Ph.D.

from the University of Houston, Texas. Prior to joining State University of New York at Binghamton, he worked for NASA. His current research interests include knowledge management, IS outsourcing, and virtual organization.

E.R. Jessup is Associate Professor of computer science at the University of Colorado at Boulder (UCB), USA. She earned her Ph.D. in computer science at Yale University. Her research interests are in the design, analysis, and implementation of algorithms and efficient software for matrix algebra problems. She has been actively involved in undergraduate education, beginning with her role as co-developer of an award-winning, NSF-funded, undergraduate curriculum in high-performance scientific computing. Most recently, she has worked with the Institute for Women and Technology to expand its Virtual Development Center to UCB.

David King is undertaking his Doctorate in Information Systems with the University of South Australia. He lectures in subject areas such as distributed systems, business information systems and information system security and control. David earned his B.A. and M.A. degrees in Accounting and Management Information Systems and has extensive executive working experience in these areas. He is a Microsoft Certified Professional in TCP/IP and also a Novell Certified Administrator. Since 2000, David has presented at the ACIS, IFIP, IRMA, ItiRA, and PACIS conferences. His future research interest lies in the areas of e-governance in Africa and in other developing countries.

Jerzy Kisielnicki received his Ph.D. from the Warsaw School of Economics (S.G.P.i.S.) He is a full Professor of Management and Head of the Department of Information Systems in Management and Faculty of Management at Warsaw University, Poland, and the Head of the Department of Organization and Management at the School of Economics and Law. His interests are organization and management, systems analysis, management information systems, process innovation (re-engineering), strategic management, and transition systems organization and management in the market economy. He is a member of and the representative for the Information Resources Management Association and the Institute for Operations Research and the Management Science TIMS-ORSA. Dr. Kisielnicki is a member of the Board of Organization and Management in Polish Academy of Science and is the head of the Scientific Council of Polish Society of Systems Information. He has had about 220 publications.

Jinyoul Lee is an Assistant Professor of Management Information Systems at State University of New York at Binghamton, USA. He received his Ph.D. from the University of Nebraska - Lincoln. His research interests include virtual organization, knowledge management, and enterprise resource planning implementation. His recent research is especially focused on enterprise integration and virtualization in the context of social structuration processes.

Zhang Liyang Graduate Student at the Department of Information Management, Peking University, China. B.S. from Peking University. Research interests include information resources management.

Wayne A. Long is currently Emeritus Professor of Management with The University of Calgary's Faculty of Management, Canada, where he co-founded the New Venture Development Program. His experience and research is in the fields of entrepreneurship and new venture creation and development is extensive. His publications appear in a wide variety of media and include a book co-authored with W. Ed McMullan entitled *Developing New Ventures: The Entrepreneurial Option*, (Harcourt, Brace, Javanovich, San Diego, CA, 1990). His consulting experience in recent years has been focused on the design and development of innovative programs for facilitating business start-up, development and growth, as well as innovative approaches to entrepreneurship education. Clients have included governments, educational institutions, and businesses. In addition to 10 years of industry experience, Wayne Long has taught at the university level and conducted research in business and entrepreneurship for almost 30 years. He consults with institutions and organizations internationally regarding entrepreneurship education, training, and program development.

Monika Magnusson is a Ph.D. Student at the department of Information Technology, Karlstad University, Sweden. She is conducting research in the area of electronic commerce. Her main research interests lie in small business adoption, implementation methods and change management. She is participating in several research projects one-commerce, one of them particularly addressing small and medium-sized enterprises. Monika teaches courses in Information System Development and Analysis of Change at the undergraduate level.

Julianne G. Mahler is Associate Professor of Government and Politics in the Department of Public and International Affairs at George Mason University, USA. She has worked extensively in the area of organization theory and public management, conducting research on organization culture in several federal government agencies. Her most recent research is on agency learning and the evolution of policy technologies. She has published numerous articles on decision-making, measuring customer satisfaction, organization culture, and learning. She is co-author of *Organization Theory: A Public Perspective*, with Hal Gortner and Jeanne Nicholson. She currently directs the masters program in Political Science. Her B.A. in Political Science is from Macalester College and her M.A. and Ph.D. are from SUNY at Buffalo.

Lai Maosheng is a Professor and Ph.D. Advisor at the Department of Information Management, Peking University, China; Chief Member, Council of China's Information Association; Chief Member, Council of the China Society for Sci-Tech Information; Chief Member, Council of the Chinese Association of Information Economics; Member, Academic Commission, the China Society for Sci-Tech Journalism; Director of the National Institute for Information Resource Management (Beijing). Research interests include information resources management, information storage and retrieval, information policy and law, and information economics.

Fiona Meikle is a Senior Lecturer in Information Management at Leeds Metropolitan University, UK. Her main research interests include business strategy and e-commerce development. Other research interests center on criminology and she is in the process of beginning a Ph.D. in this field. She is currently consulting on the development of a Web-enabled database for a major European health project. She has published papers and presented at conferences.

Thomas O'Daniel is a Lecturer in the School of Business and Information Technology, Monash University (Sunway Campus), Malaysia. His previous experience includes lecturing positions in management and information technology at several universities, electronic commerce application development, and more than 10 years in the financial services industry. Research interests focus on information management and the administration of mission-critical systems. His work on models of business-value for electronic commerce has been published in a book and articles in several well-known journals.

Shan-Ling Pan is Assistant Professor in the Department of Information Systems of the School of Computing at the National University of Singapore. His primary research focuses on the recursive interaction of organizations and information technology (enterprise systems), with particular emphasis on issues related to work practices, cultures and structures from a knowledge perspective. Some of his previous research has been published/forthcoming in *IEEE Transactions on Engineering Management, Communications of ACM (CACM), Information* *and Organization, Journal of Strategic Information Systems (JSIS), European Journal of Information Systems (EJIS), Decision Support Systems*, and the *Journal of Organizational Computing and Electronic Commerce (JOCEC)*.

Anand Ramchand is a Postgraduate Candidate in the Department of Information Systems of the School of Computing at the National University of Singapore. His current research interests focus on the management of knowledge strategies and initiatives in knowledge-intensive organizations.

Priscilla M. Regan is an Associate Professor in the Department of Public and International Affairs at George Mason University, USA. Prior to joining that faculty in 1989, she was a Senior Analyst in the Congressional Office of Technology Assessment (1984-1989) and an Assistant Professor of Politics and Government at the University of Puget Sound (1979-1984). Since the mid-1970s, Dr. Regan's primary research interest has been the analysis of the social, policy, and legal implications of organizational use of new information and communications technologies. Dr. Regan has published over 20 articles or book chapters, as well as *Legislating Privacy: Technology, Social Values, and Public Policy* (University of North Carolina Press, 1995). As a recognized researcher in this area, Dr. Regan has testified before Congress and participated in meetings held by the Department of Commerce, Federal Trade Commission, Social Security Administration, and Census Bureau. Dr. Regan received her Ph.D. in government from Cornell University in 1981 and her B.A. from Mount Holyoke College in 1972.

Don Schauder (M.A. Sheffield, M.Ed., Ph.D. Melbourne) is Professor of Information Management in the School of Information Management and Systems, Monash University, Australia. He is also Associate Dean (Research) of the Monash Faculty of Information Technology. Don is Chair of the Information & Telecommunication Needs Research Group, and of the Centre for Community Networking Research. He has been Director of several libraries, most recently RMIT University Library. As one of the pioneers of electronic publishing in Australia, he founded INFORMIT Electronic Publishing (now part of RMIT Publishing). He was co-founder of VICNET: Victoria's Network, based at the State Library of Victoria. Throughout his career he has maintained an active commitment to information access for people with disabilities. His teaching and research focus on the development of information products and services that benefit individuals, organisations and society; facilitating the transfer of knowledge among people; and reducing the "digital divide" between the information rich and poor.

Ada Scupola is an Assistant Professor at the Department of Social Sciences, Roskilde University, Denmark. She holds a Ph.D. in Business Administration from the same department, an M.B.A. from the University of Maryland, College Park, USA, and an M.A. in Information Systems from the University of Bari, Italy. Her research interests are in the impacts of EC technologies on organizations and industrial structures, adoption and diffusion of IT and electronic commerce, electronic commerce in SMEs, and strategic management of IT. She has been a visiting scholar at several international universities, including the Center for Research in Electronic Commerce, University of Texas at Austin, USA.

Tatsumi Shimada is Professor of Information Management in the department of Business Administration of Information at Setsunan University, Osaka, Japan, where he teaches courses on management information systems and information ethics. He received his Ph.D. in Business Administration from Osaka City University. His research interests include electronic government, strategic outsourcing, and information ethics. His publications include "The Impacts of Information Technology of Organizations in Japanese Companies" in *Management Impact of Information Technology* (edited by E.Szewczak, C.Snodgrass, & M.Khosrowpour, Idea Group Publishing, 1991), and "IS Outsourcing Practices in the USA, Japan, and Finland: A Comparative Study," *Journal of Information Technology* (with U.M.Apte, M.G.Sobol, T.Saarinen, T.Salmela, A.P.J.Vepsalainen, & S.Hanaoka, Vol.12, Dec., 1998).

Paul Turner was a research fellow at CRID (Computer, Telecommunications and Law Research Institute) prior to joining the School of Information Systems in Belgium where he worked on a variety of European Commission projects in the field of electronic commerce, telecommunications and intellectual property rights. Paul's strong research focus in the field of electronic commerce continues both in his work as senior research fellow at the University of Tasmania, Australia, and in his concurrent position as research manager for the Tasmanian Electronic Commerce Centre.

Virpi Kristiina Tuunainen is currently a Professor at the Helsinki School of Economics, Department of Management, Findland, Information Systems Science, and a Project Manager at LTT Research Ltd., Electronic Commerce Institute. She holds a Ph.D. and an M.A. from Helsinki School of Economics and Business Administration. She is author or co-author of many publications in international journals such as *MIS Quarterly* and *The Journal of Strategic Information*

Systems. She serves also on the editorial board of many journals such as JITTA, Scandinavian Journal of Information Systems, and Electronic Markets.

Kiyoshi Ushida is Director, Land Survey Section, Bureau of City Planning, ex-Director in charge of information system guidance, Office of Information Technology, Bureau of General Affairs, in the Tokyo Metropolitan Government, Japan. He received his M.S. at the Graduate School of Policy Science at Saitama University.

Edward Watson is the E. J. Ourso Professor of Business Analysis and Director of the SAP UCC and Enterprise Systems Programs at Louisiana State University, USA. Dr. Watson's interests include ERP and e-Business systems implementation and organizational impact, logistics information management, process engineering and performance analysis. Dr. Watson's doctoral and master's degrees are in Industrial Engineering from Penn State, and his B.S. in Industrial Engineering and Operations Research is from Syracuse University. He has published in such journals as Decision Sciences, Decision Support Systems, IEEE Transactions on Computers, International Journal of Production Research, Interfaces, European Journal of Operational Research, and Communications of the Association for Information Systems. He is active in the information systems and decision sciences communities and is a regular contributor and speaker at related conferences and workshops.

Ruediger Weissbach achieved his M.A. in communication sciences in 1986. Subsequently he worked as a freelancing scientist. From 1987 until 1992 he was engaged at an IS department in the electrical industry. In 1993 he changed to a building society, where he is responsible for information technique and information systems. Besides this function, he has worked as a Lecturer at several universities since 1990 and took his Ph.D. in information sciences in 2000 at the Free University of Berlin, Germany. The main aspects of his scientific work are communication processes in organizations, the impact of IS on organizations and IT management, especially in SMEs.

Dianne Willis is a Principal Lecturer in Information Management at Leeds Metropolitan University, UK. She is currently completing a Ph.D. in the use of e-mail as a communication mechanism in work organisations. Her other research interests include sociotechnical issues surrounding the implantation of new technology in business and social environments. She is currently involved in a large UK research project on e-business, which will be published in December 2002. She has published articles in journals and books and has presented at conferences. As a member of the BCS Sociotechnical group, she has co-edited two books titled, *The New SocioTech: Graffiti on the Longwall* and *Knowledge Management in the SocioTechnical World: The Graffiti Continues*.

Fu Xin is a Graduate Student in the Department of Information Management, Peking University. B.A from Beijing Foreign Studies University. Research interests include information organization and retrieval and information resources management.

Keiichi Yamada is an Associate Professor of Faculty of Business, Marketing and Distribution at Nakamura Gakuen University, Japan. His research covers corporate strategies, organizational theory, management information systems, and information technologies, etc. His current research focuses on the strategies for interorganizational competition and cooperation – especially on the strategic alliances as cooperative relationships, and interorganizational network organization as interorganizational linkage.

Yurong Yao is a Doctoral Candidate and Research Associate in the Department of Information Systems and Decision Science at Louisiana State University, USA. She has articles published in books and several conference proceedings. She received her B.Sc. in International Business and Computer Science and Engineering, and M.Sc. in Computer Science and Engineering from Shanghai Jiao Tong University in China. Her research interests include applications service provisions, electronic government, and strategic issues of information technology.

Teoh Say Yen is a Researcher affiliated with the IT Business Unit of the School of Business and Information Technology, Monash University (Sunway Campus), Malaysia. She has recently completed a broad survey of the use and value of Internet B2B for businesses in ASEAN.

Index

V

W

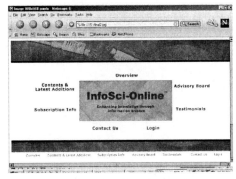